Trust without Borders

A Study of Psalm 37

Pamela J. Alexander

WESTBOW
PRESS®
A DIVISION OF THOMAS NELSON
& ZONDERVAN

Copyright © 2016 Pamela J. Alexander.

All rights reserved. No part of this book may be used or reproduced by any means, graphic, electronic, or mechanical, including photocopying, recording, taping or by any information storage retrieval system without the written permission of the author except in the case of brief quotations embodied in critical articles and reviews.

WestBow Press books may be ordered through booksellers or by contacting:

WestBow Press
A Division of Thomas Nelson & Zondervan
1663 Liberty Drive
Bloomington, IN 47403
www.westbowpress.com
1 (866) 928-1240

Because of the dynamic nature of the Internet, any web addresses or links contained in this book may have changed since publication and may no longer be valid. The views expressed in this work are solely those of the author and do not necessarily reflect the views of the publisher, and the publisher hereby disclaims any responsibility for them.

Any people depicted in stock imagery provided by Thinkstock are models, and such images are being used for illustrative purposes only.
Certain stock imagery © Thinkstock.

ISBN: 978-1-4908-9879-7 (sc)
ISBN: 978-1-4908-9881-0 (hc)
ISBN: 978-1-4908-9880-3 (e)

Print information available on the last page.

WestBow Press rev. date: 05/20/2016

Bible Versions Used

Scripture quotations taken from the New American Standard Bible®, Copyright © 1960, 1962, 1963, 1968, 1971, 1972, 1973, 1975, 1977, 1995 by The Lockman Foundation. Used by permission." (www.Lockman.org)

Scripture taken from the New King James Version. Copyright 1979, 1980, 1982 by Thomas Nelson, inc. Used by permission. All rights reserved.

Scripture quotations taken from the Holy Bible, New Living Translation, copyright 1996, 2004. Used by permission of Tyndale House Publishers, Inc., Wheaton, Illinois 60189. All rights reserved.

Scripture quotations taken from The Message. Copyright (c) by Eugene H. Peterson 1993, 1994, 1995, 1996, 2000, 2001, 2002. Used by permission of NavPress Publishing Group.

Scripture taken from the King James Version of the Bible.

Scripture taken from The Living Bible copyright © 1971 by Tyndale House Foundation. Used by permission of Tyndale House Publishers Inc., Carol Stream, Illinois 60188. All rights reserved. The Living Bible, TLB, and the The Living Bible logo are registered trademarks of Tyndale House Publishers.

Scriptures taken from the Holy Bible, New International Version®, NIV®. Copyright © 1973, 1978, 1984, 2011 by Biblica, Inc.™ Used by permission of Zondervan. All rights reserved worldwide. www.zondervan.com The "NIV" and "New International Version" are trademarks registered in the United States Patent and Trademark Office by Biblica, Inc.™ All rights reserved.

Scripture taken from the Amplified Bible, Copyright © 1954, 1958, 1962, 1964, 1965, 1987 by The Lockman Foundation. Used by permission.

Contents

Dedication ix
Acknowledgements x
Foreword xi
Preface xiv
Introduction xviii
Psalm 37: A Psalm of David xix

Chapter 1:   The "Dirt" on Dirt: Cultivating the Land 1
Chapter 2:   Hurry Up and Wait –
             "It shouldn't-oughta be this hard!" 26
Chapter 3:   Inheritance: Blessings of the "Now and Not Yet" 52
Chapter 4:   Matchless, Scandalous Grace 85
Chapter 5:   Sweet Intimacy of Prayer: Harps, Golden
             Bowls and "Camel Knees" 114
Chapter 6:   Trust without Borders 144
Chapter 7:   Surrounded by Strongholds 174
Chapter 8:   Perfect Peace 209

Closing Thoughts 233
Teaching Suggestions 234
Endnotes 245

Dedication

Thanks to my Sweetheart for giving me hours-on-days-on-weeks-on-months of time to write this book. Such a wonderful "the glass-is-half-full" type of guy to release "the glass-is-half-empty" woman I often am with the freedom to write all hours of the day and night! As "iron sharpens iron," my husband Jimmy has been my most inspiring, dedicated and challenging counsel in my life. He is truly the love of my life that won't let me get by with anything! Most aggravating for years, I am now so thankful he was piercingly pursuant of the Godly woman he knew I could, should and would be. Truly, truly, I can never thank him enough for *literally praying me through the deep, dark night of my soul*, helping me pick up the pieces of my life and rebuilding it with me. I am thankful to laugh out loud with him on earth and praise the LORD beside him eternally. I love you husband!

Acknowledgements

Through my life many gracious and wise believers have crossed my path, and to all of them I say, "Thank You" for sharing your love and wisdom with me, grooming me, exhorting me and loving me. Scripture states "All things work together for good to those who love God, to those who are called according to His purpose" (Romans 8:28). I would not be who I am without all their input.

Thank you, Paige Henderson, for taking time to write so eloquent a Foreword for this book. You blessed me with your forthrightness that nailed it on the head!

Each and every testimony or story in this book holds a special place in my heart. Many people will be blessed, healed and ministered to, the Lord glorified, and jewels will be added to each of your individual crowns for what has been shared:

Jimmy Alexander
Nathan Alexander
Vickie Boone Watson
David and Karen Mains
Holly Ogden
Karen Jordan

Jennifer Alexander Wright
Suzanne Wallace
Debbie Morris
Majid Babakhanian
Kerry Bond
Austin Lewter

Special thanks to the lovely ladies who helped me edit, review content and study the materials: Cindy Hall, Jeannie Summers Lyons, and Nancy Miller. Your skills, encouragement and comments were blessings to me!

Thanks also to my beautiful granddaughter Megan for the author photography session. And to my beautiful sisters: Billy Rae Montana, who gave love and time to help me with the details of our bed and breakfast and spent so much time with our Mom; and, Patricia Eagle, whose masterful love of writing inspired me to continue on when I despaired to give up.

Foreword

All it takes is faith and trust...and a little bit of pixie dust! One of my favorite animated tales gives a lightweight, cartoon take on trust. Sprinkle a fine dusting of something outside yourself and you'll have all you need to accomplish all you want. That would be a great plan, if only it worked!

The truth is there is no dust or product of any kind to buy and apply to your heart that will open it up to crossing the border of *known* and wandering unfettered in a life of pure trust into *unknown*. To not go with the Lord when He gives a vision, a dream, a new creative idea, or a new way of doing something causes you to miss the Great Adventure, shut down and shut out by your own inability to trust.

Our lack of trust doesn't keep us safe; it makes us useless in the Kingdom of God. Trust is the bedrock of obedience. We will not obey the Lord if we do not trust Him. And if we don't trust Him then He will not accomplish "on earth as it is in heaven" in our lives. We use all kinds of euphemisms and phrases to deflect the truth of why we won't move, or go, or create, or leave; but in the end it just comes down to a very simple, confining seed: lack of trust.

My husband and I experienced our own head-on collision with trust in 2002 when the Lord interrupted a perfectly bland and predictable life with a wildly out-of-the-box vision for ministry. There we were, minding our own business, living our own lives when God poured out a plan for a ministry that was going to shake it all. Income and insurance, security and personal space were going on the chopping block. I remember sitting in my pantry (literally) wrestling with a deep desire to be both securely "normal" and wildly obedient.

Been there? Then you know what it feels like to be stunned by the reality that you don't trust God like you thought you would when you grew up. You understand completely the words of the father in Mark

9:24 who came to Jesus for the healing of his son: "Lord, I believe; help my unbelief."

Right there in print is the trust battle. In the same sentence is both belief *AND* unbelief, holding hands. Wanting to trust, but seeing the circumstances, what we see with our eyes crashes into what we want to see with our hearts You believe fully that God can, but wonder deeply if He will. Knowing very well that what you've heard from the Lord is good and true, but also knowing that there is no way you can pull it off. And that's the heart of the matter: you can't pull it off. *You* can't. But <u>*He* can</u>.

Trust isn't trust if you can do the thing. Trust becomes trust when you reach into your pockets of ability and strategy and creativity and favor and find that all you have is the lint of your own limits. If you can pull this thing off, then you don't need to trust.

"Faithful is He who calls you, and He also will bring it to pass," (1 Thessalonians 5:24 NASB). Some of that bringing to pass involves giving you the capacity to believe when you don't. I wish the record would indicate more pious responses on my part to the directions of the Lord, but more likely mine matches that of the dad in Mark 9 who said "I do trust You, but I don't."

How do you get to a place of trust, real and deep and sustaining? Come clean; be honest. Then pack your "want to" on top of your "I can't do this" and hike out of your unbelief.

And that's where Pamela Alexander and her story come to help you.

Pamela takes the reader from uncertainty to hope in eight chapters. Her book is the map of the journey of trust from its most fundamental definition to its fullest practice, from point A to point B. Then all points beyond are yours to explore – limitlessly.

This book is not a read for those who are just cerebrally curious. If you just want to peruse the pages and absorb more information about God-things, then put this book down and move on. But if you want to dig in and "know that you know" the essence of trust, belief and obedience, grab a fork! From the initial chapters that define and clarify what trust is and isn't to the last that exposes the strongholds attacking and diluting your trust in God, you are in for a fine five-star buffet.

Go as far as you dare, but dare to go all the way. Be honest and be diligent; actually do the work of uncovering the issue of trust. Like the Mark 9 dad, want to believe more than you don't; and be brave enough to ask for and seek God's help.

Consider Pamela's story therapy for the soul as you learn to live with borderless trust. Then hide and watch the glory of the Lord!

Paige Henderson,
Co-founder, Fellowship of the Sword Ministries

Preface

Gardening has been a love of mine since early childhood living on alfalfa acreage fields, with a chicken coop, a mean rooster, and lots of room to explore. Granddaddy always had a garden, telling stories as we walked along, poking the ground with his cane, dropping seeds into the poked hole, and then pushing dirt over them with his foot. Granny cooked, canned and pickled everything the garden produced.

Later I helped Dad with his bountiful garden in the West Texas town of Abilene (no small task in that heat!). Mom wasn't into gardening, but she cooked and prepared all the delicious bounty that Daddy grew.

Dad retired from the Air Force in Abilene and began driving for North American Van Lines, leaving me to mow our large corner lot yard, care for the flowerbeds and tend his garden. Weeding, watering, pruning and picking became my job, developing even deeper my love for gardening. From early marriage until now, I have always attempted to have a garden wherever we've lived. Most were nothing to brag about, but all demonstrate my heart to keep trying! Some were extremely successful; most needed much help, and certainly a greater amount of time than I granted them. God began teaching me many lessons and farming scriptures through these experiences.

My business education degree (with English minor) has only been used twice in very small colleges: a business college in downtown Dallas, and at a girls' college while living in Tehran, Iran, in the mid-1970's. Many short-term and odd jobs have come my way through my life, but my most rewarding job, still on-going, has been *motherhood*.

I threw myself into mommy-hood 100% loving it all: the good, the bad and the ugly. Rooms were painted, decorated, equipped, cleaned and fumigated! Clothes were sewn, bartered, sold and purchased; hair washed, brushed, de-liced and de-tangled! I was a Brownie leader, Girl Scout leader and Cub Scout Den leader (twice!). We cooked, camped, created, painted, tied knots, sang songs and laughed until we thought we would pop telling stories around campfires. I scolded, sang songs, found special crayons, pencils, paper and lunch boxes (even melting some I had hidden in the oven – it's a loooong story!); loved, hugged, spanked, paddled, and made each one a unique baby book, scrapbook and a bound book of blessings. Often I was exasperated, exhilarated, initiated, but always in wonder of the responsibilities God had placed upon Jimmy and me to parent our four children. It was very serious business to me to "train up our children in the way they should go, so when they were old they would not depart from it" (Proverbs 22:6).

In January 1980 while on our 11th-wedding anniversary trip we felt the Lord spoke to our hearts to open a bed and breakfast, and it was a real diversion to me. While dining at a catfish restaurant in Uncertain, Texas (yes, you read correctly), my husband got a puzzled look on his face and exclaimed, "I think we're supposed to do this." "Have a catfish restaurant?" I gasped! "No. God just spoke to my heart that we are supposed to have a bed and breakfast," he answered.

That summer while visiting dear friends in Clemson, South Carolina, early one morning God led me to read Psalm 37. It spoke of trusting in Him, delighting in Him, and He would give the desires of one's heart. Repeatedly it mentioned dwelling on the land and inheriting the land. As I read, my heart quickened with excitement that God was confirming through this psalm of finding the land we had always desired and operating a bed and breakfast on it. Doubtfulness jumped right in with both feet: "Well, there are probably many psalms that speak of owning, dwelling, and inheriting land." Perusing all 150 psalms in those early dawn hours, I could find only one other that mentioned inheriting land. Psalm 37 immediately became our verse for our calling to operate a bed and breakfast.

We thought it would be immediate but in God's wisdom and timeline it took years. From "the calling to the arriving at the land" it was thirteen very long years. In those thirteen years we repaired a broken marriage, grew in leadership of our neighborhood church, adopted our fourth child, helped start the Vineyard Christian Fellowship

Church of Dallas, matured in leadership there, and learned how to pray and wait as we never had before.

God blessed me with mentors along the way that "cultivated" my life by planting seeds, watering, feeding and pruning. For ten years I sat under the Bible teaching of Mrs. Betty Brinson, one of the wisest women I've ever known. Often I wished she had not been so repetitive in her teaching – "didn't she realize she taught that last week?" But she spoke "it" over and over and over, and now I speak those same words and phrases repeatedly when I teach and talk and walk along the way. Through her diligent training, I perfected my testimony to share with others in thirty seconds, three minutes, thirty minutes or three days, depending on the situation.

My friend and peer, Suzanne Wallace, wife and co-pastor with John at Redeemer's Fellowship and later the Vineyard Christian Fellowship of Dallas in the 70's–90's, shared her practical wisdom and conversational prayers, helping me grow tremendously. She listened well to God and had a heart to obey at all cost. Linda Attaway, our Vineyard associate pastor's wife, also hears God's voice adamantly. She is a very practical and no-nonsense woman from whom I gleaned wisdom and am thankful God allowed me to learn from her. My dear friend Sharon Bendy and I were co-leaders of Women's Ministry at the Vineyard Christian Fellowship for years until Jimmy and I moved to our land. We spent many hours planning Bible studies, retreats and women's events during those years. Both she and her husband Bob, who built the Guest House *and* the Main House of our Bed and Breakfast, influenced our lives tremendously. And so with June Hines, Betty Bodine, Bonnie Harlow, Corinne French, Lin Barnes and so many others who blessed me during healing and growing years.

A particular healing ministry that helped shape my life, as well as Jimmy's, our marriage, and almost every member of our immediate family is *Fellowship of the Sword*. All these ministries have helped "work all things together for good" in my life.

Many verses of the Bible are my favorites, but Psalm 37 is the "life verse" of our land and our bed and breakfast. It is in verse three that God speaks of cultivating (NASB), and thus the title of the first week of study will involve *cultivating the dirt* of life.

Please join me with my dirty, gardening fingers of life as we explore the Psalm 37 that I love, and learn how to trust in God!

Introduction

Years ago my husband and I had felt God leading our hearts to own and operate a bed and breakfast and were led to Psalm 37 within a short time of that calling. This precious Psalm began to teach us how to wait upon the LORD for the finances to purchase country acreage, how best to prepare and build a B&B, be trained in the art of hospitality, and grow us in His wisdom. We began to learn these things while in God's waiting room for over fourteen years before we actually purchased and moved to the land to open our B&B! Since that time we have read Psalm 37 over and over year in and year out, praying over each verse as God has groomed us, taught us and stretched us in ways we would have never imagined. It has also given us great comfort and strengthened us beyond our earthly wisdom.

In *Trust without Borders* I examine how God desires our hearts to trust Him with ALL of our being, showing that when we worship Him in that obedience, "He who calls you is faithful, who also will do it" (1 Thessalonians 5:24). Studying through Psalm 37 and other scriptures will show that:

- *Trust* is our gift back to God, and He is pleased by the beauty of a trusting heart.
- *Trust* defines the meaning of living by grace rather than works.
- "Is it *trust* only when we get our way?"
- How do *trust* and entering His *rest* co-mingle?
- Gratefulness is a foremost quality of a trusting follower of Christ.

My heart is for the deep need of people to *learn to pray and to trust God; really trust God through the empowerment of the Spirit*. Come fellowship and explore Psalm 37 and God's word with me in learning how to trust God with everything and every need in your life.

Pamela Johnson Alexander

Psalm 37: A Psalm of David

¹ Do not fret because of evildoers, nor be envious of the workers of iniquity.
² For they shall soon be cut down like the grass, and wither as the green herb.
³ Trust in the Lord, and do good; dwell in the land, and feed on His faithfulness.
⁴ Delight yourself also in the Lord, and He shall give you the desires of your heart.
⁵ Commit your way to the Lord; Trust also in Him, and He shall bring it to pass.
⁶ He shall bring forth your righteousness as the light, and your justice as the noonday.
⁷ Rest in the Lord, and wait patiently for Him; do not fret because of him who prospers in his way, because of the man who brings wicked schemes to pass.
⁸ Cease from anger, and forsake wrath; do not fret—it only causes harm.
⁹ For evildoers shall be cut off; but those who wait on the Lord, they shall inherit the earth.
¹⁰ For yet a little while and the wicked shall be no more; indeed, you will look carefully for his place, but it shall be no more.
¹¹ But the meek shall inherit the earth, and shall delight themselves in the abundance of peace.
¹² The wicked plots against the just, and gnashes at him with his teeth.
¹³ The Lord laughs at him, for He sees that his day is coming.
¹⁴ The wicked have drawn the sword and have bent their bow, to cast down the poor and needy, to slay those who are of upright conduct.
¹⁵ Their sword shall enter their own heart, and their bows shall be broken.
¹⁶ A little that a righteous man has is better than the riches of many wicked.
¹⁷ For the arms of the wicked shall be broken, but the Lord upholds the righteous.
¹⁸ The Lord knows the days of the upright, and their inheritance shall be forever.
¹⁹ They shall not be ashamed in the evil time, and in the days of famine they shall be satisfied.
²⁰ But the wicked shall perish; and the enemies of the Lord, like the splendor of the meadows, shall vanish. Into smoke they shall vanish away.
²¹ The wicked borrows and does not repay, but the righteous shows mercy and gives.
²² For those blessed by Him shall inherit the earth, but those cursed by Him shall be cut off.
²³ The steps of a good man are ordered by the Lord, and He delights in his way.

24 Though he fall, he shall not be utterly cast down; for the Lord upholds him with His hand.
25 I have been young, and now am old; yet I have not seen the righteous forsaken, nor his descendants begging bread.
26 He is ever merciful, and lends; and his descendants are blessed.
27 Depart from evil, and do good; and dwell forevermore.
28 For the Lord loves justice, and does not forsake His saints; they are preserved forever, but the descendants of the wicked shall be cut off.
29 The righteous shall inherit the land, and dwell in it forever.
30 The mouth of the righteous speaks wisdom, and his tongue talks of justice.
31 The law of his God is in his heart; none of his steps shall slide.
32 The wicked watches the righteous, and seeks to slay him.
33 The Lord will not leave him in his hand, nor condemn him when he is judged.
34 Wait on the Lord, and keep His way, and He shall exalt you to inherit the land; when the wicked are cut off, you shall see it.
35 I have seen the wicked in great power, and spreading himself like a native green tree.
36 Yet he passed away, and behold, he was no more; indeed I sought him, but he could not be found.
37 Mark the blameless man, and observe the upright; for the future of that man is peace.
38 But the transgressors shall be destroyed together; the future of the wicked shall be cut off.
39 But the salvation of the righteous is from the Lord; He is their strength in the time of trouble.
40 And the Lord shall help them and deliver them; He shall deliver them from the wicked, and save them, because they trust in Him.

~ Chapter 1 ~

The "Dirt" on Dirt: Cultivating the Land

Day 1 ~ *"Trust in the Lord and do good; dwell in the land, and cultivate faithfulness" (Psalm 37:3).*

God, open up our hearts and minds to Your scriptures today as we begin to dig into Your word and what it means in our lives and how it applies to us personally. We ask for understanding and that You would grant us wisdom. In Jesus' name, amen.

<u>Cultivate</u>: (1) to prepare and use soil or land for growing crops; (2) to break up the surface soil around (plants) in order to destroy weeds, prevent crusting and preserve moisture; (3) to grow (plants or crops) from seeds, bulbs, etc.; (4) to improve or develop by various techniques; (5) *to improve by care, training or study; refine (as to cultivate one's mind)*; (6) *to promote the development or growth of*; (7) *to seek to develop familiarity with; give one's attention to: pursue.*[1]

One of the first things a gardener must do before beginning a garden is to cultivate the soil. The soil must be worked by tilling, plowing, and breaking up the dirt. Clay or compacted soil must be aerated and use more composted, richer soil whenever possible. There are many types of soil: clay, compacted, sandy, rich and fertile, depleted, black, red, brown, cracked, dry, soggy. A gardener must know not only the type of soil but also what is lacking in the soil in case enrichment needs to take place. Even a small plot requires more than a hoe, requiring tilling the soil with a plow or modern-day tiller. Larger plots need a tractor to till the earth and prepare the rows for planting.

The "Dirt" on Dirt: Cultivating the Land

Please look at Hosea 10:12–13. There are four instructions in verse 12 that the reader or receiver is to do. Please list them here:

1)

2)

3)

4)

What do you think it means to "sow for yourselves righteousness," or with a "view to righteousness" (depending on your version)?

What does the phrase "reap in mercy," or "reap in accordance with kindness," (depending on your version) mean to you?

Can you explain what it means to "break up fallow ground"?

Remember the previously mentioned point that one of the first things a gardener must do is cultivate the soil? Fallow ground is soil or land left uncultivated. After we sow righteousness, reap mercy, break up our fallow ground and seek the LORD, how long did verse 12 say we should wait for the LORD? Take some time to explain what that might mean to you:

In Hosea 10:13 four things are mentioned that we, in our own flesh, do and have done wrong. Please list them below:

1)

2)

3)

4)

Now explain what we did to cause those things to happen:

Oooooooh, because we trusted in our own way!

Take a moment here to think about what kind of soil you are and journal your thoughts below. Are you hard clay, hardened by past events; or compacted with no way to breathe? Are you sandy and loose so that nothing can be permanent, or rich and fertile? Are you depleted of nutrients and anything healthy, or encouraging? Maybe you are swamp-like or soggy; burdened and overwhelmed? Write out your thoughts:

Any gardener experiences pride and joy when the dirt is tilled, loose, easily dug, and softly sifted through the fingers. It is then that the seeds or young plants can be added with confidence and hope that the plants will have a chance to grow and produce the crops desired. Gardner God allows the Holy Spirit to dig and till in our hearts as soon as we become believers. The work begins instantaneously when

The "Dirt" on Dirt: Cultivating the Land

we accept Jesus as our Savior. There is always much work to be done to become loose, fertile soil that can fall between His fingers.

Years ago at the high school our teens attended I sat in the auditorium reading Proverbs 4:23 written across the entire stage above the curtains: "Keep thy heart with all diligence, for out of it are the issues of life" KJV. How far we have come from allowing Scriptures to be written above a school stage!

As Christians, we need to keep watch over our hearts and over our spiritual lives. Sin is insidious and may seem harmless in the beginning, but its end brings destruction and separation from God. We must not allow it to germinate in the soil of our hearts. Instead, we are to break up the hard places in our lives and sow seeds of righteousness so that we will reap the fruits of faithfulness and mercy. Ask God to show you how to soften any places in your spiritual life that have become hardened so that the soil of your heart will be ready to receive seed that will bear much fruit.[2]

In 1 Thessalonians 5, the apostle Paul shares wisdom concerning the hope of our resurrection with encouraging words, many one-line exhortations and instructions. Several final verses contain wonderful hope: *"Now may the God of peace make you holy in every way, and may your whole spirit and soul and body be kept blameless until our Lord Jesus Christ comes again. God will make this happen, for He who calls you is faithful"* (1 Thessalonians 5:23–24 NLT). Now read it again a little slower; then slowly one more time. Other translations are just as point-blank powerful: **God will do it, not us!**

According to Philippians 2:12, we are to ". . . work out our salvation with fear and trembling . . ." NASB. We are responsible for discipline, choices and sharing the joy of our Savior. In the Amplified Bible's version of Philippians 2:12–13, we see the same phrase and thoughts: ". . . work out (cultivate, carry out to the goal and fully complete) your own salvation with reverence and awe and trembling (self-distrust: with serious caution, tenderness of conscience, watchfulness against temptation, timidly shrinking from whatever might offend God and discredit the name of Christ). [Not in your own strength] for it is

Trust without Borders

God Who is all the while effectually at work in you [energizing and creating in you the power and desire], both to will and to work for His good pleasure and satisfaction and delight." Write in your own words what verse 13 is expressing:

We must exhibit responsibility, but the grace of our Lord and Savior is what makes us righteous. Nothing we do can make us holy (that is NO thing). Our choice to choose Jesus Christ as our Savior brings us to God, but it is God who makes us holy in every way. ". . . God will make this happen . . . ." What a burden is lifted off our shoulders when this realization is understood! What a wonder it is to tremble in self-distrust so that we can trust in the God who will make this happen!

List several hindrances that occur to you that prevent your believing this righteousness can happen:

Faith accepts God's testimony in a trusting, childlike manner, and salvation as a free gift. The Law was given to lead us to Christ; thus, any use of the Law as a means of earning our salvation is a distortion. By nature mankind presumes to seek salvation by works. It seems offensive to the flesh to believe we cannot. But God's Word says it is an offense to Him to believe we can.[3]

The word cultivate was defined seven ways in the beginning paragraph of today's lesson. Take some time to review the italicized last three definitions and think of ways in your own life that you could apply them. How could your life be improved by care, training or study? How could your mind be "refined"? What would it mean to promote development or growth in your life? How could you develop

The "Dirt" on Dirt: Cultivating the Land

familiarity with God? How do you give attention to God or pursue Him? Reference those many questions in listing your thoughts below:

✪ Finally, memorize Psalm 37:5 today: "Commit your way to the LORD; trust also in Him and He shall bring it to pass." Write it on a card or sticky note so it can be seen all day. My friend Suzanne calls sticky notes brain cells. So, keep it on a brain cell and say it repeatedly, asking God to fulfill it in your life.

Close out today's lesson by asking God to work the soil of your heart. Say out loud and remind God as you pray that *God will make this happen, for He who calls you is faithful.*

Oh, Master Gardener, we offer You the soil of our lives. Please cultivate it according to Your will; break up the hardened soil so that it will be ready for the seeds You will plant within our hearts. Thank You for fulfilling Your work of faith, with power, in our lives. We ask this in Your name. Amen.

Trust without Borders

<u>Day 2</u> ~ *"Commit your way to the LORD; trust also in Him and He shall bring it to pass" (Psalm 37: 5).*

Lord, we humbly come before You thanking You for what You do and have done in our lives. We confess that we have tried "to hold it all together" way too long. Please allow the Holy Spirit to help our hearts submit to You in all that we do. Help our "soil" to soak You in as You teach us today, Lord. Amen

We truly must realize and *always remember* that we are works in progress. Today let's take a look at Deuteronomy 7:21–23. In these and the surrounding passages, God was speaking through Moses of entering the land of promise He had told the Israelites about prior to their leaving Egypt, and how they were to drive out the inhabitants of that land. God's instructions are very detailed as Moses describes them to the Israelites.

How was the LORD going to clear out the nations? _____ ____ _____. *Not* quickly, but little by little. He promised to go before them; He told them He would be in their midst. Oh, what an incredibly awesome truth!

Now let's return again to Philippians 2 reading verses 5–13. What is the main theme of these verses?

Was there a struggle searching for the main thought of those verses or was it obvious? Did you zero in on verse 8 which mentions He humbled himself? These verses exemplify the ultimate, highest humility. They explain that "Jesus Christ, even though He existed in the form _____ _____, did not regard _____ with God a thing to be grasped, but *emptied* Himself, taking the form of a bond-servant . . ." (Philippians 2:5b–7a, NASB).

The "Dirt" on Dirt: Cultivating the Land

In your own words, what does *"emptied Himself"* mean?

As my cowboy friend Hal would say, "Pamela gal, I reckon that means there was nothing (NO thing) left in him of himself." That is humility. So, re-reading <u>your</u> list of hindrances from Day 1 to believing that *God will make this happen*, are there things listed that interfere with humility? Feel free to elaborate on them here, in your own words and thoughts.

✪ Take some time right now to stop and prayerfully ask God to help you get rid of those hindrances. Pray that "God will make this happen."

What is the opposite of humility? _____. Yessiree! Pride with a capital P! Whenever we have to work harder to be better, never feel we are good enough, have an "I can do better" attitude, strive for never-ending self-improvement, or always feel guilty, then we are not allowing God to make this happen.

In 1 Thessalonians 5:23: This would be accomplished by whom?

Also, what would that One be doing? (I'm looking for three words here).

_____ _____ _____

And how would that happen?

God Himself, making you holy; and not just a little bit holy, but *entirely*! "The God of peace make you holy in *every* way . . .," preserving you or keeping you blameless until the Lord Jesus returns again! Are you having some doubts that this is possible? Or, glory hallelujah, are you shouting for joy? Write your thoughts about this here:

Again from 1 Thessalonians 5:24: Who will bring this to pass?

What descriptive word does this verse use to describe this one who will bring it to pass?

Examine these similar scriptures to those just studied and briefly summarize each one:

2 Timothy 1:12

The "Dirt" on Dirt: Cultivating the Land

Philippians 1:6

Deuteronomy 7:9

1 Corinthians 1:4–9

2 Thessalonians 1:11–12

I love verse 11 that says God will fulfill the work of faith *with power*, fulfill every faith-inspired effort, and give power to accomplish all the good things your faith prompts you to do. It helped me realize He called, inspired and directed me to write this Bible study and gave me the power to do it!

Hebrews 10:23

The word hope used here is the absolute assurance that what God promised He will deliver.

✪ Congratulations! What an excellent amount of study accomplished today digging into those detailed scriptures! Close out today's study time reading Psalm 37:5–6. Spend a few "Mary" moments at the feet of Jesus in prayer and ask that God will fulfill the work of faith *with power* in your life.

"Now to Him who is able to keep you from stumbling, and to present you faultless before the presence of His glory with exceeding joy, to God our Savior, who alone is wise, be glory and majesty, dominion and power, both now and forever." Amen,

Jude 24–25.

Heavenly Father, Thank You that You hold ALL things in Your hands, because that means we do not have to! Help us trust You to present us faultless before the presence of His glory. Help us to learn how to sit at Your feet. In the name of Jesus, amen.

The "Dirt" on Dirt: Cultivating the Land

Day 3 ~ *"Do not fret because of evildoers, nor be envious of the workers of iniquity. For they shall soon be cut down like the grass, and wither as the green herb" (Psalm 37:1-2).*

Lord, today would You help us garden in Your word to cultivate what You would have us study, learn and apply in our lives? Thank You. Amen.

The New American Standard version of Psalm 37:3 says to "Trust in the LORD and do good; dwell in the land and cultivate faithfulness." What part of the definition of cultivate given at the beginning of Day 1 could you use here?

After studying the detail of the Day 2 scriptures and Psalm 37:3, can you see how when we truly understand that "God will make it happen," we can more easily trust in the LORD? When we understand that it is not we who control or make things happen *but the LORD who indeed makes everything happen* (John 1:3), then we can cease being anxious and learn to trust in Him. Consider this thought: *"The presence of anxiety means the absence of humility."*

No, slow down – don't rush here. Think about that thought. We all may experience anxiety at times for various reasons. However, when we dwell in anxiousness, constantly being anxious about everything, then we do not trust God or the one He has entrusted to care for us. We are trusting in ourselves, our pitiful anxiousness, or manipulative ways to work out situations instead of God.

That is *not* humility. It is pride, Dear One. Oh. That "P" word again. Pride is the absence of humility. Humility is emptying ourselves and allowing God to fill us. It is setting aside our thoughts and the way we think or decide that the world should be run. Instead, we turn trustfully to God and ask for His way, His deliverance, His discernment: "For God has not given us a spirit of fear, but of power and of love and of a sound mind" (2 Timothy 1:7). The heart converted from mistrust to trust in the irreversible forgiveness of Jesus Christ is redeemed from the corrosive power of fear.[4]

✪ Step aside here with the Lord and ponder things that may cause anxiousness. What do you try to hold tight control over? Prayerfully ask God to open the eyes of your heart to show you areas you are unwilling to release to Him. Ask Him to help you trust Him. Ask Him to help you cultivate faithfulness.

Trust is an action, a conscious choice. Trust should be unwavering and needs to be unconditional, but sometimes doubt does creep in. Doubts cause us to work at the issues in our own strength, sometimes because of perfectionistic tendencies. Look at what God told Job about that perfectionism in Job 22:3: "Is it any pleasure to the Almighty that you are righteous (perfect)? Or is it any gain to Him that you make your ways perfect?" KJV

In other words, "How's that working out for you to take care of all these issues in your own strength?"

Is it trust only if we get our way? Do you need to read that sentence once more? Take a look at how Isaiah worded it in Isaiah 12:2: "See, God has come to save me. I will TRUST in Him and not be afraid. The Lord God is my strength and my song; He has given me victory" TLB.

Truth has been planted within our lives, but in difficult times it is often hard to stand firm, stand tall, stand still and trust in God. When

The "Dirt" on Dirt: Cultivating the Land

we do firmly plant our stand with God, however, the pieces of that trust will begin to return. Please review 2 Corinthians 4:8–10 with me: . . . we are afflicted in every way, but not crushed; perplexed, but not despairing; persecuted, but not forsaken; struck down, but not destroyed; always carrying about in the body the dying of Jesus, that the life of Jesus also may be manifested in our body" NASB.

Let's review some of those words for a few moments, writing examples of how these words have happened to you or made you feel in your life:

Afflicted: pushed down; hard pressed; hard pressure; intense

Crushed: crowd into a narrow place; a violent crowding; squeeze into; alter

Perplexed: doubt; uncertainty

Despairing: giving up hope; utter loss of hope or a cause of such loss

Persecuted: harassed in a manner to injure, grieve or afflict; to cause to suffer because of belief

Forsaken: abandoned; to give up, renounce, quit or leave entirely

Destroyed: to ruin or demolish; to put out of existence

Wow! Certainly none of those words are simple or easy, especially if we have had to deal with them in our lives. *Just a little side note here on abandonment. Having adopted and raised three abandoned children, and having done many years of lay-ministry marriage counseling for couples with my husband, that word abandonment mentioned above in the "forsaken" section is a really big, strong and difficult demonic stronghold. Spiritual issues of abandonment are not just for abandoned children. Issues of abandonment can stem from a sudden death of a spouse, child, parent, family member or friend; loss of a close friendship or job; infidelity, etc. If you specifically had difficulty with that word in any area of your life, seek someone whom you can trust and have some dedicated prayer. You will be glad you did. I'll get off my soapbox now.

✪ Today was a shorter lesson to allow you time for a review of the many scriptures you have researched the last several lessons, and for contemplation with Him. Close out your time today by reading Psalm 37:1–6. Ask the Lord to help you especially realize verses three and five in your life. See you tomorrow!

The "Dirt" on Dirt: Cultivating the Land

Father, we are so hungry. We want to feed on Your faithfulness so You will give us our heartfelt desires. Please help us commit our ways to You so that You can bring them to pass. In the righteous light of Your name, amen.

Day 4 ~ *"Delight yourself also in the LORD and He shall give you the desires of your heart" (Psalm 37:4).*

Father, thank You that You are the God of the breakthrough! Thank You that You are cultivating our hearts, breaking up the fallow ground and planting new seeds in our lives. Be near us as we delve further into learning how to trust You. Amen

Read again Psalm 37:3. When we trust in the LORD and do good, we can simply and more believably cultivate faithfulness because the One who is faithful will make it happen. The New Living Translation says we "will live safely in the land and will prosper." That word prosper doesn't necessarily mean financial, but being blessed of God with security, health, close family ties, and prosperity in your spiritual walk. Would we not want to prosper in any way that God would open up for us?

Let's take a trip through several translations of Psalm 37:3b:

"Then you will live *safely in the land and prosper.*" NLT
"Dwell in the land and *cultivate faithfulness.*" NASB
"So shalt thou dwell in the land, and *verily thou shalt be fed.*" KJV
"Dwell in the land and *feed on His faithfulness.*" NKJV

These are varying phrases of the same verse that lead to the same meaning. The roots of these translations all lead back to *trustworthiness, faithfulness, stability, steadiness, permanence, truth, sureness, to be true,* as well as many others.

So, if we trust in the LORD and do good (accomplish, finish, practice), then we will live securely, steadily, truthfully and faithfully in the land (the place we abide).

The *land* can mean a physical place where we live or it can be a spiritual land (a spiritual meaning). Name several places you would like to abide (live) physically:

The "Dirt" on Dirt: Cultivating the Land

Now name some spiritual places where you would like to abide (i.e., peace, wisdom):

I want to abide here: "He who dwells in the shelter of the Most High will abide in the shadow of the Almighty" (Psalm 91:1 NASB). There is plenty of room under His shadow if you decide to join me.

Think on some ways you could cultivate faithfulness or prosper in the land:

Blessed One, there is no one greater that we can trust; no one who is more faithful than our God! There is no human being that can stand up to that kind of test when it comes to trusting. As humans, we will all fail at some point, but not our Sovereign God! Not our Savior, who gave up His equality with God to humble Himself on the cross by His shed blood on our behalf! There is none other!

At a Christian Motorcyclists Association women's conference I met Kerry Bond, a talented worship leader for CMA from Missouri. She sang a beautiful song called *Restored* written from a poem she penned after attending the 2012 Missouri CMA Women's Conference where Holly Ogden shared a story she had written. Holly and her husband, John Ogden Jr., are evangelists for the CMA. Our north Texas area is within their jurisdiction, so as CMA members, my husband and I are fortunate to hear them speak at various conferences and training sessions.

Just a tiny bit of history here: John Ogden Jr., was a rebel-rouser in his younger years, often disappointing his parents, John, Sr., and Becky Ogden of Arkansas. After "he fell in love with Jesus," he eventually met and married Holly – much to the delight of Becky. He and Holly have served as evangelists for several years now and often share their insights, issues and struggles of life when they speak. Holly shared the piece below in 2012:

"When You came into my life, You took my shattered heart and wrapped Yours around it. You made me a new creation, but I had yet to realize it. As we have walked together through the years, some of the shards of my old heart pressed through Your new heart and came into the open. The choice I had to make was what to do with these shards. Do I press them back into Your heart and hide from them, or do I offer them to You, though they are a terrible thing to offer to someone I love so much?

"As I cradled this latest piece, remembering the pain it represented, the dreams lost, the innocence shattered, You held out Your hand for it. Though I knew it was best to give it to You, I held on a little longer. This particular piece had a significant role in defining my old heart. Tarnished and ugly, I turned the piece over and allowed those old emotions to roll over me: loneliness, pain, rejection, the feeling that no one would ever rescue me, that no one would ever notice and save me; invisibility. These were deep wounds. Could I just give them up?

I felt I was to trust You, with whispers to my heart that I was precious to You.

"Ashamed, I handed this piece over to You. The minute it touched Your hand it transformed into a rainbow that shot off into the distance.

"'What just happened?' I asked?

"Then I realized You promised to make beautiful things out of me and my heart if I would just trust You with them. That shard was not me, nor was it meant for me to carry. God had been waiting for the day I would be willing to hand it to Him. Now it had turned into a rainbow, the fulfillment of a promise; a promise that He will never leave me. His Word promised that He will come to my rescue; and promised that I will never be invisible to Him. I knew I had to continue to let down my heart and step out of my box, and that I would find God faithful to be right there with me. I knew He loved me." [5]

The "Dirt" on Dirt: Cultivating the Land

Holly shared this story at the 2013 CMA Women's Conference at June Hunt's The Hope Center in Plano, Texas. Out of Holly's story, Kerry Bond shared this song it inspired:

Restored

The shattered pieces of my life and all that I defined as right,
The things I cling to, the things I hold to;
Is it really worth the fight?
Every piece and every part and the secrets of my heart,
Have been my burden, have been my pain, have been
my solace and my shame. But you say . . .
"Trust Me, simply Trust Me; Trust Me. . ."

I'll hold this piece a little longer, with the bitterness I harbor
Until I truly let it go. Then You quickly let me know
That every piece and every part and the secrets of my heart
Are not my burden anymore, peace resides here;
I've been restored.
It's handed over, it's been remade;
It's fulfilled promise; it's an open cage.
He'll never leave me; He'll always guide
me, and I can still hear Him say. . .
"Trust Me, simply Trust Me; Trust Me . . ."

Every piece and every part, and the secrets of my heart
Are not my burden anymore, peace resides here,
I've been restored.

Words and Music by Kerry Bond, 2012
Used by Permission[6]

Not long before the 2013 CMA Women's Conference John Jr. had a terrible motorcycle accident that nearly severed his nose from his face. Holly received a call that he had been in an accident but wasn't told the severity other than his nose had been broken. Upon arriving at the hospital, she learned that it was much more than a broken nose; it was almost a completely severed nose that required extensive surgery to repair, with no promise of ever functioning properly again.

However, prayers were being lifted up all over the world to the "throne of the God that heals." John's nose was completely peeled back; all under-skin and tissues were exposed and hanging out in many directions. Surgery was performed by a surgeon that stated this was one of his most complicated surgeries in his 40-year career, but then prognosis was that it wouldn't heal properly . . . or infection would set in . . . or it would take months for the swelling to diminish or it might heal deformed.

We serve a mighty God – and *John walked out of the hospital <u>in a day</u>* instead of weeks, the swelling lessened in record time and within six weeks proof that he had major surgery on his nose was barely visible! Examine Isaiah 61:2–4: "And the Lord will provide for those who grieve in Zion– to bestow on them a crown of beauty instead of ashes, the oil of joy instead of mourning, and a garment of praise instead of a spirit of despair. They will be called oaks of righteousness, a planting of the Lord for the display of his splendor" NIV.

This couple chose to trust God to see them through this challenging time. They had to trust Him for restoration in whatever form it took. For John, it was a trust for a physical healing; for Holly, it was trust for an emotional healing. The trauma of dealing with the emotions from the accident had sent her heart reeling. In the end, God prevailed. John's nose was restored, and Holly handed her anxiety and pain over to God and He brought restoration to her heart.

✪ Close today by asking God to help you cultivate faithfulness, to help you prosper in the land. Remember, "He who calls you is utterly faithful and He will finish what He has set out to do" (1 Thessalonians 5:24, Phillips). Read Psalm 37:1–11 to complete today's study. Delight yourself in the abundance of peace.

Thank You, LORD, that You are faithful and true. Please teach us to listen intently for Your voice and strengthen us to be obedient to answer it. Amen.

The "Dirt" on Dirt: Cultivating the Land

<u>Day 5</u> ~ *"But the salvation of the righteous is from the LORD; He is their strength in the time of trouble" (Psalm 37:39).*

O, Lord, now that we are beginning to have an inkling of thought about how to trust You to live securely in "the land," help us to begin to understand our "land." Amen

The Hebrew word for *land* (erets) in Psalm 37:3 means the earth (at large or a land); a field, country, nations, the earth or the world.[7] When we dwell in the earth, in the world trusting in Him, it is much more likely we will cultivate faithfulness because we *trust the One who is faithful.*

When my husband and I were planning, dreaming and waiting to move to our land where we felt led by God to build and open our bed and breakfast, my husband mentioned several different times that he wanted to get a beagle once we settled there. We moved from the big, busy city of Dallas, Texas, to the quiet, country setting during the fall, and I was soon able to locate a beagle to give him for Christmas. We have enjoyed three beagles now and totally love their sweet dispositions and even temperaments.

One of our guests was an artist who selected a place in our back meadow to sketch for a while, settling on a nice spot near the edge of the woods. While she was working on her artwork, she saw and heard our Bentley Beagle howling in the meadow as he came upon the scent of a rabbit. He and the rabbit would crisscross across the pasture, the rabbit scurrying one way and Bentley going the other (just like in the cartoons!), with Bentley always lagging just a few seconds behind the bunny. After zigzagging for a few minutes, the rabbit ran under a log. Bentley finally caught up with the rabbit and stood barking in front of the log. His howl deepened as he kept thrusting his head at the log, never quite 100% sure that he wanted to go into the crevasse under the log to get the rabbit. Our guest laughed out loud when after several minutes the rabbit's foot appeared from underneath the log and slapped Bentley in the face! Bentley stood stunned for a few seconds, barked a few more barks, and then walked away in defeat.

Since they are hunters, Beagles love to dig in the dirt hunting moles or digging a rabbit out of its hole. They will seriously dig until the hole gets quite deep, their heads all the way into the hole, back end sticking up in the air, dirt furiously flying backward, but usually resurfacing unsuccessfully with dirt-covered nose and face.

Aren't we like that? I have prayed that you would have that devotion to digging into God's word; that there would be a hunger so deep that the digging would continue until your searching and your prayers would unearth answers for you. Precious One, God wants to be found! And, often it is easier to let go and literally let God step in to what you are so desperately holding on to.

God takes the compost of our refuse, adds heat, moisture and air, and uses it to make a bountiful and beautiful garden. At the end of 2 Samuel 24, David had sinned against the LORD and a plague had come against the people. Upon his repentance, David was instructed to erect an altar to the LORD on the threshing floor of Araunah the Jebusite. David went to Araunah and asked to buy the threshing floor, which in those days was important for threshing out of the grain, a major part of a village's sustenance and economy. Araunah offered to give it to King David, but David wisely chose to purchase the threshing floor, the oxen and the entire area instead, ". . . I will not offer burnt offerings to the LORD my God which cost me nothing" (v. 24, NASB).

Confessing and repenting (turning from) our sins and wrong-doings always seems difficult to do. But the beauty, peace and restfulness that follow are always worth it! This threshing floor was on Mount Moriah, a hill in the region of Moriah and is the mount where Abraham offered Isaac to the LORD (Genesis 22:2). This is important because the city of Jerusalem developed from this location, and a valley called the Kidron Valley went through this region. Solomon later built the temple of the LORD there (2 Chronicles 3:1), with the pinnacle of the

The "Dirt" on Dirt: Cultivating the Land

temple overlooking the Kidron Valley. In later Old Testament days, refuse was often thrown into this valley, and in 2 Chronicles 29:16, idols were carried out of the temple Solomon had built and thrown into this valley as well. The valley of Kidron separates the old city of Jerusalem from the Mount of Olives to the east. The city eventually built up around the valley, the junk was cleaned up, and compost and waste thrown there grew into the beautiful valley it is today.

This week the chapter opened with definitions of the word *cultivate*. Let's close with some definitions of *dirt:* (1) any unclean or soiling matter, as mud, dust, dung, trash, filth; (2) earth or garden soil; (3) anything common, filthy, or contemptible; (4) dirtiness, nastiness, corruption, etc.[8]

Can you think of some dirt you have been sweeping under the rug for way too long? Maybe there are some idols that have begun to take your loyalty, or some refuse mounting up in your life. Take some time right now to journal about it and prayerfully bring it to the Lord.

Rather than cultivating the dirt of our past, of our sinful flesh, let's ask *the God who will make it happen* to cultivate that faith within us with His power. Rather than dig around in the traumatic trouble of anxiety, manipulation and control, let's "trust in the LORD, and do good; dwell in the land and cultivate faithfulness."

✪ To close this week's study, allow time to re-read Psalm 37:1–6 and v. 39 several times. Don't rush, but instead read the verses slowly and dwell on verses or thoughts that help you ponder on the things you have brought to the Lord this week. Practice the verse(s) you may have memorized. Let them refresh you. Share them with others in conversation, because as you "delight yourself also in the LORD, He shall give you the desires of your heart."

Father, We want to lay all the dirt, dust bunnies, filth, nastiness and heavy bags of trash at Your feet. If anyone involved in this study does not know You as their personal Savior, we ask that You would stir their heart right now. We ask that You fulfill every desire for goodness and the work of faith within us with Your power. By Your Spirit, confirm to us there is NO thing that we can do to separate us from the love of Christ, and that there is also NO thing we can do to make You love us more. Help us know that You loved us before we were even born and Your grace is sufficient for us. Thank You for Your grace. Thank You for Your love. We praise Your Mighty Name, Jesus! Amen and amen.

~ Chapter 2 ~

Hurry Up and Wait –
"It shouldn't-oughta be this hard!"

Day 1 ~ *"For they shall not be ashamed who wait for Me"* (*Isaiah 49:23*).

Heavenly God, Creator of the Universe and the earth therein, help us wait for You today. Even when we sit still, our lives and the activities that revolve within them spin around us. Please allow the Holy Spirit to calm our hearts, still our thoughts and fill us with Your presence. In Your precious name we pray, Lord. Amen.

One of the Tangles of Life

Hurry up, go-go, rush-rush to town.
Hurry up; rush, rush;
The world wears a frown.
People pass up so much
love and happiness and joy to
hurry up and go, go
and rush to stand around.

Pamela Alexander[1]

When my husband and I were dating, it was always fun to be going and doing and getting details lined up for all our dating activities. I didn't realize at the time that he was a man of many letters: Type A (controlling, strong, leadership tendencies), ADHD (Attention Deficit Hyperactive Disorder), strong-willed and very outgoing. Once married, it seemed there was an over-abundance of activities and busy-ness but occasionally I just wanted to slow down. The rush and the thrill were certainly fun, but now "let's just sit and enjoy the peacefulness of the sunset." Not only was life constantly on-the-go, but we had to arrive early so a rush accompanied every activity. Plus, once we got "there," we usually had to stand around because no one else had arrived yet. It was very frustrating to me, thus the writing of the above poem. We have since learned to compromise on times of departure and the rush of the details.

With God it seems I tend to do the opposite. I want Him to hurry up, give me the details and answer the requested prayer. Doesn't He realize that the time is running short? Doesn't He know there is no money left? Can't He see that child needs "such-and-such"? Surely He should understand that *I need* this thing done!

When my good friend Lin's first grandson was about three, his Mommy had told him he couldn't have another cookie. While Mommy was in another room tending to little baby sister, he came to Grandma and said, bending slightly and gripping his hands into fists, "Grandma, *I neeeeed* a cookie!" We are like that little boy. We are to "Rest (be still) in the Lord and wait patiently for Him" (Psalm 37:7). But while He is not looking, we grip our fists and go to our friends, family, our funds or our big ideas, and we try to solve the issue at hand. We try to convince our Pastor, our spouse, our friends, our children – anyone who will listen – that we *neeeed* whatever it is we think is the answer, when what we need is not be ashamed to wait on the Lord.

What is the cookie you currently need?

In your heart, how do you feel God has asked you to wait?

Hurry Up and Wait – "It shouldn't-oughta be this hard!"

How successful were you?

When one of our daughters was in the throes of potty training her toddler, the little one decided she wanted to be in the bathroom and on the toilet alone – without Mommy in there to supervise. One day after quite a long wait outside the door, our daughter asked, "Are you finished yet?" No answer came. She waited just a little longer then asked again, "Are you through now?" A little voice came from the potty behind the closed bathroom door: "Wait for it . . . wait for it." Sayings like this from our toddlers often make us laugh, but I wonder if God is humored as well by our shenanigans, delays, excuses and procrastinations given while we impatiently wait – or disobediently "don't wait."

In my life there have been some very lame, lying or ridiculous excuses to avoid waiting for something that "I wanted NOW!" or "didn't want now," and I was certain some action should be done immediately to avoid something extreme. But, as comes with maturing and age, I began to realize that if God is in "it," "it" is worth the wait. It never works to rush God nor deliberately delay things to avoid His instructions.

It was five years between the time God gave our hearts the dream of having a bed and breakfast and finally finding the land on which to build. Most of those five years were spent looking at structures already built. But the desire of our hearts was to be in the country, and most properties we found were in small country towns. When we did find the land that seemed to fit all the criteria, we knew it was God's gift because of the timing, the cost, our finances and the location. Since it was spring, as soon as we had completed the contract for the land, we put our Dallas home up for sale and figured we would move before school started in the fall. Nope! Fall came and went; winter slid by, and spring arrived again. Then another complete year passed and our home still hadn't sold. We often prayed with our church leadership as well as our small group, but our house didn't sell. By now we had the architectural plans drawn up, the builder lined up and many items purchased for decorating the guest rooms of the B&B.

Our three older children were ready for high school and finishing middle school, so we made the decision to stay in our Dallas home and allow them to graduate with their friends. Many of those praying for us said it would not be outside God's will for us to rent our home and move to the land to begin building the bed and breakfast, but we just didn't have peace about doing that. We did not feel good about "stepping out before the Ark of God." If it was truly His word to us to have a bed and breakfast, then we didn't want to step out one foot before He released us.

"For the vision is yet for the appointed time; it hastens toward the goal, and it will not fail. Though it tarries, wait for it; for it will certainly come, it will not delay" (Habakkuk 2:3 NASB).

We stayed in Dallas almost seven more years, helping start the Vineyard Christian Fellowship of Dallas, adopting our fourth child, and allowing our marriage to heal. God's timing is always perfect!

Before moving on to the next thoughts and scriptures, consider how you think God would want you to wait on Him, or even ways you already use to wait on Him.

If something has tarried for you recently, did you try to rush God?

OR ~ can you describe how you were able to wait for it?

Hurry Up and Wait - "It shouldn't-oughta be this hard!"

Now dig into several scriptures to help learn how to wait better on the LORD. Write out the scripture and then paraphrase it in your own words.

Psalm 27:14

Psalm 37:7a

Psalm 37:9

Jeremiah 14:22: "Can the idols of the godless nations cause rain? Can the sky water the earth by itself? You're the one, O God, who does this. So you're the one for whom we wait. You made it all; you do it all," Message. (This was long so I wrote it out for you).

✪ Close with Psalm 25:5

This verse most likely is difficult for most of us if we truly take it to heart. How do we "wait all the day"? Pray and ponder over this verse as you close out today's study. Take a jab at memorizing either Psalm 25:5 or Psalm 37:9.

Lord, help our hearts to be humble before You, for You are the God of our salvation, the God who saves us, the only God who can save us from anything. Help us to wait on You "all the day." Amen

Hurry Up and Wait - "It shouldn't-oughta be this hard!"

<u>Day 2</u> ~ *"Rest in the LORD, and wait patiently for Him; do not fret because of him who prospers in his way, because of the man who brings wicked schemes to pass. Cease from anger and forsake wrath; do not fret - it only causes harm. For evildoers shall be cut off; but those who wait on the LORD, they shall inherit the earth" (Psalm 37:7-9).*

Father, many of us are so weary, so fretful today. Please continue to teach us how to wait upon You, how to lay down our anger at the foot of the cross, how to wait instead of fretting. Please forgive us and reveal to us today how we are inheritors of the entire earth! Such a vast inheritance . . . if we can learn to embrace such little, bitty words: "rest and wait." In Jesus' name, amen.

Webster defines *rest* as: Rest as by lying down, esp. as in sleep; to cease from action or motion; to be free from anxiety or disturbance; to remain confident: *TRUST*.[2] There are other listings as well, but the ones listed here certainly line up with the Hebrew word for rest, *menuchah* (meh-noo-chah): Resting place; place of stillness, consolation, peace, rest; a quiet place; also the condition of restfulness. This word is derived *from nuach*, a verb meaning "to rest, soothe, settle down, comfort."[3]

Recently I was blessed to turn a room in our house into a studio where I am able to write, work on my hobby of calligraphy, do some scrapbooking, sewing and study. It is my place of respite, a get-away from the hustle and bustle of the bed and breakfast, guests, and the busy-ness of life. It is named "Studio A" after a Greek word for rest, *anapauo*, (an-ap-ow-oh), (from *ana*, "up," and *pauo*) "to make to cease."[4] The word describes a cessation from toil; refreshment, an intermission. *It is my intermission from work.*

The room has been repainted, shelves added, my calligraphy table rescued from twenty years of living in the laundry room with sheets, towels, soaps and various phases of laundry covering it, and a rocking chair placed in front of a small, soft rug. When I get to escape there I feel such comfort; the weariness and burdens just roll off my shoulders and my breathing becomes deep and steady. It takes great discipline to make my visits regular because it is hard to get there.

Take a moment to read Isaiah 28:12: "This is the resting place, let the weary rest" NIV. Write what that means to you at the moment:

When our children were younger we used to joke that if we couldn't find one of them just go into the bathroom and shut the door. At least one or two would always come knocking on the door almost instantly! Now it's the business phone or the doorbell; the same way with our dinner. It doesn't seem to matter if it is 5:30 or 8:30, if we sit down to eat, guests arrive or the phone rings. But that is why we need to learn to rest in Him – for that state of restfulness. That is why we learn that in Him we can remain confident: we can TRUST. No matter what is happening around us, the menuchah can give us the foundation we need to maintain a "condition of restfulness." No matter what is happening around us, trusting God provides the foundation needed for a state of restfulness.

Do you believe that? What would you need to change, have to change, to be able to have a condition of restfulness?

Did you happen to mention trusting in the LORD instead of yourself? Look at Isaiah 11:10: "And in that day there shall be a Root of Jesse, who shall stand as a banner to the people; for the Gentiles shall seek Him, and His *resting* place shall be glorious."

This verse is actually speaking of the last days when all the nations of the earth gather to His banner. Did you know that is one of the names for our God? *Jehovah-Nissi* means "the LORD my banner." It

Hurry Up and Wait - "It shouldn't-oughta be this hard!"

emphasizes that God is our rallying point and our means of victory; the one who fights for His people.

Think back to Day 1 of *The "Dirt" on Dirt* chapter to the 1 Thessalonians 5:23–24 verses we studied. In that lesson think back to who did the work or the fighting for us. _____. Have you been asking Him to do it – to fight for you?

Look at Zechariah 4:6b: "**Not** by might, nor by power, but <u>by my spirit</u>, says the LORD of hosts."

What part of this verse puts the responsibility upon your shoulders? . Yep, about that much! It, too, stresses He is the One who fights for us; the One who will make it happen . . . by His spirit.

The first time I read the Bible completely through, one of my very favorite verses became Exodus 14:13–14. Would you look it up please? I memorized it in the New American Standard version and usually quote it without 13b. However, the Egyptians mentioned in verse 13b certainly represent the issues, problems, and strongholds we fight against.

"But Moses said to the people, 'Do not fear! Stand by and see the salvation of the LORD which He will accomplish for you today; for the Egyptians whom you have seen today, you will never see them again forever. <u>The LORD will fight for you while you keep silent</u>'" (Exodus 14:13–14 NASB).

Standing by and seeing the salvation of the LORD work for you is simply living with God in your life; His life in you – instead of trying to be in personal control. The entire Bible gives us guidelines that help build our lives on His precepts, His principles. Precepts, ordinances and practices can very easily become just dead religious ceremonies if we practice them in our own self-will. But if we stand by, stand firm and stand back, the salvation of the LORD will fight for us. That is trust with a capitol T! Not to fear, but to stand firm and let the power of His spirit do the work for us. That is the only way – that is trust. That, is Trust.

And those "Egyptians" . . . those evil strongholds and dark, hidden places in our hearts . . . to never see them again forever is my goal for all of them! Each time God reveals one to me by the power of His Spirit, my prayer asks Him to shine His light in that part of my heart, in my spirit, so that no darkness can remain in that area. ***Where His Light is allowed to live no darkness can survive or exist.*** Those who fear the darkness have no idea what the Light can do! "Even so, come, Lord Jesus!" (Rev. 22:20, NASB).

✪ Commit Exodus 14:13–14 to memory today for the end of today's lesson. Think of some situations where <u>if you stood firm</u> and let the LORD fight for you, <u>if you kept silent</u> and let the LORD fight for you – what might happen in those situations.

✪ We will close out today with another of my favorite passages from Habakkuk 3:17–19 which teaches us to wait on the LORD:

> *"Though the fig tree should not blossom, and there be no fruit on the vines; though the yield of the olive should fail and the fields produce no food; though the flock should be cut off from the fold and there be no cattle in the stalls, Yet I will exult in the LORD.*
> *I will rejoice in the God of my salvation.*
> *The LORD God is my strength, and He has made my feet like hinds' feet, and makes me walk on my high places."* NASB

When we lived in Iran the electricity would often go out, traffic was crazy and crowded, groceries were constantly short of demands; the religion was oppressive; language was always a problem and finding supplies was a significant challenge. Here was my paraphrase of the above scripture:

Hurry Up and Wait - "It shouldn't-oughta be this hard!"

"Though there be no eggs in the entire capital city of Tehran,
and no turkey found for Thanksgiving;
though the yield of our electricity should fail and
the grocery store has no grape jelly for the kids;
though our stateside phone connection is filled with static
so that I can't hear my mom's voice
and there has been no milk for days,
Yet I will exult in the LORD.
I will rejoice that we found Cheerios this morning!
The LORD God is my strength, and He has made me find a taxi
before my hyper five-year-old son grew weary and went berserk,
And He makes me walk home safely to our apartment."

Lord God, please help us stand and watch as You work in our lives. Help us keep silent while You go about Your work. Please help us take "every thought captive to the obedience of Christ." Reveal to us Your deliverance, Lord, as we thank You in advance! In the name of Christ Jesus, amen.

Day 3 ~ *"But those who wait on the LORD shall renew their strength. They shall mount up with wings like eagles; they shall run and not be weary; they shall walk and not faint" (Isaiah 40:31).*

O, Lord, we are learning, but there is so much resistance against us from the world and our enemy, Satan. We do ask to be renewed in Your strength, that Your Holy Spirit help us wait upon You. Help our hearts to wait upon You for there is no other. Help us crawl up into Your lap and rest in Your presence. In God we trust. Amen.

Day 2 ended learning and practicing how to "stand firm" in the salvation of the LORD; asking God to shine His beautiful presence into our hearts which casts out the darkness of evil. Those are not easy things to do. Those are things that we learn by practicing and repeating over and over; in effect, "taking every thought captive to the obedience of Christ" (2 Corinthians 10:5, NASB), and diligently "practicing the presence of God." When we ask God to illuminate areas of our heart so that evil and dark things cannot abide there, we then begin to feel calm, at rest, peaceful. Philippians 4:7 says that it is a "peace that surpasses *all* understanding." When that peace is within me, I am at rest. Do you feel that way?

Strongholds are first established in the mind, and that is why 2 Corinthians 10:4–6 tells us to take every thought captive to the obedience of Christ. Behind every stronghold is also a lie – a place of personal bondage where God's Word has been subjugated to any unscriptural idea or personally confused belief that is held to be true. Behind every lie is a fear, and behind every fear is an idol. *Idols are established wherever there exists a failure to trust in the provisions of God* that are ours through Jesus Christ.[5]

How have you practiced bringing your thoughts to the Lord and practiced being in His presence?

The Exodus 14 scripture memorized yesterday speaks of a time when the LORD struck Egypt with ten plagues, then struck with death all the firstborn in the land of Egypt (sparing Israelite lives but not Egyptians), the Israelites had received gold, silver, brass and precious jewels from the Egyptians, and Pharaoh finally released them to leave Egypt.

Over a million Israelites are now standing at the Red Sea with a rugged, older Moses at the front of the group, when approaching from behind them come Pharaoh and his soldiers with horses and chariots because Pharaoh has changed his mind. Remember now that the Israelites have been in servitude for over 400 years, have just experienced freedom, and are now trapped between the angry, warring Pharaoh and the waters of the Red Sea. Surely you would have been terrified, too, and thus, they are crying out to Moses for help. Moses answers the people with Exodus 14:13–14 in a great belief of trust, not knowing what God would do for them. In verse 15 God tells Moses to quit crying out to Him, but instead to tell the children of Israel to go forward. He then tells Moses to lift up his rod and stretch out his hand over the sea to divide it, and all the Israelites walk across the sea on dry land. Amazing!

Dr. David Jeffress, author and pastor of First Baptist Church, Dallas, Texas, calls this a *"Red Sea Moment*: An impossible situation through which God delivers you." Red Sea Moments:

- Are designed by God for a distinct purpose in your life.
- Are necessary for our growth because we are forced to trust in God instead of ourselves, others or circumstances.
- Prepare us for future challenges by heading us through – not out of – the situation. Sometimes He will take us out of the situation, but *usually He supernaturally leads us through them.*[6]

Is that not incredible? As if the experiences of ten plagues, the angel of death and Pharaoh allowing them to exit Egypt after plundering the wealth of the Egyptians of gold, silver, brass and jewels were not enough, the Israelites have now begun a journey to the Promised Land with an inspiring, awesome, miraculous water show! But almost immediately they began to grumble about everything – legitimate complaints, but obviously the previously mentioned miracles and wonders were short-lived in their minds. Ever been there? Haven't we all!

They set up camp and Moses treks up the mountain where in 40 days (and many chapters of Exodus later) he receives the Ten Commandments, instructions for the tabernacle and other important points of instruction from God Himself. But at base camp, 40 days of freedom for a people who have had no freedom for over 400 years proves too much to bear. They think Moses is not returning, so they melt their plundered gold into an idol and party so hardy that God says in His wrath He will destroy them all!

Moses petitions God to spare this people that He has miraculously brought out of bondage, reminding God of His covenant promises to Abraham, Isaac and Jacob; that they would be His descendants and inherit His promised land *forever.* So ". . . the LORD relented from the harm which He said He would do to His people" (Exodus 32:14), and He said to Moses, "My Presence will go with you, and I will give you *rest*" (Exodus 33:14). The *rest* God is talking about here is not a good night's forty winks. This rest is to give comfort, confident trust, and freedom from anxiety, disturbance, and fear. What a forgiving God!

Take a look at Matthew 11:28–30 in the New Testament. These verses speak of the *anapauo* mentioned in an earlier lesson: a cessation from work, an intermission. Write out these verses and prayerfully meditate over them:

Don't those verses make you *want* to learn from Him so you can have rest for your soul? Do you think that part of that learning is trusting Him to "lean not on your own understanding"? (Proverbs 3: 5). Notice that the Matthew 11 verses instruct us to "take My yoke upon you and learn from Me." With His yoke, He will be guiding us – not us taking the lead! He will direct our paths, He will guide; "He who calls you will be faithful, who also will do it." It's those verses again from 1 Thessalonians 5:23–24: If we trust Him to handle the work for us, the "God of peace Himself shall sanctify you completely. . . ." As our oldest son says, "That's what I'm talkin' about!"

Hurry Up and Wait - "It shouldn't-oughta be this hard!"

Let's study one more set of verses in Galatians 6:1–5 and some specific words before we move on: "Brethren, even if a man is caught in any trespass, you who are spiritual, *restore* such a one in a spirit of gentleness; each one looking to yourself, lest you too be tempted. Bear one another's *burden*s, and thus fulfill the law of Christ. For if anyone thinks he is something when he is nothing, he deceives himself. But let each one examine his own work, and then he will have reason for boasting in regard to himself alone, and not in regard to another. For each one shall bear his own *load*" NASB.

The word *restore* in verse 1 is like setting a broken bone back in place. Having had eight broken bones in my life since age six on, I understand the process of setting them back into place. It does take time for their proper growth and healing! The latter part of that verse reminds us not to become arrogant as we help our brother in his or her situation.

But the comparison of two words in verses 2 and 5 are the subject of our study here. The word for *burden* in verse 2 is like a ship's cargo, a massive amount of items being stored, transported, or both. Compare that *burden* to the word *load* in verse 5 which there means a word similar to backpack. It is impossible to carry a ship's cargo on our backs, but not too difficult to support a backpack. A backpack can be dealt with by prayer, discipline and help, but a ship's cargo will take us down!

Please read through Numbers 11:10–17. Moses is depressed because of the grumbling and complaining of the Israelites and he cries out to God. God answers him to gather some specific wise men around him so that ". . . He will take of the Spirit who is upon you and will put Him upon them; and they shall bear the *burden* . . . so that you shall not bear it all alone," NASB. Beloved, it is worth waiting upon God to change a ship load of cargo to a backpack!

Because God had such favor for Moses, He forgave this rebellious group of Israelites. After God had given the Law of the Ten Commandments, instructions for the tabernacle and of the priestly order and ordinances to Moses to present to the Israelites, He wanted the people then to conquer the land He had promised them. Twelve spies were sent out to see what the land was like and how the Israelites could go about conquering it. The report the spies gave upon their return was factual: the land was fruitful, the population was mixed, and the cities fortified. However, ten spies said that they should not go into the land to conquer it because the people were too strong for them. Only two said, "We should by all means go up and take possession of it, for we shall surely overcome it" (Numbers 13: 30, NASB).

The congregation then began to whine, moan and grumble that they would all be killed. In our family when any of us began to whine like that we called it "O, woe is me! We'll never make it." One child did it so often we called him Eeyore (from *Winnie the Pooh*). The LORD was ready to strike down the Israelites after all that grumbling. Please take the time to read this long passage of Numbers 14:1–38 to close out today's lesson. It will help set the stage and our understanding for the next lesson.

✪ Begin to memorize Psalm 37:7a by reading it over and over. Also, go back and review verses you have already started memorizing. Soak them into your memory. The Lord will bring them to your mind at the least expected times!

Heavenly Father, please forgive us for the incessant whining we grumble throughout our days. May Your Spirit fill us with an appreciation for the blessings and favor You show to us. We ask You to grant us a spirit of grace. Please help us to think "outside the box" so we can begin to see things from Your perspective. In the name of Jesus, amen.

Hurry Up and Wait - "It shouldn't-oughta be this hard!"

<u>Day 4</u> ~ *"For yet a little while and the wicked shall be no more; indeed, you will look carefully for his place, but it shall be NO more. But the meek shall inherit the earth, and shall delight themselves in the abundance of peace" (Psalm 37:10-11).*

*LORD, we pray that You would shine Your light within our hearts, minds, and spirits by the power of the Holy Spirit. Let Your light illuminate the hidden crevices within us where the "wicked" and the "Egyptians" tend to hide, as well as the strongholds that hold and support them. We **CHOOSE** to trust You today as Your Light displaces the evil thoughts and patterns, whether they are conscious to us or unconscious. Help us "come to ourselves" so that we realize we are children of the King, and we can delight in the abundance of Your peace. Amen.*

We ended the last session with God's declaration that the adult Israelites would not enter into the land of Promise, nor have the promise of His rest. God then turned them away from a quick two-week route to the Promised Land, and they spent 40 years wandering in the wilderness (one year for each of the 40 days the spies were in the land). Everyone who disbelieved that God would give that land to them died in the wilderness; only Joshua, Caleb and the younger generation actually crossed into the promises God had for them.

Now let's jump to the New Testament to read from the first and second chapters of Hebrews which demonstrate <u>*all that Christ is and what He has done for us*</u>:

- He fulfilled all prophecies as the Son of God
- He is the Word of God
- He has sat down at the right hand of God, showing His completion and God's acceptance of His sacrificial work
- He is exalted above the angels
- He is all Righteousness
- He is the Creator of the heavens and the earth
- He is crowned with all glory and honor
- All things are in subjection under His feet

- He is not ashamed to call us brethren
- He is in the midst of our assemblies singing praises to God, putting His trust in God
- He accomplished destruction of the devil and delivered those who believe in Christ from the fear of death (The destruction of Satan does not mean he is annihilated, but that his power is curbed in the lives of believers committed to Christ.)
- He took on the nature of mankind, not the nature of angels
- As our High Priest, He is our representative to God
- Because He physically, mentally and emotionally suffered for us, He is able to aid those who are tempted
- As an apostle, Christ represents His people[7]

Therefore, (which my friend Suzanne says we need to see what the "therefore" is there for) today we will read in Hebrews 3:1–19 concerning that lack of rest. Please turn to that passage and take time to read it slowly and carefully, "chewing" on the verses because they are deep.

The "therefore" is there because of the above list that shows who Christ is and what He has done for us. The first several verses of chapter 3 tell us that Jesus Christ was faithful to God who appointed Him and thereby is counted worthy of *more* glory than Moses because Moses was a servant and a member of the house; Christ, however, is both the builder *and* the Lord of the house. He is the fulfillment of all that Moses foreshadowed.[8]

Use Hebrews 3:7–11 to list at least three reasons why God showed His wrath toward the Israelites:

Verses 7–19 show very specifically that the ultimate reason the Israelites could not enter into the Promised Land was because of their unbelief (v. 19). Unbelief is caused by a hardened heart, which is caused by the deceitfulness of sin; departing from the living

Hurry Up and Wait – "It shouldn't-oughta be this hard!"

God.⁹ When we abandon our Christian faith, we are turning away from God. Enjoying a living, active, continuing faith in Jesus Christ requires a continuance in faith, an active relationship, not just a one-time experience. A relationship requires activity on both sides: some inquiry, communication, and obedience.

The author of Hebrews is trying to show that their unbelief in the wilderness – their spirit of disobedience – resulted in the wrath of God keeping them from the promised rest in the new land God wanted to give them. This wrath may seem harsh to some, but God's desire of this Hebrew people He had called into being through Abraham, then Isaac and then Jacob was because He wanted a people set apart unto Himself. He could have called any nation, any people; but He had called an idol-worshipping, Gentile named Abram who did not know this God, telling him that if he would believe in God: "I will make you exceedingly fruitful; and I will make nations of you, and kings shall come from you. And I will establish My covenant between Me and you and your descendants after you in their generations, for an everlasting covenant, to be God to you and your descendants after you" (Genesis 17:6–7).

Look up and read 1 Peter 2:1–10, then write down "who you are" as mentioned in vv. 5, 9 and 10:

1 Peter 2:9 tells us that God calls us "a chosen generation, a royal priesthood, a holy nation, His own special people . . . ." God's desire was to have a people set apart from all other nations, holy unto Him. That requires belief and obedience. Dear One, that is still His desire!

When we as believers of Jesus Christ, God's son of our salvation, believe that He can do what He says He will *and* can do through His word, then, with obedient hearts we can choose to obey Him. *We want to choose to search Him out*, to search His word, the Bible, to know and learn and to receive His wisdom. When we do that we begin to heal, to mature and grow in our faith. It is in those processes of obedience that we are blessed – and <u>we receive *rest* for our souls</u>!

Look up the following verses, writing them out first, and then paraphrasing them:

Psalm 130:5–6

Lamentations 3:25

Isaiah 8:17

Sometimes the condition of our heart separates us from the Lord, and there is an interval of time we wait before we return to His presence. The length of that interval is related to the level of our obedience.

Several verses confirm that our hearts are His when we become believers. The apostle Paul speaks to believers in Romans 4:6–8 when he quotes (King) David as saying "Blessing is upon the man to whom God reckons righteousness apart from works; . . . *Blessed is the man whose sin the LORD will not take into account*" NASB.

The apostle John also speaks of our position of righteousness in Christ in 1 John 3:19–21 by saying God is greater than our heart. We may be too self-condemning or too lenient when we look at our own lives, but God assures us that He is all-knowing and all-loving.

Hurry Up and Wait - "It shouldn't-oughta be this hard!"

✪ Read Psalm 37:10–11 that began today's lesson. Pray over these verses and ask God to help you trust Him to begin the eradication of anything dark or wicked that you *choose* to surrender to Him.

O, LORD, we ask that Your Holy Spirit will reveal the hidden things in our hearts that are hindering us from inheriting your peace and experiencing your rest. Please help us to <u>choose</u> to surrender those dark things so Your Light will move in. We thank You in advance for what you are going to do. In Your precious name, Jesus, amen!

Trust without Borders

<u>Day 5</u> ~ *"Therefore the Lord will wait, that He may be gracious to you; and therefore He will be exalted, that He may have mercy on you. For the Lord is a God of justice; blessed are all those who wait for Him" (Isaiah 30:18).*

Lord God, All week we have studied on how to wait for You, and this verse speaks of how You will wait for us. Thank You! Thank You that You are gracious and merciful to us as children of the King. Help us, we pray, to learn to trust You as a just God. In the name of Jesus, amen.

Yesterday's Day 4 lesson ended with Hebrews 3:19 specifically showing that the ultimate reason the Israelites could not enter into the Promised Land was because of their unbelief.

Remember from Day 2 that Webster defines *rest* as lying down, especially as in sleep; to cease from action or motion; to be free from anxiety or disturbance; to remain confident: **TRUST**; place of stillness, repose, consolation, peace, rest; a quiet place; the condition of restfulness; to rest, soothe, settle down, comfort.

Read slowly and carefully now in Hebrews 4:1–13 about the *rest* God offers us. There is a promise of entering His rest that is not an easy or obvious one, but it is a precious one. The "promise" of God of entering His rest is through Jesus Christ. By the grace of His forgiveness and the mercy extended to us by His death, we have the choice of receiving Him as our personal Savior, thereby receiving the promise of His rest.

Since Jesus is the promise of entering God's rest to we who believe (v. 3a), what is keeping *you* from receiving that rest?

In Hebrews 3:7–11 Israel tested the Lord God and because of their hardened hearts chose not to enter the land promised to them. Those verses and example become a solemn warning to us as believing

Christians to not pass up what God has offered us through His son, Jesus Christ. In Christ, the believer who totally surrenders to the lordship of Jesus and is filled with His Spirit will experience His rest. This rest found in Jesus Christ is through the grace of His salvation through faith, not by works or doing good works to be good enough.[10] That is trust. It began when Jesus spoke these words to His disciples:

"Gathering them together, He commanded them not to leave Jerusalem, but **to wait** for what the Father had promised, 'Which,' He said, 'you heard of from Me; for John baptized with water, but you will be baptized with the Holy Spirit not many days from now. . . . But you shall receive power when the Holy Spirit has come upon you . . .' " (Acts 1:4–5 and 8, NASB).

Hebrews 4:9–10 says, "There remains therefore a rest for the people of God. *For he who has entered His rest has himself also ceased from his works as God did from His*." There it is. That is restful to me because I don't have to work to be good enough for God to like me, choose me, accept me or love me. The Holy Spirit within me works powerfully for me . . . so I can rest!

Pastor Duane Sheriff of Duane Sheriff Ministries says, "I am nothing, I have nothing, I can do nothing, I know nothing; but with God I am everything," which he draws from verses in 1 Corinthians 2. Without God we are nothing – we have no rest. With God we have everything, including rest! Some of us after getting saved and receiving His power then take over and do everything ourselves. How's that working out for you?[11]

Take some time to chew on the Hebrews 4 verses and journal your thoughts on this rest:

The one who trusts in Christ rests in what God has done for him. He has ceased striving to achieve salvation by his own efforts, and in daily life has begun to learn a dependence upon the Holy Spirit's help.[12] Remember that the heart converted from mistrust to trust in the irreversible forgiveness of Jesus Christ is redeemed from the power of fear,[13] as we saw in 2 Timothy 1:7: "For God has not given us a spirit of fear, but of power and of love and of a sound mind."

Hebrews 4:11 challenges us to be diligent to enter that rest so we don't fall as the Israelites did by disobedience. How do you think verse 12 explains how to keep from falling into disobedience?

This verse encourages us to confess the word of God to keep us from falling into disobedience. In this verse the Bible describes itself: "The word of God is living and powerful." The term for *word* here is the Greek word *logos*, which commonly indicates the expression of a complete idea and is used in referring to the Holy Scriptures.[14] How awesome it is to know that the word of God is living and powerful, sharper than any two-edged sword; that it pierces and is a discerner of thoughts and intents!

✪ In closing today read this powerful passage from Isaiah 43:1–21 and think on the awesome deity of the God of all creation:

Hurry Up and Wait - "It shouldn't-oughta be this hard!"

¹ ...But now, thus says the Lord, your Creator, O Jacob, and He who formed you, O Israel, "Do not fear, for I have redeemed you; I have called you by name; you are Mine!

² "When you pass through the waters, I will be with you; and through the rivers, they will not overflow you. When you walk through the fire, you will not be scorched, nor will the flame burn you.

³ "For I am the Lord your God, the Holy One of Israel, your Savior; I have given Egypt as your ransom, Cush and Seba in your place.

⁴ "Since you are precious in My sight, since you are honored and I love you, I will give other men in your place and other peoples in exchange for your life.

⁵ "Do not fear, for I am with you; I will bring your offspring from the east, and gather you from the west.

⁶ "I will say to the north, 'Give them up!' and to the south, 'Do not hold them back.' Bring My sons from afar and My daughters from the ends of the earth,

⁷ Everyone who is called by My name, and whom I have created for My glory, whom I have formed, even whom I have made."

⁸ Bring out the people who are blind, even though they have eyes, and the deaf, even though they have ears.

⁹ All the nations have gathered together So that the peoples may be assembled. Who among them can declare this and proclaim to us the former things? Let them present their witnesses that they may be justified, or let them hear and say, "It is true."

¹⁰ "You are My witnesses," declares the Lord, "and My servant whom I have chosen, so that you may know and believe Me and understand that I am He. Before Me there was no God formed, and there will be none after Me.

¹¹ "I, even I, am the Lord, and there is no savior besides Me.

¹² "It is I who have declared and saved and proclaimed, and there was no strange *god* among you; so you are My witnesses," declares the Lord, "and I am God.

¹³ "Even from eternity I am He, and there is none who can deliver out of My hand; I act and who can reverse it?"

¹⁴ Thus says the Lord your Redeemer, the Holy One of Israel, "For your sake I have sent to Babylon, and will bring them all down as fugitives, even the Chaldeans, into the ships in which they rejoice.

¹⁵ "I am the Lord, your Holy One; the Creator of Israel, your King."

¹⁶ Thus says the Lord, Who makes a way through the sea and a path through the mighty waters,

¹⁷ Who brings forth the chariot and the horse, the army and the mighty man (they will lie down together and not rise again; they have been quenched and extinguished like a wick):

¹⁸ "Do not call to mind the former things, or ponder things of the past.

¹⁹ "Behold, I will do something new, now it will spring forth; will you not be aware of it? I will even make a roadway in the wilderness, rivers in the desert.

²⁰ "The beasts of the field will glorify Me, the jackals and the ostriches, because I have given waters in the wilderness and rivers in the desert, to give drink to My chosen people.

²¹ "The people whom I formed for Myself will declare My praise." NASB

We adopted two of our children while living in Iran and an interpreter working in Jimmy's office helped us with *ALL* the adoption legalities and necessary interpreting, spending hours on our children's behalf. We lost contact with him for over 35 years but recently he found us through the internet. He was not a Christian when we knew him years ago, but he and his family escaped from Iran during revolutionary times and he became a Christian during that time. He said he had always been impressed with the joy we displayed to him and the gratefulness of our hearts. During a very dangerous part of his escape while on a night train he bowed his head in weariness. A "man" sat across from him and began asking him if he knew God. He answered "yes" but the man challenged him that he did not. Majid shared what was happening, how he had lost almost all their money when it fell into the water while they were crossing into a boat, how their passports had been taken by some smugglers and that he had no hope. The man encouraged him and said, "Your passports will be returned to you, you will be accepted into the country where you seek asylum, and the money you have will be sufficient for you." Then the man offered to pray for our friend who welcomed the prayer, but when Majid opened his eyes the man was nowhere to be found. It was at that moment that Majid became a Christian, and when he shared this information with us during his visit to the states recently the above scripture from Isaiah 43:1–3a came to my mind. As I read it to him from the new Bible we had just given him, he wept passionately because it sounded like what the "man" had prophesied to him. Isn't God incredible? His wonders never cease to amaze me! [15]

Testimony of Majid Babakhanian, Fellow Brother in Christ Jesus!

O, Holy One, creator of the entire universe, thank You for teaching us how to wait. May we be filled with your Holy Spirit every day so that more of You fills us and less of us is there to leak out. Thank You for so lovingly pursuing us. You are precious, Jesus! Amen.

~ Chapter 3 ~

Inheritance: Blessings of the "Now and Not Yet"

The Bedroom

We call it "the Bedroom," a little spot on the curve of the driveway where our dogs, and sometimes the cats, have found the first light of the sun on cold winter mornings. We will glance out the windows during our busy bed and breakfast prep and there they will be, all huddled together in one little spot of sun shining through the trees. Later, as the area widens with the waking of the morning, they will move over closer to the yard, stretched out full body and basking in the sun's warm glow.

Often on overcast mornings I see them sitting there together, shivering, seemingly wondering why it is not warm "in the bedroom." Bentley the bent-tailed Beagle will run off to play, bay or torment the cats in a chase. But Miss Allie, at 16 (or around 100 in dog years), just sits patiently and waits for the warm glow she loves so much. We've had many cloudy, misty, rainy days this winter, and I've seen her give it a chance, only later to mosey toward the garage where we keep a warming light on for her. I watched her this weekend; it was 40° when we woke up, 40° at lunch, and 40° when the sun set.

Allie sat there for a long time; I'm sure with memories of the warm "bedroom." She would look around, shift position and stare off to the direction from where the bright light usually comes. Bentley came and went, along with both cats, while she so patiently waited. As I rinsed coffee pots, refilling with water for the next pot to perk, I would check on her – still there; still waiting. Finally by the time breakfast was served I saw her wandering toward the garage. She had given the wait a good try, but the chill and mist had finally gotten to her.

I'm often like Allie, liking the warmth and comfort of doing the same things. Often I "sit, go, and do" in the same way – waiting when it doesn't happen in the normal spin of things. This year our congregation was encouraged to have more than a "view" of our lives for the New Year. Instead, in this year have a vision, and not only a vision, but write it down and pray over the vision. It could be more than one thing – but write anything received down and pray over them, expecting answers. This process is from the Bible in Habakkuk 2:1–3:

1. "I will stand on my guard post and station myself on the rampart; and I will keep watch to see what He will speak to me and how I will reply when I am reproved.
2. The LORD answered me and said: 'Record the vision and write it on tablets that the one who reads it may run.
3. For the vision is yet for the appointed time; it hastens toward the goal, and it will not fail. *Though it tarries, wait for it*, for it will certainly come, it will not delay. . . .' " NASB.
4. Early this January I *did* write down my "vision," a vision for myself, my family members, and our bed and breakfast. I have returned to the "writings on the tablet" many times, repeatedly praying over them. The amazing thing is that within days answers began to come – major answers; awesome answers!

It is good to sit in the "bedroom" warmed by the glow of the sun. There are also times to move on. Write down the vision; pray over the words and wait – for it will certainly come!

Pamela Alexander [1]

Inheritance: Blessings of the "Now and Not Yet"

Day 1 ~ *"Wait on the LORD and keep His way, and He shall exalt you to inherit the land . . ." (Psalm 37:34a).*

Abba, Father, we are Your children, adopted into Your family because of the work Jesus accomplished on the cross. Everything is possible for You. We are saved by grace because of Your extended mercy to us. We were worthy of none of those things but because of them we are now partakers of all the glorious riches of Your Kingdom. Thank You for washing us clean and saving a place at Your table for us. Exalt us, O LORD, to inherit Your land. In Jesus' precious name, amen.

When my parents reached their early 70's they took the wonderful and careful initiative of drawing up and organizing one document of trust for their wills, finances, home, land, vehicles, investments, insurance, etc. It consolidated everything and everyone into one place of management. In that process they discussed the appointment of the executor of their wills and the Trust, eventually appointing me as the Executor, Power of Attorney and Power of Health Attorney. Approximately five years before Dad's death he began turning responsibilities of that Trust over to me as the Executor/Power of Attorney. Fortunately for my two sisters and me, we never had to call those titles into effect for over sixteen years! Knowing all the details and having all the files and information in order made my job much easier than if no preparations had been completed. For once in my life I was so very thankful for my engineer-minded, organized, detailed Dad, because my obsessively organized Mom knew nothing about the financials!

For several years my responsibilities were next to nothing, more centered on their health care and chauffeuring them to medical appointments, and gathering everything for taxes. While it was very convenient to have everything consolidated, as tax prep became my responsibility I realized how disjointed things actually were. There was a clause in the Trust stating that if my Father "became unwilling or unable" to execute decisions they would fall to Mom. Mom promptly told me she was unwilling, so the entire can of worms fell to my lot immediately. We had to update the Power of Attorney and send that paperwork to every investment company. Another "rabbit trail" took over a year of calls, paperwork and deep prayers trusting God to refund the money of an investment company sued for selling its product to my Dad and others that were too old for that type of insurance.

The responsibilities of large amounts of paperwork, taxes, learning the lingo and re-mailing "this-that-and-the other" was not only time consuming but extremely overwhelming! There were also "Sanballots" along the way (from the book of Nehemiah 2:19 and on), but thankfully I also had great "Nehemiah's" to help me, and we fought side by side with one hand on the financial info and one hand on our weapons (prayer & God's Word!). Many encouragers arose along the way including friends, workout buddies, church members, my husband and our tax preparer. After Dad and Mom both died, the process of handling their financial details was much less complicated (not that it is ever easy!). I was encouraged when the tax preparer told me that he had taken several months off after his brother died just to work on his brother's finances – and he has a master's degree in taxes!

"See, God has come to save me. I will trust in Him and not be afraid. The Lord God is my strength and my song; He has given me victory" (Isaiah 12:2 TLB).

Receiving an inheritance is almost always bitter sweet: sorrowful that the loved one is no longer with us, but thankful that a blessing has been passed on. One of the Old Testament Hebrew words for "inherit" is *nachal* meaning: inherit, inheritance, possess, have, divide, heritage, possession.[2] Our English equivalent adds: obtain by inheritance, be an heir.

In the *Hurry Up and Wait* chapter we studied in Hebrews 3 and 4 about how the Israelites forfeited on the *rest* that God had planned for them. Let's "back up the bus" and read some background of how the Israelites "came to be" by turning to Genesis 11:27–31 and continuing into chapter 12:1–8.

Inheritance: Blessings of the "Now and Not Yet"

Abram burst onto the scene about five generations after the famous Tower of Babel and the splitting up of earth's one-language civilization. Now speaking different languages and dispersed all over the earth, Abram's family (known later as Abraham) went out from Ur of the Chaldeans to the land of Canaan to dwell in Haran (current-day Syria). There are some very specific, power-packed instructions from the LORD to Abram in chapter 12:1–3. Read those verses carefully again and list the four parts of the LORD's instructions of verse 1:

1.

2.

3.

4.

How would you have reacted, or what would you have done if you had heard these powerful, awesome words from the God of all creation? Be honest . . . could you just pack up and "go to a land that I will show you"? Journal your thoughts:

Years ago when Jimmy and I were in our mid-twenties and our first child was four years old, Jimmy came home from work to tell me of the possibility of his corporation setting up an office in a middle eastern country. At that time it was not a much-talked-about country (although it is now on the nightly news), and the move for us was still just a bleep on the possibility window. But I knew instantly in my heart that we were going. That spring he would come home day after day saying "it's still up in the air." By June I began buying larger sized clothes for our son, stocking up for him, and making various kinds of lists and plans. One day he came home with a large notebook detailing all sorts of information about this country as well as instructions for obtaining our passports and work visas. We were going! Although it was to a totally unknown part of the world for us, we had expectant faith that we were supposed to go. That time of my life gives me a tiny inkling of how Abram must have felt. The impressiveness of the call of God trumps the fears of the unknown – *if* one has the faith to trust God! If it was important enough for God to choose us out of many other families, then my God was big enough to carry us through the two years of being stationed there, and for whatever reasons He had planned for us.

Abram's family worshipped other gods, but the LORD God Jehovah called him out by name to give him these instructions. It must have been incredibly awesome because Abram changed in his faith from believing many gods of the day to believing the one, true, living God. He is later called the father of faith because he exhibited exemplary faith through-out his entire life, growing steadily in his faith even though he did not see immediate fulfillment. He put his hope in the God who spoke to him. He put his trust in the God of all creation. Mark your place in Genesis 12 and go to Hebrews 11:1 in the New Testament. Take time to write the one-sentence verse here:

Faith is akin to the Latin *fidere*, to trust. It is belief, a loyalty to and trust in God, trusting Him in a childlike manner. Fidelity to the way of trust will lead to the same place it took Job[3]: *"Though He slay me, yet will I trust Him"* (Job 13:15). Faith is a firm belief or conviction in something for which there is no visible proof. In this verse it is exhibiting complete confidence concerning a future reward. Try your hand at paraphrasing the Hebrews 11:1 verse:

Inheritance: Blessings of the "Now and Not Yet"

Having a conviction to believe in things unseen that represent God, His glory, His purposes and His calling for us is not easy. The topic could be and has been many a complete book on its own, but for us it will be a launching into the understanding of the call God ushered unto Abram and the "why" that made Abram trust in Him. Somewhere along the way, in the life of the maturing Christian, faith combined with hope grows into trust.[4]

Now go back to Genesis 12:2–3 where God moved from instructions into blessings He explains to Abram. List the blessings of verse two here:

1.

2.

3.

4.

Whoohoo! I'm in! The Hebrew word for bless is *barach* (bah-rahch), meaning to bless, salute congratulate, thank, praise; to kneel down.[5] In Old Testament days and even into more recent centuries, people would kneel when preparing to bless or receive blessings, whether to their king on his throne or to God in heaven. A blessing can confer prosperity or happiness upon. Take some time to journal your thoughts on how Abram must have pondered such magnanimous blessings!

These blessings can't be passed over lightly and obviously God doesn't dole out "I will make you a great nation" to just anyone. But this, my friend, is where God began to choose a people set apart, a people holy unto Him. From this man Abram came forth a people, a nation, that God would call His own. Verse 3 finalizes the word from the LORD:

1.

2.

3.

With these verses God charged Abram to leave the idols of his family and his country so that God could make him and his long lineage of descendants into a holy people, a messianic nation which ultimately would bring salvation to *all* the families of the earth, to *anyone* who would call upon the name of the LORD.

✪ End today's lesson by memorizing Hebrews 11:1. Don't panic; it's short. Deeply consider how your belief in God and His son, Jesus, is affected by this verse. What is the "substance" that you hope for? What is the "evidence of things not seen"? How deep is your faith? Do you trust the evidence that is not seen?

LORD God, we want to believe in You. Please help our unbelief. Help us examine the substance that we hope for. Reveal to our spirits the evidence of things not seen. In Jesus' name, amen.

Inheritance: Blessings of the "Now and Not Yet"

Day 2 ~ ". . . but those who wait on the LORD, they shall inherit the earth" (Psalm 37:9).

O, LORD God, You have made the heavens and the earth by Your great power. You bless those who bend their knees to You, so in humble obedience we bow. Help us to understand the blessings You bestow to us. In our Father's name, amen.

Today return to Genesis 12:4 which says Abram departed as the LORD had spoken to him. He was 75 years old. Not a young rooster to begin the journey to a new land, for new purposes, to hear from an unknown God and decide to serve Him with all your heart. Quite a feat if you ask me! He journeyed to the land of Canaan where God spoke again, (v. 7): "To your descendants I will give this land." I love it when God confirms a word that He has spoken to me. For example, this book was written on trust, but it always helped me to have confirmation from those closest to me. Amen? Amen!

What does the second part of verse 7 say?

Building an altar to the LORD is not something that we as Christians do anymore because Jesus offered Himself on the altar of the cross for each of us, once for all, so that we no longer are required to do so. However, I have learned in my life that when a major word is spoken to me by the LORD, it is important for me to write it down, preferably in a journal so I can refer back to it. Be encouraged to journal specific words and instructions, or special prayers you feel God has emphasized to you, like Joshua 24:21–28 that speak of remembering what God has done:

Your journal will be like the stone in verse 27 to help be a witness so you won't deny that it happened, that God spoke to you or that you had a dream, a vision, or a prophecy spoken over you. Those written remembrances will let you depart to your own inheritance; depart to the riches and rich blessings that God has in store for you.

Read through 1 Samuel 7:10–12, especially verse 12 and write out your thoughts.

Samuel took a stone and named it Ebenezer, saying, "Thus far the LORD has helped us." Ebenezer means "stone of help." I call these kinds of journal entries "stones of remembrance." It seems we humans have very, very short memories when it comes to remembering instructions from God, but loooonnnnng memories when it comes to hurts, negative things, and not being willing to forgive. Frequently I have re-read journal entries of words the LORD has given me. So many times I have been encouraged; many, many times those words have breathed new life into me, saving me from the lies the enemy is whispering, speaking or shouting all around me. We have been called to be obedient! We can't hold on to the mountain of the problem – but we can hold on to a stone, a rock, a piece of the mountain – with all the strength we have. How are you holding on? What is God doing in your life today? When your problem seems as big as or bigger than a mountain, call out to Him and say, "God just _give me a piece_ of the mountain!"

1. What are you entrusting to Him?
2. Take inventory of what you trust Him for today.
3. Acknowledge emotions. They are God-given.
4. As challenges arise, find a moment alone to pray. This enables peace to overflow you.
5. **Trust is a decision.** God will push you back from doubt to strengthen you to believe.
6. Trust is built on stones of remembrance on what He's done.

Inheritance: Blessings of the "Now and Not Yet"

> 7. Trust is "holding on when everything around you is letting go. An active decision."[6]

Years of Abram's life pass through several more chapters, when in Genesis 15:1–5 God gives him assurance. Read over these five verses for a few moments.

Abram's name was eventually changed to Abraham when God confirmed his everlasting covenant and blessings to him at the young age of ninety-nine! He received an awesome, fantastic inheritance that was beyond imagination! Read about this amazing covenant in Genesis 17:1–8 before we continue on.

Since our bed and breakfast is in the country we can often enjoy some incredibly beautiful views of the stars, the moon and planets, and even shooting stars. It's amazingly different than when we lived near downtown Dallas! How would it have registered with you if God had told you your descendants would be as numerous as the stars?

God did give a son to Abraham and Sarah when he was one hundred years old! (Genesis 21) But God tested Abraham with a test of ultimate faith that he was to lay Isaac, his only son by Sarah, on an altar to God as a sacrifice. I must confess I don't think I could have done it. As strong as I think I am, I honestly don't know if my faith would have been strong enough to obey, unless God had audibly spoken to me as He did to Abraham. But Abraham did believe. God called out to him to stop, and then provided a ram in the thicket.

The basic premise of biblical trust is the conviction that God wants us to grow, unfold, and experience fullness of life. However, this kind of trust is acquired only gradually and most often through a series of crises and trials. Through the indescribable anguish on Mount Moriah with his son Isaac, Abraham learned that the God who had called him to hope against hope was eminently reliable, and that the only thing expected of him was *unconditional trust*.[7]

This great old man models the essence of trust in the Hebrew and Christian scriptures: *to be convinced of the reliability of God.*[8]

Anytime you make a decision to act on faith in something God has called you to do, the enemy will most certainly come against you. But if you keep your faith in the ONE who called you to do it, He will be strengthening you to do it. You will continue to grow, and God will continue to bless.

The act of trust is a ruthless act. Search your heart for the Isaac in your life – name it and then place it on the altar as an offering to the Lord and you will know the meaning of Abrahamic trust.[9] Scriptures say that Abram believed God. Find and write out the following two verses so we can discuss them:

Genesis 15:6

Galatians 3:6

God took into account, or added up, everything that Abram's belief meant to Him. When God added it all – summed it all up – God determined it was equal to righteousness. Wow!

Is our belief, when added up, equal to righteousness? Is my belief, when added up, equal to righteousness? Is your belief, when added up, equal to righteousness? To paraphrase the prophet Daniel in his book, "You have been weighed in the balance and found lacking . . . ." – unless we are believers in the Lord Jesus Christ (Daniel 5:27). As Christians we have been covered over by the robe of righteousness and have Christ in us, the hope of glory!

Galatians 5:17 calls our "flesh" carnal, inbred, and worldly tendencies of fallen humankind. These inclinations are the most immediate

Inheritance: Blessings of the "Now and Not Yet"

enemy of the believer who desires to live a life under the leading and empowering of the Holy Spirit. The Word says the desire alone to do good is not enough to overcome our flesh (Romans 7:21). We are called to war against the flesh – it's like a tug-of-war as our fleshly body and thoughts yell out for indulgences, and the Holy Spirit draws us to righteousness.

Victory will only result when we: abide in a right relationship with our Lord Jesus (v. 25), understand that true strength is found in our weakness (2 Cor. 12:10), and continually submit to the unction and urging of the Spirit (Ephesians 5:18).[10]

In the New Testament, James 2:23 says Abraham was called "the friend of God." I want that kind of relationship with my Father, don't you? That close, personal relationship that speaks of security, rest and peace with Abba Father. Years ago our church sung a song about our old names being changed to new names we would now be called:

> *"I will change your name. You shall no longer be called wounded, outcast, lonely or afraid.*
> *I will change your name.*
> *Your new name shall be: Confidence, Joyfulness, Overcoming One; Faithfulness, Friend of God, One who seeks My Face."*

D.J. Butler © 1987 Mercy / Vineyard Publishing [11]
License Permit #168482, Music Services, Brentwood, TN

In the Day 1 lesson this week we backed up the bus to see how the Israelites were called into being by God who wanted a people holy unto Himself. In *Hurry Up and Wait* we studied how they grew as a nation in bondage in Egypt for over 400 years and escaped from that country by passing through the Red Sea, but were eventually not permitted to enter into God's rest. Now take a look at Numbers 13 and 14 for background on what happened, starting with chapter 13, reading all the verses. Don't worry if you can't pronounce all the names – we won't have a test on them.

Trust without Borders

Let's review the specific instructions of Moses in verses 18–20. Some of us may have attention deficit, but how many distinct points did Moses make in these verses? List below what you found:

Now go back to Numbers 13:1–2: "And the LORD spoke to Moses, saying, 'Send men to spy out the land of Canaan, which *I am giving to the children of Israel;*'. . . ." In verse 3 "Moses sent them from the Wilderness of Paran *according to the command of the LORD* . . . ."

What do you specifically note about the italics in the above verses?

Hopefully, you noted that *the LORD said He was giving the land*; it was His command.

So, the spies did spy out the land for forty days and returned with incredible bounty, including delicious grapes on a pole carried by two spies. Yum! Their report in verses 26 and 27 was accurate and quite positive. But then we have a downturn in verses 28 and 29. What did a spy named Caleb have to say in verse 30?

"We can do this!" Caleb gave a great pep talk to say they were well able to take the land, but then the "Negative Ten" spiraled the people down again with their remaining fearful report. To close out today's lesson you can read or review Numbers 14:1–38 that we studied in Day 3 of the *Wait* chapter. Be attentive especially to the only other positive spy, Joshua, who spoke out in verses 7–9.

✪ Now come aside and rest awhile. Give yourself time to get alone with Daddy God, Abba. Ask to come into His presence and then ask

Inheritance: Blessings of the "Now and Not Yet"

to let you hear His voice. Journal His loving responses to you and enjoy the relationship. "But those who wait on the LORD, they shall inherit the earth" (Psalm 37:9).

Daddy, we understand there is a necessary spirit of obedience in our relationship with You. But we also know there is an everlasting love that You long to pour over us. For that, we wait. Reveal that love to us in ways we have never known and help us to realize we are a "friend of God." Amen.

Day 3 ~ *"But the meek shall inherit the earth, and shall delight themselves in the abundance of peace" (Psalm 37:11).*

Heavenly Father, whose report will we believe? We admit we often feel fear because the world presses in all around us. It is so hard to think beyond what we can see, things that we know, what we can understand with our finite minds. Please help us believe in You, Creator of the universe. In the name of our Savior, Jesus, amen.

At the Crossroads

At three and four years old my nephews Branden and Brett, only nine months apart, came to live with us. Branden was a very sensitive little boy, the kind that would find the person in the room that was hurting on the inside and just go sit by them.

One Sunday we took the boys to our large, Episcopal church on a day of baptisms. Intrigued, the boys asked about them. We explained that baptism started with a decision to become part of God's family by letting Him wash away all the bad stuff we had ever done so that His Spirit could come live in us, then give our life to Jesus so He would live in our heart forever and be our King. This excited the boys so much that for months they begged us to let them be baptized so they could belong to Jesus forever! At five and six years old they were baptized in a private service, with about twenty-five witnesses, smiling ecstatically the entire time because they knew they now belonged to Jesus forever!

About a year later the boys and I were shopping for a birthday gift. I was holding Branden's sweet seven-year-old hand when he asked, "Aunt Debbie, will I ever have my own home?" He had really missed his parents that week. I answered, "Why yes, Branden! Did you know that Jesus is building a house just for you with Him in heaven and that as soon as it is ready He will come and bring you to it?" He looked at me in unbelief and said, "Jesus is building a house for ME?!" Startled by how important that

Inheritance: Blessings of the "Now and Not Yet"

was to him I responded, "Yes, Branden, He is building a house just for you." He was overwhelmed and amazed Jesus would do that just for him.

The following March many changes had happened in the boys' lives, one being their mother had come home and they were now living with her. One night Branden came over to spend the night and burst through the door saying, "AUNT DEBBIE, GOD IS IN THIS HOUSE!" I answered, "Yes Branden, God is in this house; this is His house!" He had such deep thoughts for such a little boy. When I leaned over to hug and pray for him as I tucked him in that night his body was trembling, and he said he was afraid. We prayed and he fell asleep. Later when I checked on him, I was startled to feel small tremors moving through his body. The next day I mentioned it to his mother who had also noticed them several times – so a doctor's appointment was made.

I will never forget the day of the diagnosis when the doctor had Branden, his mother and me come into the office, looked right at Branden and said, "This child is dying." Branden, sitting on my lap, looked at me with huge wide eyes and said, "Aunt Debbie am I dying?" I told him Jesus was bigger than the doctor and covered his ears, but I could not believe what I had hearing.

Branden had a rare condition that can occur when a child has a measles vaccination while their immune system is depressed. Branden apparently had a cold when he had his shots, and the antibodies of the vaccine had built up in his spinal fluid. Only seven children in the United States had this condition at this time. The room became nightmarishly ethereal, and I just needed to get him out of there.

As I began praying I felt the Lord told me He was healing Branden, but the illness progressed so quickly that within a few months Branden had become a complete invalid. He continually had several types of seizures, always about three seconds apart, except while he was sleeping. My days off were spent helping the hospice nurse bathe and care for him. I would pick up this now nine-year-old and take him outside just so he could touch the grass and see the sky. I would rock and sing *Jesus Loves Me* to him constantly as that one song gave him immediate comfort. I went home exhausted at every level, got on my knees and prayed, still hearing over and over the Lord telling me He was healing Branden.

But things just got worse. When I fasted and prayed, I always felt the Lord's reassurance that He was healing Branden. I stood on it. But soon Branden was in the hospital and his small, frail body began shutting down. The family had a counselor come to speak with me because they felt I was in denial. But I continued to stand on what I had been told by the Lord.

The following morning a nurse called to say there seemed to be a miracle they could not explain. Branden was sitting up eating and talking with everyone, and all of his symptoms seemed to be reversing. As I hung up the phone a vision went before my eyes of Jesus and Branden in heaven with their backs to me. Jesus had his hands outstretched, showing him all of heaven. Branden started jumping up and down, his head bobbing all around and I heard him say, "This is so cool, man!" and he took off running for heaven as fast as he could. Jesus laughed over Branden's great delight!

As I came out of the vision I thought, "No, that can't be right. I just got this phone call from the nurse saying that his illness is reversing." By the next morning everything had changed again and Branden was dying. I was briefly allowed to see him, but he was gone within five minutes. I had to make a split second decision: God was still who He said He was and even though I did not understand, I would worship Him and choose to trust Him; or ~ God had let me down, had not met my expectations, and therefore I could not trust Him anymore. I chose the first.

God is who He says He is and He is faithful! Branden saw his home in that vision and I know he is OK, healed and running all over heaven! When I get to heaven and get to be with him again, he will be able to tell me about all the things he has been learning. I don't have to understand all of God's ways and I never will. But "though He slay me, yet I will trust in Him" (Job 13:15, KJV).

Debbie Morris, Kingdom Culture Ministry, Dallas, Texas[12]

Branden believed in Jesus for salvation, trusting in Him with the knowledge that the Lord was building him a house in eternity. After being diagnosed with his illness, knowing he had a heavenly home gave him comfort as he grew weaker and closer to his death. Branden believed God and received a great inheritance! Debbie also trusted

Inheritance: Blessings of the "Now and Not Yet"

God, making a choice to believe Him even when the healing was to be an ultimate healing and not an earthly one as she thought she had understood. She, too, knows her inheritance is in eternity and not here on earth.

In Matthew 5:5 Jesus said, "Blessed are the meek, for they shall inherit the earth." Usually we think of a meek person as being mousy, weak and quiet. The word meek, however, means *power under control*. When we use *His* power under the control of the Holy Spirit, "we will inherit the earth!" Today we will see how two of those twelve spies used their meekness to inherit the earth.

Yesterday in Numbers 13 we read of ten spies who gave a fearful, negative report about conquering the land of Canaan. One spy, Caleb, spoke out positively saying they would be able to conquer the land promised to them. The only other spy to speak *positive* words, Joshua, spoke out in Chapter 14:7–9. The highlights of those verses that stand out specifically are verses 8a, 9a and the last phrase of 9:

- "If the LORD delights in us, then He will bring us into this land and give it to us. . . ."
- "Only do not rebel against the LORD, nor fear the people of the land. . . ."
- ". . . the LORD is with us. Do not fear them."

What do you say are the highlights of what Joshua said?

The verses of Numbers 14:10–25 are extremely interesting because they go the gamut from the glory of the LORD appearing in the tabernacle before all the Israelites, to Moses pleading a pardon for the Israelites, to the LORD laying down the sentence of them not seeing or entering the land He had promised to them. It was over.

Return to our study of Psalm 37:12–15, reading them and writing in your own words how they would apply to the verses just studied in Numbers 14.

Those verses pretty well sum up what we just studied in Numbers 14. In our society and this day and time we sometimes feel sorry and have empathy for those who have done wrong, have broken the law, and sometimes even for the whiners. Those ten spies *did see* giants in the land; the people *were strong*; the cities *were fortified and very large*; descendants of Anak *were* there, as well as many other mighty and dangerous people. Their report was one of "a land that devours its inhabitants and we were like grasshoppers in our own sight" (vv. 31–33).

That was truthful reporting. BUT . . . did not the LORD say, "Spy out the land of Canaan, which **I am giving** to the children of Israel"?

- There was some work involved here.
- There was definitely obedience required here.
- The LORD did not say it would be easy.
- A little bit of disobedience is not obedience. A little bit of obedience is disobedience!

But, my friends, there is power and promise in God's Word: Caleb saw the same giants and walled cities as the other spies, but the ten spies brought back an evil report of unbelief. Caleb's words declared a conviction, a "confession," before all Israel: "We are well able to overcome." He had surveyed the land, a reminder that faith is <u>not</u> blind. *Faith does not deny the reality of difficulty; it declares the power of God in the face of the problem.*[13] So true!

There is a message in the spirit of Caleb's response to the rejections of his faith-filled report. Some use their confession of faith to cultivate schism, but Caleb stood his ground in faith and still moved in partnership and support for 40 years beside many whose unbelief

Inheritance: Blessings of the "Now and Not Yet"

delayed his own experience. What patience as well as faith! His eventual actual possession of the land at a later date indicates that even though delays come, faith's confession will ultimately bring victory to the believer.[14]

The congregation decided to stone Caleb and Joshua, and the LORD told Moses he was just going to "zap" the entire people right then and there. Moses pleadingly interceded for this rebellious people once again "according to the greatness of the LORD's mercy" and for His Glory known throughout all the earth. And, the LORD did pardon the people according to Moses' word.

BUT . . . what exactly did the LORD say in Numbers 14:20–24 (paraphrased)?

Finish chapter 14:26–38 and again paraphrase what happened to those who went against the LORD.

What inheritance did the rebellious Israelite's lose?

What inheritance do we lose when in our obedience we fail to rest in the LORD?

We fluctuate between castigating ourselves and congratulating ourselves because we are deluded into thinking we save ourselves. We never lay hold of our nothingness before God, and consequently, we never enter into the deepest reality of our relationship with Him. But when we accept ownership of our powerlessness and helplessness, when we acknowledge that we are paupers at the door of God's mercy, then God can make something beautiful out of us.[15] Then we inherit everything.

Remember reading in Hebrews 3:19 "that they were not able to enter because of unbelief"? Also remember in Hebrews 4:11 we are called to "be diligent to enter that rest, lest anyone fall through following the same example of disobedience" NASB. Referencing Psalm 37:11 that began today's lesson, was the congregation *meek*? Did they *delight themselves in the abundance of peace*?

✪ Close your time today by reading Psalm 37:16–22. Prayerfully consider the differences of the wicked and the righteous. Journal below your observations concerning the upright and the righteous:

Lord, help us to put our trust in You on every level, for everything and in everything. Help our heart's desire to be blessed by You so that we shall inherit the earth. In your Blessed Name, amen.

"But the meek shall inherit the earth,
and shall delight themselves in abundance of peace."
(Psalm 37:11)

Inheritance: Blessings of the "Now and Not Yet"

<u>Day 4</u> ~ *"For the LORD knows the days of the upright, and their inheritance shall be forever" (Psalm 37:18).*

LORD, You know our names; You know our every thought. Please open our hearts more and more to realize the richness of Your inheritance, on earth as it is in heaven. To You we pray, amen.

We began and ended yesterday's lesson with Psalm 37:11 that spoke of the meek inheriting the earth. In your journaling, did you decide if the congregation was *meek*? Do you think they *delighted themselves in the abundance of peace*? When we do not feel that peace in a given situation, what would be some good practices to form as habits to reach or maintain peace?

Look in Philippians 4:6–7 to see what God's word says about reaching for that peace. Verse 7 says that it is a "peace that surpasses *all* understanding." When that peace is within me, I am at rest. Do you feel that way? Do the answers given in these two scriptures match up with what you wrote above? It is important for us to remember that God does not live according to standards our society decides should be. Instead, God wants us to live according to what the standard of His Word of the Bible says should be. Why does that matter? Look up John 1:1 and paraphrase your answer:

This verse links Jesus, the Word, with the God of creation. The Word *is* Jesus Christ, the eternal, ultimate expression of God.[16] "Every word of God is pure (tested, refined); He is a shield to those who put their *trust* in Him" (Proverbs 30:5).

Modern warfare does not utilize the shield as in centuries past, but we have studied about shields in history, read about them in novels and have seen use of them in many movies. Warriors that kept together could hold their shields in a united stand to avoid arrows or balls of tar shot their way. In smaller encounters, they could form a circle and shield themselves from the enemy in a united front. Standing separately they would most likely be killed, but united, with shields together, they could better withstand the enemy's attack. When we stand united with God by putting our trust in Him, by consciously choosing to trust Him, He is a shield to us that wards off the attacks of the enemy. When there is adversity in your life, "raise the Word level;" call out to the LORD and the shield will be raised for you.

But what about the hard or extremely difficult times when God doesn't show up? What about the times when we wait for our inheritance and blessings and there is no answer? My prayer during those times is that I have the faith to trust as did Shadrach, Meshach and Abed-Nego in Daniel 3. These young men had been taken as captives from their homes and homeland to a distant, foreign land. They had been "re-trained" for several years in the ways of the new land and now worked in the court of King Nebuchadnezzar. Please read the details in Daniel 3:1–30 before answering some questions below.

Was it a simple choice not to be obedient to Nebuchadnezzar's decree?

Were there others listed in verse 7 besides these three who decided not to bow to the statue?

Although Nebuchadnezzar became enraged, he did offer a second chance to the three young men to bow before the statue, threatening death by fiery furnace if they remained rebellious to him. Then he pridefully stated, "And who is the god who will deliver you from my hands?" To this question they answered boldly: "If that is the case, our God, whom we serve, is able to deliver us from the burning fiery furnace, and *He will deliver us from your hand*, O king (Nebuchadnezzar). But if not, let it be known to you, O king, that we do not serve your gods, nor will we worship the gold image which you have set up" (vv. 17–18).

Wow, I pray for that boldness daily! In any danger or threatening occurrence we should immediately, first and above all, seek the LORD. After sincerely calling upon His name, praying for God's

Inheritance: Blessings of the "Now and Not Yet"

mercy, help, healing and safety, there is also wisdom in praying with others close to you. Review Proverbs 15:22 and paraphrase it:

That does NOT include gossiping or repeating negative, fearful words or thoughts over and over. But it does include prayerfully, trustfully seeking God's face and His wisdom. That is the heart of trust in any circumstance.

Obviously God did answer their prayers and mightily saved the men from the fiery furnace. It does not always happen that way or the way we think it should happen. Research the following scriptures for insight into that thought: Hebrews 11:1–40 through 12:1–2 (paraphrasing vv. 35–40).

Jeremiah 29:11–14a

Isaiah 55:8–9

We often presume that trust will dispel the confusion, illuminate the darkness, vanquish the uncertainty and redeem the times. But the crowd of witnesses in Hebrews 11 testifies that this is not the case. Our trust does not bring final clarity on this earth. It does not still the chaos or dull the pain or provide a crutch. When all else is unclear, the heart of trust says, as Jesus did on the cross, "Into Your hands I commit my spirit" [17] (Luke 23:46, NASB).

God wants us to live according to the standard that Jesus Christ set during his life and ministry here on earth: one of total obedience as we studied in Philippians 2:5–8 in Day 1 of *The "Dirt" on Dirt*.

When we begin to understand and live out Philippians 4:6–7, then verse 8 tells us what to think about in order to achieve the *"peace that passes all understanding . . ."* NIV. List those eight things here that we are to think and meditate on:

Take some time to read Psalm 37:23–31. Our steps are ordered by the LORD, and none of our steps shall slide when we are thinking and meditating on the eight things listed above: things that are true, noble, just, pure, or lovely; things of good report, virtuous and praiseworthy. These verses say when we are meditating on these things God delights in our way! Verse 24 says "we may fall, but we shall not be utterly cast down; for the LORD upholds us with His hand." How encouraging is that? Here are scriptures that speak of Him covering us with His shield and upholding us with His hand. Of course we will fall; we live in a fallen world and all the sinful junk we began with in this life and added to our lives along the way are in constant need of laying at the altar. It's a process. We are forgiven when we accept Jesus as our Savior and LORD, but we will always be *working out our salvation with fear and trembling* as long as we occupy life on this earth.

Throughout my life as a Christian there has been continual growth, mainly because of being a "work in progress." Even if we start later in life, it is a choice given to us and *it is never too late to start praying, growing in God's word and seeking Him!* When Jesus carried our sins on the cross, He submitted Himself to God making that salvation not only available to us, but when we accept His salvation, it makes us

Inheritance: Blessings of the "Now and Not Yet"

heirs with Him. Being heirs gives us all authority under heaven to do even greater things than He did here on earth! Just try to imagine that!

We can't be wimps! Matthew 11:12 instructs us that, "The Kingdom of Heaven suffers violence, and the violent take it by force." You aren't begging, you aren't crying and you aren't persuading; you are coming to take what is legally yours according to the Word of God. This powerful reign (*suffers violence*) that Jesus set up while on earth requires of us an equally strong and radical reaction. "The violent" then who *take it by force* are people of keen enthusiasm and commitment willing to respond with radical abandonment to the message and dynamic of God's reign.[18] That *radical abandonment* is the "violence." May we all live with keen enthusiasm and commitment as we trust in God each and every day of our lives! As Daniel 11:32b instructs: "The people who know their God shall display strength and take action" NASB.

We have permission to invade the enemy's territory because as heirs we have the authority Jesus has given us. Satan has permission to invade our territory too, but he doesn't have the authority! According to Hebrews 10:19–23, we can go boldly before the throne of God accessing the power of the Holy Spirit we have been given. So . . . let's get going.

✪ Ponder and pray for the boldness to trust the LORD in all situations. After all, He is who He says He is and can do what He says He can do. He is LORD of all!

Please end your lesson today by reading this sweet letter we received from our son Nathan a few years back. It speaks of our cherished *inheritance:*

"I feel that I am supposed to thank you all for something specific in my life and sense that I am to share this with Jason, Samantha and Jennifer too. As I continue to seek God and truly open my heart to His will, it seems the Holy Spirit has been bringing to my memory songs of praise and worship from my childhood.

All these songs, every one of them, were songs I heard because of Mom and Dad's influence, either at home, in the car, at church or at church camps. Additionally, I'm getting full songs of praise and worship during the day, in my dreams, immediately when I wake, while I'm playing sports. I've also been getting very detailed visions or dreams of exactly where I was when I heard these songs, like in the Astro van, while Mom was cooking dinner, driving with Dad to Sears to get chocolate-covered peanuts, playing jacks with Samantha on the dining room floor, at Six Flags with Jason at Christian concerts, and so forth.

So what does this all mean? I believe it means the Lord used Mom and Dad to fill my heart, and yours, with praise and worship so we could enter into the presence of the Lord. All those years of listening to Christian music at a young age and into teens I was learning how to connect directly to God. I have a vision of a treasure chest in my heart, and all these songs of praise and worship have been in there like little mustard seeds. They are no longer small seeds!

Thank you for the gift of learning how to enter into the Lord's presence; *you have given me an inheritance that is priceless!* I look forward to passing along this special gift to my children. (These are just a few of the songs I remember: *The Building Block, Are You Living in an Old Man's Rubble?, Hosanna;El Shaddai, Lord I Lift Your Name on High, As a Deer, Thank You for Giving to the Lord*)."

Nathan Alexander, Used with Permission [19]

LORD of all, we humbly bow before You and ask that you show us any golden statue we may be kneeling before, consciously or unconsciously. Please anoint us with Your spirit of boldness. Cover us with Your shield of protection. We ask that You take this cup away from us; but let it be as You, not we, have it be done (Mark 14:36). In the name of the mighty Shield over all, amen.

Inheritance: Blessings of the "Now and Not Yet"

__Day 5__ ~ *"The righteous shall inherit the land, and dwell in it forever" (Psalm 37:29).*

Our Father, our Shield over us, help us to live richly in Your inheritance, on earth as it is in heaven. Help us understand and accept the blessings of Your kingdom that is "here, but not yet." For Yours is the power and glory forever. Amen.

Shadrach, Meshach and Abed-Nego made some hard choices – and lived to tell about them. Now look at a bad choice in Luke 15:11–24 that needed later correction.

What was asked for in verse 12?

The younger son asked for his portion of the inheritance early, and the dad gave it. The son then left his father and his home, squandered all his inheritance and very soon ended up slopping in the pig pen with a very empty stomach.

Explain the first phrase of verse 17 in your own words:

Have you ever "come to yourself" in your life?

Trust without Borders

I have, and it was after slopping around in the pig pen also! Sometimes it's a short stay in the pig pen; other times it is years. Those around us often see it long before we can. These verses show us what a loving, forgiving Father we have when we "come to ourselves" and return home. When there is an acknowledgement of wrongs done against Him and turning with repentance of heart, our Father is always and immediately there with arms wide open. Re-read verses 18–20: What did the son decide he would say to his father?

Write specifically what the son was going to say as he practiced in his mind in verse 19a:

"I am no longer worthy to be *called* your son." *Called* is the word for summon or invite, especially used concerning God's call to participate in the blessings of the kingdom.[20]

When we become believers in Jesus Christ, we are called to participate in the blessings of His kingdom. Sometimes, however, when we walk in a prodigal lifestyle, we feel estranged from our heavenly Father – but He is still our Father.

I love those verses because God has received me just like that. The prodigal had a prepared confession that he was going to give to his father if his father would even allow him to speak to him. I bet he practiced that confession over and over on his return from that foreign, distant land. Then as he approached his father's property I imagine that the prodigal got a little nervous. What do you think?

But, as you read in verse 20, his father saw him *when he was still a great way off.*

Inheritance: Blessings of the "Now and Not Yet"

One of our children was a prodigal for seven very long years. We would receive a telephone call occasionally but could always tell from the conversation that she was not ready to return home. Then there was that one very special day – a phone call with real conversation, no attitude in the inflection of her words, no excuses, no asking for anything. I knew she was sincerely and honestly ready to return home; and I welcomed her home – even though she *was still a great way off.*

Before the prodigal could even speak it, his father fell on his neck and kissed him. God knows our every thought! Back in the pig pen – when the son's true conversion experience took place – the Father forgave him with an irreversible forgiveness. The moment our hearts repent, the Spirit knows our confession. There is importance in verbal confession as scripture teaches: "For with the heart one believes unto righteousness, and with the mouth confession is made unto salvation" (Romans 10:10). Remember that we have studied about working out our salvation with fear and trembling. My belief is that the confession spurs our hearts in the turn of repentance. Write out what the father says in verse 24:

Dead stuff doesn't move. It's stinky, lifeless and cannot get up and change directions. A prodigal is "dead" in the life of the family they have left. But, when they return, they ". . . are alive again; lost but now are found." Repentance is realizing a need to turn and go in the opposite direction from the way we have been going. When we genuinely repent, confess to God and to others, we are restored to our heavenly Father and instantly receive the blessings of His kingdom!

The importance of this parable of the prodigal son is that the Father's love toward us is everlasting. His love for us never ends. His inheritance of eternal life is still for us – even after we have done foolish things, if we will only return home. Wallowing in shame, remorse, self-hatred and guilt over real or imagined failings in our past lives betrays a distrust in the love of God. It shows that we have not accepted the acceptance of Jesus Christ and thus have rejected the total sufficiency of His redeeming work.[21] The sign you can trust will be the slow, steady and miraculous transformation from self-rejection to self-acceptance rooted in the acceptance of Jesus Christ.[22] "Is it possible that each time we stumble, fall, and rise again, God can barely bear the bliss of it?"[23]

There was something incredibly awesome, overwhelming and time-consuming about writing this chapter on *Inheritance* in this book on *Trust*. By the time chapter five was reached, I kept trying to close it out . . . but each day it remained unfinished. There were mistakes, duplications, numerous revisions, lost work and computer glitches, but it wouldn't "close out." One evening after losing a large portion of what I thought was some saved work, I left my computer and sat in my rocking chair, praying with tears streaming down my face. "What is it, Lord, about this chapter? Why can't it finish?" As I continued pondering and praying I felt like the Lord answered, "Because this chapter is like My inheritance – it never ends." Oh my, I thought – that's it! His inheritance of love to us *never ends!* His incredible, everlasting, never-ending love to us cannot be outdone. It is His immeasurable joy if we will accept it.

"And I pray that Christ will be more and more at home in your hearts, living within you as you trust in Him. May your roots go down deep into the soil of God's marvelous love; and may you be able to feel and understand, as all God's children should, how long, how wide, how deep, and how high His love really is; and to experience this love for yourselves, though it is so great that you will never see the end of it or fully know or understand it. And so at last you will be filled up with God himself" (Ephesians 3:17–19, TLB).

Inheritance: Blessings of the "Now and Not Yet"

Father, it surely means more to You for us to say, "I trust you," than for us to say the words, "I love you." Please pour Your Spirit over us so we can begin saying, "I do believe; help my unbelief," with total acceptance. To the LORD of all, amen.

> "All things are possible to him who believes."
> Immediately the boy's father cried out and began
> saying, "I do believe; help my unbelief."
> (Mark 9:23–24, NASB)

~ Chapter 4 ~

Matchless, Scandalous Grace

SCANDAL OF GRACE

Grace what have you done?
Murdered for me on that cross.
Accused in absence of wrong.
My sin washed away in Your blood.
Too much to make sense of it all.
I know that Your love breaks my fall.
The scandal of grace. You died in my place.
So my soul will live.

Oh to be like You. Give all I have just to know You.
Jesus there's no one beside You.
Forever the hope in my heart.
Death where is your sting?
Your power is as dead as my sin.
The cross has taught me to live
and mercy my heart now to sing.
The day and its troubles shall come.
I know that Your strength is enough.

The scandal of grace. You died in my place.
So my soul will live.
And it's all because of You Jesus.
It's all because of You Jesus.
It's all because of Your love that my soul will live.

United, Zion CD by Hillsong, ©2012 [1]
License Permit #552711, EMICMGMUSIC

Matchless, Scandalous Grace

<u>Day 1</u> ~ *(In spite of iniquities and transgressions, the Lord is eager to bless us)* "...*Therefore the Lord will wait, that He may be gracious to you; and therefore He will be exalted, that He may have mercy on you. For the Lord is a God of justice; blessed are all those who wait for Him*" *(Isaiah 30:18).*

Heavenly Lord, We are at the mercy of Your grace, and for that we are eternally grateful. Please pour Your wisdom over us, Lord, so that we can begin to comprehend the scandalous, matchless grace that You have given to us who call upon Your name. To You we humbly bow our knee and pray and say thank You. Amen.

Webster defines *grace* as unmerited divine assistance given man for his regeneration or sanctification.[2] That is an excellent definition for a secular dictionary, don't you think? The Greek word for grace, *charis*, means unmerited favor, undeserved blessing. It is from the same root as *chara*, "joy," and *chairo*, "to rejoice." *Charis* causes rejoicing.[3] It is the word for God's grace as extended to sinful man and it signifies unmerited favor, undeserved blessing; a free gift.[4] God's grace, unmerited favor, is that indeed – a manifestation of His power, exceeding what we could achieve or hope for by our own labors. God's grace becomes His enablement or empowerment to achieve His plan, endure hardship, or access Him.[5] Both *grace* and *charis* cause me to rejoice because two of my younger granddaughters, Ashlyn and Lily, respectively, have these words as their middle names.

In 2 Corinthians 12:9 the apostle Paul had a "thorn in the flesh" given to him by a messenger of Satan. Please look up this verse and write the Lord's answer here:

No one knows for certain what this intense difficulty was, but Paul had asked the Lord three times that it might depart from him (v. 8).

The answer means that the Lord's grace and strength will be sufficient in times of weakness, struggles or illnesses, and in times of sorrow. Do you remember the main point of 1 Thessalonians 5:24? *God will make it happen.* Are we beginning to get the grasp of that verse yet? It is hard, isn't it?

Remember that 2 Corinthians 12:9 says, "My grace is enough for you. When you are weak, My power is made perfect in you" NCV. This isn't referring to the moments when we feel inadequate or recognize that we lack in some way (although those moments are covered by grace too). Can you imagine *any* circumstance in which we would measure up next to Jesus? By God's standards, our "rooms will never be clean" because His standard is absolute and constant perfection. Measured against the strength of God, we are always weak. We are always in need of His grace to be enough for us. Jesus said, "Without Me, you can do nothing" (John 15:5). By "nothing," He means *nothing*! His grace is enough for every assignment, every calling, and every moment – from our lowest lows to our highest heights. We desperately need His grace, and He provided it for us – for free!

Worldly reassurance, whether genuine, real, actual or obvious, cannot create trust for us. Nothing we try to hold on to or sustain in any form or fashion can guarantee any certainty of trust for us. Trusting in Jesus, the Savior of our souls, requires us to hand over our *complete* self, trusting with confidence of what He can accomplish for us (1 Thess. 5:24 again!). When the stifling and craving of any reassurance happens, then trust happens. Anything before that stifling or craving is not trust. It is still working in our own strength.

"Come to Me, all who are weary and heavy-laden, and I will give you *rest*. Take My yoke upon you, and learn from Me, for I am gentle and humble in heart; and *you shall find rest for your souls*. For My yoke is easy and My load is light." (Matthew 11:28–30 NASB; italics mine). Several lessons back I mentioned converting one of the smallest guest bedrooms of our bed and breakfast into my studio. Do you remember that it was called Studio A and that the "A" represented

Matchless, Scandalous Grace

the Greek word *anapauo*? Do you recall what that word meant? Yes, that's it: rest.

When we grasp the fact that the Lord calls us to come to Him, lay down our heavy baggage at His feet, and He will give us *rest*, then we have learned to trust. It is His grace that offers that peaceful trust to us, but it has to be our choice to accept that peaceful trust. It doesn't just mysteriously happen one day. It is a choice to trust Him – *a choice*.

In the chapter *Hurry Up and Wait* on Day 5 we studied Hebrews 4:1–13 about the *rest* God offers us. We learned that the promise of entering His rest was not an easy or obvious one, but it was a precious one. God's promise of entering His rest is through Jesus Christ. By the grace of His forgiveness and the mercy extended to us by His death, we have the choice of receiving Him as our personal Savior, thereby securing the promise of His rest.

Look up and read Hebrews 4:9–13, which explains what we can receive and who can receive something special from God:

Only by grace and grace alone are we qualified to pursue the dreams God has given us. It's not our spirituality, depth, prayer life or preparation. It is by *His* grace that we are enough for the task. There are no more qualifications to wait for. There is *nothing* to stop you from pursuing His dream for your life. God says you're more than enough to do what He's called you to do – so do it! You may go out and play now.[6] When we determine to choose to trust Him, then *our room is clean and we can go out and play*.

There is freedom, liberty and grace in Christ as shown in Galatians 5:5: "For we through the Spirit eagerly wait for the hope of righteousness by faith." The word *hope* here is not just an optimistic outlook or wishful thinking without any foundation, but a confident expectation based on solid certainty. Biblical hope rests on God's promises. *Hope* is never inferior to faith, but is an extension of faith. Faith is the present possession of grace; hope is confidence in grace's future accomplishment[7] (and the middle name of my youngest granddaughter, Ivy Hope Alexander!).

There is also another way we can be confident of that freedom from the shackles of sin. Write out Romans 8:15 and then write your insights and thoughts about it also. For some it will be easy; for others quite difficult.

If it was difficult for you to be reconciled to a heavenly Father, I pray that you will continue to approach Daddy at other times during your time of prayer. Always remember He is not to be compared to *any* earthly father. He is our Heavenly Father.

If what you ask for in prayer is not within God's will, His timing or His answer, then *His grace will be sufficient for you!* His grace is ALWAYS sufficient for us, but sometimes we do not perceive it. Would you look up Job 33:14 and write out this short, powerful verse?

We earthlings are quite "dull around the edges" aren't we? God is always speaking and communicating with us . . . *but man does not perceive it.* Just because we can't understand His delay, can't hear His voice, or are dull to how He speaks through His word, it does not mean He is not speaking. If there is a default, I can guarantee you it's not on His end!

Matchless, Scandalous Grace

✪ Close today's lesson meditating on how God has spoken to you in your life about His grace, especially remembering Ephesians 2:8–9: *"For by grace you have been saved through faith, and that not of yourselves; it is the gift of God, not of works, lest anyone should boast."* Journal your thoughts before you close in prayer:

God of all comfort, thank You that You are our sufficiency! Thank You that Your Word tells us Your grace is sufficient for us. Now we ask that You help our hearts to believe it. In Your gracious name we pray, amen.

Day 2 ~ *"Ho! Everyone who thirsts, come to the waters; and you who have no money, come, buy, and eat. Yes, come, buy wine and milk without money and without price. Why do you spend money for what is not bread, and your wages for what does not satisfy? Listen carefully to Me, and eat what is good, and let your soul delight itself in abundance"* (Isaiah 55:1-2).

Daddy God, Yesterday we cleaned our rooms with Your help and then "went out to play." We're back because our rooms got dirty again. Take us deeper now, we ask. In Your gracious name we pray, amen.

The saved sinner is prostrate in adoration, lost in wonder and praise. He knows *repentance is not what we do in order to earn forgiveness; it is what we do because we have been forgiven*. It serves as an expression of gratitude rather than an effort to earn forgiveness. Thus the sequence of forgiveness and then repentance, rather than repentance and then forgiveness, is crucial for understanding the gospel of grace. But many of us don't know God and don't understand His gospel of grace. Many think God sits up in the heavens like a big statue, impassive, unmoving, and hard as flint.[8]

The cross at Calvary tells us in 1 John 4:10, "In this is love, not that we loved God, but that He loved us and sent His Son to be propitiation for our sins." That word *propitiation* means that Christ's sacrificial death on the cross appeased the wrath of God on account of sin and makes forgiveness possible. His death not only "wiped out our sin" but provided a covering for our sin. Take a moment to write John 15:13 in your own words:

Propitiation is God's mercy and grace in action to put us in a right relationship with Him. A believer living by grace rather than living legalistically has made a decision to turn from mistrust to trust. The most important characteristic of living by grace is trust in the redeeming work of Jesus Christ. I am free to trust when I believe that God is present and at work in my life and that I am loved like a little child is by his father. That makes a profound difference in the way I relate to myself and others; it makes an enormous difference in the way I live.[9]

When we wallow in guilt, remorse and shame over real or imagined sins of the past, we disdain God's gift of grace. Preoccupation with self is always a major component of unhealthy guilt and recrimination. It stirs our emotions, churning in self-destructive ways, closes us into a mighty stronghold of self, leads to depression and despair, and preempts the presence of a compassionate God. The language of unhealthy guilt is harsh. It is demanding, abusing, criticizing, rejecting, accusing, blaming, condemning, reproaching and scolding. It is one of impatience and chastisement. Christians are shocked and horrified because they have failed. Unhealthy guilt becomes bigger than life. Yes, we often feel guilt over sins. But healthy guilt is one which acknowledges the wrong done and feels remorse, but then is free to embrace the forgiveness that has been offered, focusing in, then, on the realization that all has been forgiven and the wrong has been redeemed.[10]

There is not one single one of us without dark shadows of some type of wrong in our background! But God's grace and mercy is always bigger! Because His grace is always bigger, we then need to shift our focus from "What have I done?" to "What can *He* do?" "Let us therefore come boldly to the throne of grace, that we may obtain mercy and find grace to help in time of need" (Hebrews 4: 16). That verse has NOTHING to do with us except coming boldly to the throne of grace!

Dietrich Bonhoeffer said: "He who is alone with his sin is utterly alone. It may be that Christians, notwithstanding corporate worship, common prayer, and all their fellowship in service, may still be left to their loneliness. The final breakthrough to fellowship does not occur, because though they have fellowship with one another as believers and as devout people, they do not have fellowship as the un-devout, as sinners. The pious fellowship permits no one to be a sinner. So everyone must conceal his sin from himself and from the fellowship. Many Christians are unthinkably horrified when a real sinner is suddenly discovered among the righteous. So we remain alone with our sin, living in lies and hypocrisy. The fact is that we are sinners!"[11] As Christians, we actually are no longer sinners, but we are righteous believers in Christ that still have the fleshly capacity to sin.

The meaning of Bonhoeffer's above quote is that because of God's grace offered to us for past, present and future times of committing a sin, we should not be banished from receiving forgiving fellowship when we have repented, confessed and turned from our offense. Staying "utterly alone" with our sinful flesh gives full access to enemy invasion to oppress and taunt us with temptations causing only a deeper spiral in our life. Confessing to others brings light into the darkness so Satan has to flee.

Meditate for a while on times you may have stayed utterly alone, too afraid or embarrassed to confess to anyone. Journal your thoughts here:

We must always walk the fine line of not distorting God's grace to us by emphasizing only God's love and forgiveness – but ignoring Jesus' call to walk in wholehearted obedience to the Lord. To do that would be to distort the purity of the message of grace, thereby causing everything else in one's spiritual life to become blurred. The apostle Paul spoke of a time in 2 Timothy 4:3–4 when many who say they believe in Jesus as Lord would believe unsound doctrine: "For the time will come when they will not endure sound doctrine, but according to their own desires, because they have itching ears, they will heap up for themselves teachers; and they will turn their ears away from the truth, and be turned aside to fables." Can you relate this scripture in any way to our current time in history?

To me it smacks of the passage in Judges 21:25: "In those days there was no king in Israel; everyone did what was right in his own eyes." Does this passage correlate with what you just wrote above?

Jesus always emphasized remaining grounded in biblical truth. He never suggested we launch out on our own whenever we got our feelings hurt or wanted our own way. He did always emphasize approaching the message of grace through the biblical lens of scripture, with God calling us to "Love the LORD your God with all your heart, with all your soul, with all your mind and will all your strength" (Mark 12:30). That's the core of the message of grace: empowering us to walk with God wholeheartedly in love.

Jesus called Mark 12:30 "the first commandment." Thus, the Holy Spirit's first agenda is to establish the first commandment in first place in the church. And it must also be our first agenda. Wholehearted love is to be first in our response to God because it is how the Father relates to the Son and how the Godhead relates to us. We must see grace through the lens of this quality of love. To think of grace without it being anchored in the first commandment is like aiming at the wrong target. When we do not correctly interpret this first commandment, we distort the grace message. We must love Jesus on *His* terms, and He defined loving God in terms of a spirit of obedience to His commandments. There is absolutely no such thing as loving Jesus without seeking to obey His word.[12]

Some seek to love God on the terms of a humanistic culture that has no reference to obeying the Word. But loving and seeking to obey Jesus are synonymous. <u>***All***</u> of His commands are based in His love. Thus, the biblical message of grace teaches us to live righteously and to deny ungodliness as the way of expressing our love to God. "The grace of God ... has appeared to all men, teaching us that, denying ungodliness and worldly lusts, we should live soberly, righteously, and godly...." Titus 2:11–12. If you hear a teaching on grace that doesn't call you to deny ungodliness, it's not a biblical grace message – it's a distorted one.[13]

✪ Take some time to ponder and pray over John 14:15, 21 and 23, writing out what you think verse 15 means to you.

Father, help us "confess our sins one to another, that we may be healed." Be our shield to us, protecting us from the fiery darts of Satan. Please help us to desire to be protected by You more than any temptation the enemy can bring to us. In the name of Jesus Christ, amen.

Matchless, Scandalous Grace

<u>Day 3</u> ~ *"Therefore, if anyone is in Christ, he is a new creation; old things have passed away; behold, all things have become new . . . that we [our spirit] might become the righteousness of God in Him (Christ)" (2 Corinthians 5:17-21).*

Lord, Your word tells us we are new creations in Christ; that old things have passed away. But often we don't feel new or clean, refreshed or renewed. Please help us to verbally ascend to You daily, out loud (literally), in order for us to begin to believe Your word to us. Help our confession be unto our salvation. In Jesus' name, amen.

The butterfly species develops through a metamorphosis process, meaning in Greek, a transformation or change in shape. The butterfly's life cycle includes being an egg, larva, pupa and adult, each stage with a different goal. A caterpillar's job is to eat prolifically and adults need to reproduce. Depending on the type of butterfly, the life cycle may take one month up to a whole year.

The butterfly starts life as a very small, round, oval, ribbed or cylindrical egg. The coolest thing about butterfly eggs, especially monarch butterfly eggs, is that if you look close enough you can actually see the tiny caterpillar growing inside of it. The eggs are usually laid on the leaves of plants, and the egg shape depends on the type of butterfly that laid the egg.

Because their exoskeleton (skin) does not stretch or grow, they molt or shed the outgrown skin several times, staying very still for as much as a day while shedding old skin. Usually the old skin is eaten after it has been shed and underneath is a new skin that allows the caterpillar to grow. The periods between shedding are called instars. Monarch instars are fairly similar – although there is a gradual change from a tiny green caterpillar with a big black head to a larger one with white, black and yellow stripes and a small black head.

It takes about 10 days (and 5 instars) for the caterpillar to grow big enough to form a pupa, or chrysalis, which is the third stage of the life cycle. When it has eaten enough, it will start wandering around looking for a place to attach its chrysalis. Monarch caterpillars attach their chrysalises so that they hang down, sometimes attaching to a branch of the milkweed. After attaching, the caterpillar will hang upside down in a "J" shape for about a day before it makes the chrysalis, which can take as little as three minutes! The caterpillar wiggles hard, pushing its outer skin off and up. As the bundle of shed skin falls off, the green and yellow striped chrysalis stops wiggling and hangs still. It seems the caterpillar is just resting, but inside the pupa there is much action and rapid change. The new chrysalis is soft and vulnerable at first but soon hardens, becoming solid green and developing some gold spots over the next few hours.

Caterpillars are short and stubby with no wings at all. Within the chrysalis the old body parts undergo a remarkable transformation, the "metamorphosis," as tissue, limbs and organs become the uniquely colorful and beautiful parts that make up the butterfly soon to emerge. Within nine or ten days the chrysalis will be ready to hatch, usually hatching within a few hours after darkening.

In the fourth stage the butterfly emerges from the chrysalis, both wings slightly soft and folded tightly around its body, because it had to fit all its new parts inside the pupa. The new creature usually cannot immediately fly away and adjusts to its new form by quickly pumping blood into the wings and flapping the wings in order to get them working. It often waves them back and forth for several hours until they harden. Usually within a three or four-hour period the butterfly will master flying and begin searching for a mate in order to reproduce and begin the butterfly life cycle all over again.[14]

I love beautiful-winged butterflies! Their life cycle parallels with great symbolism the growth process of a Christian. Many of us have experienced our own metamorphosis, becoming new creatures in Christ, and the transformation often occurring in our life-cycle stages is also similar. Sometimes these stages of life are uncomfortable and even painful, but in the end a beautiful butterfly emerges, soaring high and rising above all of the layers shed along the journey.

As with a butterfly, we start out as small, fragile Christian "eggs." Often appearing hard-shelled when we surrender to the Lord as babes in Christ, we are instead delicate little eggs, requiring nourishment, protection and supervision until we are ready for the next phase of our Christian walk. Each tiny egg is circular or oval in shape and can easily roll away, get lost, be misplaced or crushed. Baby "eggs" in Christ need to stay together on the necessary leaf originally laid on, with other like-minded eggs and under the protective authority of their spiritual covering until they have matured. The hatched egg is not an instantly beautiful butterfly, but a peculiar looking caterpillar. It stumbles its way along, consistently growing and expanding while it eats and eats. As new Christians, most of us join a church home, sit under good, biblical teaching, read books that enhance our spirits and listen to music that nourishes our souls. As we grow in the things of God we find that certain habits, places, people and things no longer fit comfortably in our lives and we can no longer "digest" them. Like the growing caterpillar, we molt our old skin. During our Christian walk, we are constantly shedding layers of our former selves: anger, hatred, depression, stress, bitterness, habits and anything or anybody that would hinder us from moving forward.

As the Caterpillar comes into maturity to the chrysalis stage, it reaches its fullest length and weight, becoming so full that it now has to build a protective shell or cocoon to prepare for the next phase of life. God has set aside and sanctified His people to do a work in Him and there are times in our lives when we have to "cocoon" ourselves in order to hear from Him. Sometimes our world becomes "upside down" like the caterpillar that attaches and hangs upside down to begin the cocoon. That secret dwelling place is where we find shelter, strength, comfort, deliverance and healing. Our "spiritual cocoon" is a place where God takes all of those things we have shed and replaces them with His word, His creative works, His Holy Spirit and His love.

Inside the cocoon, the caterpillar goes through its major transforming metamorphosis, often becoming transparent about a day before the adult butterfly emerges. Before we can become effective witnesses, we, too, not only have to shed many layers of our former self, but God may require us to become transparent to become a living example of His greatness in our lives. As Christians some of us have been in church all our lives feasting on God's word, learning and meditating, digesting and applying. At some point, hopefully, we become so full of God's word that our cup overflows and it becomes time for us to break forth from that cocoon and soar to higher heights. At this point it's time to pour back into the earth, or sow seeds by mentoring or ministering to someone else. At this phase ministries are born, books are birthed, songs are written and the gospel is shared throughout the earth through art, music, speech, literature and dance.

Similar to the approximately 28,000 species of butterflies worldwide, we are all uniquely designed, fearfully and wonderfully made, handcrafted by the Master's hands, and varying in gifts, talents and abilities. There is no need for us to covet someone else's wings when God has a purpose for each of us. It is His perfect timing and will for all of the seasons or "stages" in our lives. What "butterfly life-cycle" stage are you in?[15]

Kerry Bond, whose song *Restored* was in the chapter on *Dirt*, got to share both Holly Ogden's story and the song it inspired at the 2013 national CMA Women's conference in Texas. But the session before she was to sing *Restored*, God gave her another song about trust while she listened to Becky Ogden talk about birds. It was the first time she had ever written a song without her guitar and she was even able to sing it without playing her guitar!

I created the bird to fly for Me; he fell but continued to try.
Now watch him soar, flying with joy,
A beautiful offering to Me.

My Heart . . . longs to hold you in My arms.
My Hands . . . are waiting to lift your load.
So hold fast, hold fast, and trust like a bird.

Matchless, Scandalous Grace

*You've been born again, you've been called to lead
A glorious life for Me.
You're on a path to make a change, but are you trusting in Me?*

*My Heart . . . longs to hold you in My arms.
My Hands . . . are waiting to lift your load.
So hold fast, hold fast, and trust like a bird.*

Written by Kerry Bond, March 2013, Used with Permission[16]

When the Japanese mend broken objects, they aggrandize the damage by filling the cracks with gold. They believe that when something has suffered damage and has a history it becomes more beautiful.[17] Review 2 Corinthians 5:17, 21b: "Therefore, if anyone is in Christ, he is a new creation; old things have passed away; behold, all things have become new . . . that we [our spirit] might become the righteousness of God in Him (Christ)." Who is the "he" that is a new creation?

That's right, it is our spirit man. Verse 21 says we possess the very righteousness of God in our spirit, which is our new, legal position in Christ – how God sees and relates to us. In Christ, all things have become new; old things are passed away. This includes being fully accepted by God, receiving the authority to use the name of Jesus and possessing the indwelling Holy Spirit – all of which enable us to resist sin, sickness and Satan; to walk in victory; and to release the works of God through prayer. The old things that passed away under this legal shift include no longer being under the *penalty of sin* nor being dominated by the *power of sin*.[18]

Earlier our legal position in Christ was mentioned. Legally we can stand before God possessing the righteousness of Christ because of what Jesus accomplished for us on the cross. Our legal standing before God is so glorious that it will never be improved upon, because we received Christ's very own righteousness instantly the day we were "born again."

Our "living condition," on the other hand, relates to *growing in righteousness progressively* as our mind is renewed, causing our behavior and emotions to be transformed by the Holy Spirit in us.[19] It is the Philippians 2: 12 verses again, the "working out our salvation with fear and trembling" that we studied in the chapter on *Dirt*.

✪ Close out today by reading John 1:17 and write it below:

O, happy day! We have been redeemed with grace and truth that came through Jesus Christ! Let that be our prayer today, Dear One.

Jesus, our Redeemer: Thank You for the grace and truth that fills us when we place our trust in You. There is NONE other who can accomplish that filling for us. We are eternally grateful! Amen!

Day 4 ~ *"The law of his God is in his heart; none of his steps shall slide" (Psalm 37:31).*

Father, allow Your Holy Spirit to pour a spirit of obedience over us as we learn to operate in Your grace. We ask that You give us discerning spirits, truthful words and obedient hearts as we grow in Your grace. To You we pray, Jesus, amen.

To trust Abba, both in prayer and in life, is to stand in childlike openness before a mystery of gracious love and acceptance.[20] Understandably, we hide our true selves from God in prayer. We simply do not trust that He can handle all that goes on in our minds and hearts. Can He accept our hateful thoughts, our cruel fantasies and our bizarre dreams we wonder? Can He cope with our primitive images, our inflated illusions, and our exotic mental castles? We conclude that He cannot and thus withhold from Jesus what is most in need of His healing touch.[21]

In order to grow in trust, we must allow God to see us and love us precisely as we are, and the best way to do that is through prayer. As we pray, the unrestricted love of God gradually transforms us. We open ourselves to receive our own truth in the light of God's truth. The Spirit opens our eyes to see what really is, to pierce through illusions so that we can discover we are seen by God with a gaze of love.[22]

Suppose someone shares with you that they have had an affair in their marriage and their spouse has just found out. They used to have a vibrant Christian life, family, ministry, life of service, and prayer life, but no longer feel His presence or have any relationship with God. They are massively embarrassed and disappointed in themselves and, therefore, are sure God could never love them.

Nothing they have done has seemed to work in their marriage and they keep doing the same stuff out of habit because there just doesn't seem to be any alternatives. Depression has set in and even though they realize they have believed the lies of Satan, they feel trapped and doomed. There seems no hope for them. "I can't get close to God," they tearfully cry to you. "How can I change so my marriage can be repaired and saved? I am so sincerely sorry for what I have done and want to rebuild my marriage, but my spouse is so angry and hurt. Surely God hates me, too."

Suppose that, like me, you have a prodigal that has been absent from your life for many years. Long and many have been the hurts, the deception, lies, the thievery; drunkenness, drug use, jail time, court visits and car trips to pick up that prodigal to bring them home time after time. Finally the day arrives that rests reality on the prodigal – and they are prodigal no more! Their countenance, attitude, speech and tone are different and they are genuine in their request to return to the family.

Now suppose you are God for just a moment: What are your feelings toward these returned, lost souls? Do you see them as having a relationship with you? Do you think that they love you? Is your heart overflowing with compassion for their feelings of exile from you? Do you see their whole life as a prayer of longing? Will you sweep them up in your arms the moment they call to you?

Take your human feelings, multiply them exponentially into infinity and you will have a hint of the love of God revealed by and in Jesus Christ. With a strong affirmation of our goodness and a gentle understanding of our weakness, *God is loving us* – you and me – this moment, <u>*just as we are*</u> and not as we should be. There is nothing any of us can do to increase His love for us and nothing we can do to diminish it.[23]

Romans 5:8 says, "But God demonstrates His own love toward us, in that while we were still sinners, Christ died for us." Of all the people attending the meal with Jesus at the Pharisee's home, Mary Magdalene was the most grateful. Remember how she poured her expensive, precious oil on His feet and then washed them with her tears? Jesus said she had the most to gain. Scriptures indicate she was the most grateful. She came just as she was, and laid her whole life at the feet of Jesus. "I do not at all understand the mystery of grace – only that it meets us where we are but does not leave us where it found us."[24]

Matchless, Scandalous Grace

In prayer Jesus slows us down, teaches us to count how few days we have and gifts us with wisdom. He reveals to us how we are so caught up with what is urgent that we have overlooked what is essential. Our response to the love of Jesus demands trust – and His response to us in Jesus Christ is a promise we can trust.[25] Look up Acts 20:32 to hear Paul's words on this promise. Write out the scripture:

What were the two things Paul says that grace is able to do?

    1) To _____ _____ _____
    2)
    3) Give you an _____

An inheritance? Where have we heard that before? Even through His grace we receive an inheritance! How precious is that? Those of us who are sanctified – who are being made holy – receive an inheritance. It is an unfinished process. Remember Day 1, *Dirt on Dirt*, when we studied *working out our salvation with fear and trembling*? Remember 1 Thessalonians 5:23–24 that taught us *God will make it happen.* Oh, Saint, it's only by His saving grace through salvation!

There are some who feel their lives are a big disappointment to God and it requires enormous trust to accept that the love of Christ can look beyond our mistakes. Read Matthew 11:29, listing your thoughts about what Jesus says:

Our Lord assumed we would be discouraged, grow weary, labor heavily and become disheartened. He knew that physical pain and illnesses, the loss of ones we love, failure, loneliness, rejection, abandonment and betrayal would sap our spirits; that days would come that would bring no comfort. He knew that during those days prayer would lack any sense of reality.[26]

But we still hide our true nature from God in prayer, like a small child would hide from a parent. We just do not believe that He would accept, or would even want to handle, all that goes on in our stress-filled lives; things like how we hate that person, our caches of bitterness, obsessive fantasies and dreams and deep thoughts of despair. It then becomes our decision that He is not able, and therefore we withhold from Jesus the deep dark things hidden within us that need especially to be laid at His feet in prayer.

✪ Close out today by reading 1 Corinthians 1:4–9; then view these bullet points to accompany those verses:

- His grace was given to us at the time of our salvation in Christ Jesus
- We were enriched in all speech (word) and all knowledge
- We are not lacking in any spiritual gift
- He will strengthen (confirm) us to the end of the age
- We are blameless – free from any legal charge!
- God is faithful to us because of Jesus Christ.

Beloved, it can't get better than that! Nothing can be compared to His grace!

"For we do not have a High Priest who cannot sympathize with our weaknesses, but was in all points tempted as we are, yet without sin. Let us therefore come boldly to the throne of grace that we may obtain mercy and find grace to help in time of need." Hebrews 4:15–16.

O, Lamb of God, thank You that we can come <u>just as we are.</u> That is matchless grace. Thank You, Jesus, Amen.

Hymn [27]

Matchless, Scandalous Grace

Words, Charlotte Elliott, 1834. Tune WOODWORTH, William B. Bradbury, 1849.

Trust without Borders

<u>*Day 5*</u> *~ "For the Lord Loves justice and does not forsake His saints; they are preserved forever, but the descendants of the wicked shall be cut off" (Psalm 37:28).*

Abba, Daddy, how blessed beyond measure are we to be able to stand in Your presence in the mystery of grace, love and acceptance. Thank you that You included us in Your family through the redeeming blood of Jesus Christ. We run to You, Daddy, and ask to sit on Your lap today as You teach us more about Your grace. In Your precious Name, Jesus, amen.

"For Mom's Book. . ."

Not really knowing my birth mother and never meeting my birth father would cause me to guess that is where the word "trust" began to disappear in my life. At a very young age I was placed in a foster home because of neglect and abuse towards my baby sister Laura and me. As a little toddler, by the age of twenty months I tried to take care of myself and my three-month old sister day after day because my mother never came home. We lived in a "day-by-day" motel in a poor area of Dallas and she would stay gone most afternoons and evenings drinking beer and doing drugs (we were later told, after my adoption). I don't remember the one day that would change my life forever; all I know is that I was taken from my birth mom by a policeman and put into a foster home. My sister was never to come back around. She died the following day at Parkland Hospital in Dallas from abuse by my birth mom.

A year and a half later I was adopted into a wonderful Christian family at the age of three. At that time I'm sure I felt like a million bucks with a new Mom, Dad, two brothers and a sister that loved me unconditionally! God had truly blessed me! As I got older I struggled with issues of anger, fear, hatred and trust. I began having nightmares by age six, and when in the nightmares my new Mom began being killed, a decision was made that I should begin counseling. The counseling seemed to work for a while when I was younger, but things just got progressively worse the older I got. God bless my parents for all the work, time, money spent, tears, prayers and effort it took to raise me.

Matchless, Scandalous Grace

I'm a very stubborn person; that can be a good and bad thing. My Mom always said, "It's a good thing when you are strong in your personality by the power of the Spirit, but not a good thing when you are stubborn in 'your flesh'." Toward the end of my middle school years and into my high school years it was definitely a bad thing! I honestly can't remember a specific thing that made me so angry all the time – it was just that EVERYTHING did. I hated my parents and I hated chores; I hated living in a B & B and having to be quiet, and I hated structure even though I desperately needed it. I felt like I was completely bullet proof – but what teenager doesn't?

I quickly began to spiral out of control. It wasn't just being late for curfew; it was being extra late for curfew and being promiscuous, partying at wild parties, even messing with drugs. I felt so rebellious and I loved it! My BIG thing was how much I hated going to church, and hated all those people. I wanted to be "free" like my friends who didn't have to attend church. Choosing to be "free" was certainly not the easy way! I began a yo-yo effect of leaving and returning home within two weeks after I graduated from high school.

My parents and older siblings tried to work and counsel with me to keep me at home, to begin junior college or work, etc. But I chose to leave my family soon afterward for the lifestyle of "the rich and famous," which is a total lie! While trying to "earn" my so called friendships, I got into drugs, alcohol and more; I was using and abusing my family, my real friends, my so-called friends and hurting innocent people along the way. I didn't care; I felt like it was owed to me. I got in so much trouble in those years: In and out of jail, arrested multiple times for shoplifting, writing hot checks, as well as getting in major debt and receiving other tickets.

I never once thought of going back to my family because my parents had always taught me God's way versus the world's way, and said they would never bail me out of jail if I chose to steal, do drugs, write hot checks, etc. I will never forget one December that changed my life forever. It was Christmas, and I was in jail because I stole a bunch of stuff and got caught. Well, of course I tried to have my parents get me out and they wouldn't but they so kindly (yes, totally being sarcastic) brought my Mamaw and my niece, Megan, and nephew, Justin, to visit me. I will never, ever forget the tears in Mamaw's eyes when she saw me; she couldn't even talk to me. It broke my heart.

I sat there and cried like a baby when my nephew Justin asked me, "Why did you do it Jenny?" I didn't have any response for him. It was just like a major slap in the face when I realized the damage I was doing to my family; the damage I was doing to an innocent child. My mom would always tell me that Justin would ask about me while I was choosing not to be with the family and ask if I still liked him, and that he would always pray for me. It mattered to me what he thought because he had always looked up to me, and I realized that it wasn't fair for him to have to think like that and not understand the reason I wasn't coming around. That was my turning point!

Going back for a quick second – I became an Auntie to the most precious boy in the world in 1996 when Justin was born. He was my world; I loved him more than anything! However, I never knew back then that this cute little blonde-headed boy would be the reason I would decide to get my life together and come back to the family.

The whole "coming back to the family" transition probably took about another year, but I was calling and coming around more. There was one more jail visit and this time my parents came to bail me out. I was finally ready to change completely and walk away from what I was doing. I will never forget that 40-minute conversation while sitting in the jail with my parents before they would even let me get in their car. It was the most terrifying thing ever! But it was great and what I needed and confirmed to me that they loved me.

I began to trust the Lord and the healing process, and began working hard to be a part of this family that the Lord had placed me in. The process was very frustrating for all of us because my selfishness had caused many hurt feelings. The most important thing for me was to apologize to each of my siblings. That was a task in itself to admit that I was wrong while regaining their trust, as well as that of my parents. I also had to pay debts that I had accumulated over the years.

Matchless, Scandalous Grace

So that resulted in ONE MORE TIME in jail. But this time it was me volunteering to clear my name. My mother drove me to the jail to drop me off. I will never forget that feeling of fear having to go in there and walk away from my mom (the one person I had been trying to get away from for all those years – ha!). I sat in the car crying, and she looked at me and asked what I was so afraid of. She said, "You've been in jail many times and it never scared you before. You were tough as snot. So why does it scare you now?" All I could think of was the feeling that I would never get out because I was happy with my new life. I began to realize the difference between the days I didn't care; I didn't think I had anything to live for. . . . Amazing isn't it? I had been in there multiple times for weeks at a time and I was never scared, but today I was shaking with fear. I still to this day can't describe that feeling. My mom prayed for me, and we sat in the car until I was ready. She then walked with me into the jail and dropped me off at the processing entrance. She hugged me and told me she would be there at the exact time they would be able to release me. Then I walked into that jail for the very last time!

It has been many years since making that long journey back home. It is the best decision I've ever made! I have a healthy, growing relationship with the Lord, my parents, my siblings, my entire family and some of my closest friends, as well as my new, sweet husband! I'm so thankful for my family that they never gave up on me even though I did on them. I'm so thankful for my parents, for all the hard choices they had to make to help me become the woman I am today! Trust is never easy, but everyone trusted in me that I was ready to change, and boy did I ever! *Because I reached out to trust the Lord, He poured His grace out to me.* There was never an easy point in this journey, but I had to stop and look at the destructive path I was taking. It was going to destroy my life if I didn't make a change. The Lord's loving and forgiving grace is what has continued to grow me into the godly woman I have become. I am beyond blessed! I couldn't have done it without His grace!

I dedicate this to my amazing nephew, Justin. Because of you I realized what I was doing wrong and now I'm back where I'm supposed to be. You loved me even when I wasn't loveable! I love you more than you will ever know!

Jennifer Alexander Wright [28]
Daughter of Jimmy and Pamela Alexander

"But as for me, I will watch expectantly for the LORD; I will wait for the God of my salvation. My God will hear me. Do not rejoice over me, O my enemy. Though I fall I will rise; though I dwell in darkness, the LORD is a light for me." (Micah 7:7, NASB)

<u>Forever **Grateful**</u>: For years Jimmy and I have discussed the concept of "gratefulness." To some it is a natural gift of being appreciative of any and all of what comes to them in life. To others being grateful is apparently the last thing on their minds. Jesus did say, "I have come so that you may have life and have it more abundantly" (John 10:10, paraphrased). Ingratitude did begin in the Garden of Eden when Eve felt ungrateful for the bountiful fruit God provided, and she just had to have the one fruit God instructed her not to eat.

Jimmy and I viewed gratefulness intermingled with faith, belief and trust in an article written in our local newspaper by Austin Lewter, now Publisher of the *Whitesboro News-Record*:

Their oldest child, Jackson, was born prematurely at 28 weeks. At seven days old doctors informed them he had suffered chronic bleeding in his brain and would probably never walk or talk. Ten days later he contracted a rare infection with only a 10% survival rate, probably not surviving through the night. A family therapist visited them in the Neo-natal ICU, but seemed to lack any real understanding of what they were going through. Austin explained they remained positive about Jackson and knew, beyond the shadow of a doubt, that he would eventually be fine. They told her that they would not take "*No*" for an answer . . . that he would, soon, be a healthy, happy little boy.

Matchless, Scandalous Grace

"After listening to his convictions for a few minutes, the therapist looked at him and said, 'It is good to remain positive but you must also remain realistic about these things.'

"'Realistic?' I replied as if she was saying that we were crazy for thinking he would recover. 'What is the definition of reality?' I asked in return. 'You are the one with a Ph.D., and you are telling me to be *realistic*. I ask you: what is your definition of reality?'

"'Well,' she stuttered, 'I guess your reality is whatever you make it.' 'That's right,' I responded. 'And OUR reality is that Jesus Christ was a man who walked the Earth. He raised the dead, cured lepers, and fed a few thousand people with a couple of fish. The days of miracles are not over, and our reality tells us that our son will eventually be fine. We *ARE* being realistic.'

"There was no way she could argue with my conviction. That was the last time she stopped by our room. The Bible teaches us that Jesus said, 'Go back and report to John what you hear and see: The blind receive sight, the lame walk, those who have leprosy are cleansed, the deaf hear, the dead are raised, and the good news is proclaimed to the poor. Blessed is anyone who does not stumble on account of me' (Luke 7:22, NIV). The days of miracles are not over. There are miracles happening every day and the sooner we open our eyes and hearts to them, the more they will reveal themselves to us." [29] Their son is now a healthy young man!

In Luke 17:11–19 Jesus healed ten lepers on His way to Jerusalem. Please stop a moment to read these verses. When only one came back to thank Him, Jesus asked where the other nine were. To have leprosy made one a total outcast from society; to be healed instantaneously should have made each one eternally grateful. Where _were_ the other nine? Research Philippians 4:11 (two versions if possible) and write the verse here:

The foremost quality of a trusting disciple is gratefulness. Gratitude arises from the lived perception, evaluation and acceptance of all of life as grace – as an undeserved and unearned gift from the Father's hand. Such recognition is itself the work of grace and acceptance of the gift is implicitly acknowledgement of the Giver. [30]

✪ I am now going to ask the "near impossible" (if we are truly honest with ourselves). List below just a few of the millions of reasons you have for being grateful:

"I thank my God always concerning you for the grace of God which was given to you by Christ Jesus, that you were enriched in everything by Him in all utterance and all knowledge, even as the testimony of Christ was confirmed in you, so that you come short in no gift, eagerly waiting for the revelation of our Lord Jesus Christ, who will also confirm you to the end, that you may be blameless in the day of our Lord Jesus Christ. God is faithful, by whom you were called into the fellowship of His Son, Jesus Christ our Lord" (1 Corinthians 1:4–9).

O God of matchless, scandalous grace, we thank You that You love us beyond our fleshly faults, and we humbly ask that You continue to grow us in Your image. Thank You for supplying all our needs according to Your riches in glory in Christ Jesus. Amen.

~ Chapter 5 ~

Sweet Intimacy of Prayer: Harps, Golden Bowls and "Camel Knees"

Day 1 ~ "... *Lord, teach us to pray . . ."* (Luke 11:1).

Lord, we have been learning how to "delight ourselves in You so that You will give us the desires of our hearts." Our desire is to learn how to sit at Your feet; how to listen for Your voice; how to engage You in conversation; how to pray Your will. Help us, Father, we ask. Amen.

In Revelation 5:8 the heavenly elders each came to Jesus with two things: a harp and a golden bowl full of incense, which represent the prayers of the saints. The harp speaks of God's music and worship songs; the bowl speaks of intercession. Worship around God's throne incorporates worship and prayer flowing together and produces a unique spiritual dynamic.[1] The following pages will list eight key points for the power of prayer in a Christian's life:

1. <u>No greater priority exists for the believer than knowing Christ through the study of His Word and the intimacy of prayer</u>.[2] Prayer catapults us onto the frontier of the spiritual life.

2. <u>Prayer is a value of the church and believers</u>. Secret, fervent, believing prayer lies at the root of all personal godliness (William Carey).[3] Take a moment to look up and write out James 5:16b, explaining what it means to you:

3. <u>To pray is to change</u>. Prayer is the central avenue God uses to transform us. Progressively we are taught to see things from His

point of view. God always meets us where we are and slowly moves us along into deeper things. John Wesley said, "God does nothing but in answer to prayer."[4] Any who have read *This Present Darkness* by Frank Peretti can understand the book illustrated the fact of how the angels were standing by to help believers but could do nothing until the believers prayed to God for help, thereby releasing the angelic messengers.

4. Prayer is a divine resource of strength for us as it was for Jesus. Below, list several important points for the following scripture: "But He Himself would often slip away to the wilderness and pray." (Luke 5:16, NASB).

5. Jesus modeled Prayer for us through the well-known Lord's Prayer which:

   a. Humbles us. (Our Father. . .)
   b. Recognizes His holiness, authority and majesty. (Who art in heaven, hallowed [or most holy] is Your name…)
   c. Takes us into the battle of spiritual warfare. (Your kingdom come, Your will be done on earth as it is in heaven…)
   d. Petitions and requests. (Give us this day our daily bread…)
   e. Teaches repentance. (…forgive us our trespasses…)
   f. Leads us into intercession. (…as we forgive those who trespass against us…)
   g. Acknowledges His sovereignty over our lives. (And lead us not into temptation, but deliver us from evil … for Yours is the kingdom and the power and the glory forever …. Amen.) (Luke 11:1–4 and Matthew 6:9–13).

6. Prayer is our primary means of communing with God.

Remember, God always meets us where we are and slowly moves us along into deeper things.[5] The more familiar we become with prayer, the more natural and child-like communion is with Him, which God intended in the first place. The more natural the prayer, the more real He becomes.[6] God wants *relationship*! He never intended stiff, formal prayers as communication with Him. Consider how Abraham, Moses and David called out to Him. There was always respect, but there was also always the love, the closeness and pursuing of the friendship.[7]

The process begins when we *search* for God in prayer, learning that we are free to question, experiment, even fail, but are always learning.[8] Scripture tells us that God wants to be found! Look up the following scriptures that prove that truth, explaining in your own words how we search for God in prayer:

Deuteronomy 4:29

Jeremiah 29:13–14a and Jeremiah 33:3

Matthew 7:7

James 4:8

The process of prayer continues when we *find* God. When we know God intimately, we experience God at work through us. We learn that our relationship with God is the most important part of knowing and doing the will of God. Without an intimate relationship with Him, we will miss what He wants to do in and through our lives.[9] Research the following scriptures, writing out what Moses was asking and what God revealed to him:

Exodus 33:18–19 and/or 34:5–8.

The process of prayer deepens when we *commune* with God. When we say, "Father" we speak with a personal God. Abba is the name the Bible uses for God, which means "Daddy." Different in meaning than just "Father," this one speaks of the close, personal relationship that is full of security, rest and peace. It is a communion involving dependence, love and assurance. Remember we studied Romans 8:15 that taught us we "received the Spirit of adoption by whom we cry out, Abba, Father."

7. Prayer is God's primary means of accomplishing His purposes through us in the world.

- In prayer God gives us His heart which is full of compassion, as is written in Colossians 3:12–13. What are seven things the Lord gives us from these verses?

How different our lives would be if we operated with the above qualities. When we commune with God we communicate intimately and *ministry will flow out of that communion,* as shown in these scriptures:

- In prayer God gives us His power (Acts 1:4, 8). Notice what that scripture did not say: not phenomena, but power!
- In prayer God gives us His direction (Acts 6:4):
  ~ leading to evangelism (Acts 10, 13)
  ~ freeing prisoners (Isaiah 61:1; Luke 4:18; Acts 12)
  ~ leading to healing (Matthew 10:7–8; Acts 28:8; James 5: 13–16)

- ~ in raising the dead (Matthew 10:7–8; Acts 9:39-41)
- ~ leading to new insight and inner strength, (2 Corinthians 12:7–10)
- ~ leading to new leadership (Luke 6, Acts 14); Jesus prayed all night before choosing His disciples.

8. <u>Learning to pray involves the actual time, practice and process of praying</u>. It is a spiritual, mental, physical, disciplined process. It is not "come aside and rest awhile," but actual work to be in His presence. "Be sober, be vigilant; because your adversary the devil walks about like a roaring lion, seeking whom he may devour!" (1 Peter 5:8).
    - ~ Ask Him for a heart to pray (1 Thessalonians 5:18–21). Jesus encouraged us to pray for the Father's will to be done on earth as it is in heaven. When we pray that way, we are praying right in line with the heart of God. This is in the center of His will and of the prophetic word of Jesus Christ.[10]
    - ~ Ask Him for help to pray. We certainly cannot hide anything from Him (He knows our weaknesses), so be honest with Him as a little child would be to a parent.
    - ~ Ask Him: "What am I to pray; what do <u>You</u> want me to pray?" *Listening is of utmost importance in prayer.* God knows our needs before we ask, but scripture tells us He wants us to ask, seek, and knock. Often, however, we are so busy asking, seeking and knocking that we fail to listen to what God is trying to say to us. "Be still and know that I am God" (Psalm 46:10). In the *Hurry Up and Wait* chapter, we studied Psalm 37:7 which taught us to rest in the LORD, and wait patiently for Him. Write the meaning of these two scriptures which accompany that verse:

Lamentations 3:25–26

Isaiah 40:31

9. Learning to pray utilizes three general types of prayers:

   A. *Worship and Personal Devotion* involve worshipful declarations of adoration, thanksgiving and praises to God. Devotional prayers focus on asking for spiritual growth and communion with God. These prayers involve meditation on God's word that turns God's word into conversation with Jesus. I love this part and often spend quite a bit of time here with the Lord. Don't rush it – just enjoy being in His presence and declaring your praises to Him, because scripture teaches us He inhabits our praises. How utterly awesome is that?!

   B. *Personal Petitions* ask for circumstances to change in some way. We are all very familiar with these types of prayers, as we ask and ask and ask, often coming with a long list. God does welcome these prayers as well, but as we mature in our prayer life, hopefully these prayers become more worshipful as we place our trust in Him to handle the requests, and we no longer try to "talk Him into the answer" that we desire. Even Jesus asked in the Garden of Gethsemane that God would "take this cup from Me; *nevertheless, not My will but Yours be done*" (Luke 22:42).

   C. *Intercessory Prayers* ask God to release His blessing, including spiritual and natural blessing, to touch others:

   a. Prayers for individuals for their salvation, healing, release of anointing or other personal needs: 2 Corinthians 1:11; Ephesians 6:19; Philippians 1:19.
   b. Prayers for a city, a church or a group of people. God has ordained intercessory prayer as the means of releasing His

sovereignly ordained blessing into a local area and into the individual lives of people. Several scriptures about this type of intercession are Isaiah 62:6 and 1 Thessalonians 3:10.[11]

10. <u>Learning to pray involves praying persistently and consistently</u> as shown in Luke 18:1–7. Explain what v. 7 infers to you:

11. <u>Learning to pray involves praying believing, in faith, without doubt</u> as is shown in Mark 11:20–24. Jesus *never* concluded His prayers by saying "if it be Your will," nor did the apostles or prophets when they were praying for others. Obviously they believed that they knew what the will of God was before they prayed the prayer of faith. Their positive prayers often took the form of direct, authoritative commands: "Walk;" "Be well;" "Stand up;" evidently leaving no room for indecisive, tentative, half-hoping, "if it be Thy will" prayers.[12]

12. <u>Learning to pray involves praying without ceasing</u>. Paraphrase 1 Thess.5:17 and Ephesians 6:18 below:

✪ We have covered detailed amounts of scripture and study in this lesson, but please take time now to sit in His presence. If time of prayer with the God of all creation is new to you, just sit still with Him today. If you are a "prayer warrior," ask Him to open up new avenues of prayer and style to you. This is a time to be on Daddy's lap and learn by His Spirit, because *"Faithful is He who calls you, and He also will bring it to pass"* (1Thessalonians 5:24, NASB).

"Lord, teach us to pray . . ." (Luke 11:1).

Day 2 ~ *Sing Praises unto our God:* "*The Levites which were the singers . . . having cymbals, psalteries and harps, . . . and 120 priests sounding with trumpets in unison with one voice to praise and glorify the Lord [came forth from the holy place]. . . . And when they lifted up their voice accompanied with trumpets, cymbals and instruments of music, and when they praised the Lord saying, 'For He is good, His mercy and loving kindness is everlasting;' **then** the house was filled with a cloud so that the priests could not stand to minister by reason of the cloud, for the glory of the Lord filled the house of God*" (2 Chronicles 5:12-14, NASB).

O, LORD, we pray for Your glory, Your Chabad, to fill our hearts, which as believers are temples to You. "Come into our hearts, Lord Jesus; there is room in our hearts for Thee." Amen

Praise brings us into worship, because praise and worship are the primary activities in heaven. Since there is no time as we know it in eternity, there is no such thing as boredom or weariness. Praise and worship have always been, and they always will be.[13] Scripture urges us to offer up the sacrifice of praise to God continually (Hebrews 13:15). The Old Covenant, of the Old Testament, required animal sacrifice on the altar. The New Testament Covenant requires the sacrifice of praise because, as Peter tells us in 1 Peter 2:9, *we are Christ's new royal priesthood.*[14] Christ's shed blood on the cross was the final atonement for sin, taking away forever the need to offer any further sacrifice.

What is praise? The psalms are the literature of worship and their most prominent feature is praise. Singing, shouting, dancing, rejoicing, adoration – all are the language of praise. Singing is meant to move us into praise. Through music we express our joy and our thanksgiving. No less than 41 psalms command us to sing unto the Lord. It helps us to center our fragmented minds and spirits to become poised toward God so that we are God-focused.

Sweet Intimacy of Prayer: Harps, Golden Bowls and "Camel Knees"

The Bible describes worship in physical terms. The root meaning for the Hebrew word that we translate *worship* is "to prostrate." The word *bless* means "to kneel," and *thanksgiving* refers to "an extension of the hand." Scripture shows us many varieties of physical postures of worship: lying prostrate, standing, kneeling, lifting the hands, clapping the hands, lifting the head, bowing the head, dancing and wearing sackcloth and ashes.[15]

In praise we see how the emotions need to totally be brought into the act of worship. Worship that is solely of the mind is unsound. Feelings are a legitimate part of the human personality and should be employed in worship. That doesn't mean worship should do violence to our rational faculties, but it does mean that our rational faculties alone are inadequate. As Paul counseled, we are to *"pray with the spirit and pray with the mind also;* (we are to) *sing with the spirit and sing with the mind also"* (1 Corinthians 14:15, NASB). We are quick to object to this line of teaching: "People have different temperaments," we argue. "That may appeal to emotional types, but I'm naturally quiet and reserved. It isn't the kind of worship that would meet my need." What we must see is that the real question in worship is not what will meet my need. The real question is "what kind of worship does God call for?" <u>*It is clear that God calls for wholehearted worship*</u>.[16]

It is as reasonable to expect whole-hearted worship to be physical as it is to expect it to be cerebral. Often our reserved temperament is little more than fear of what others will think of us, or perhaps unwillingness to humble ourselves before God and others. People do have different temperaments, but that must never keep us from worshipping with our whole being. We may, of course, do all the things described here and still never enter into worship, but they can provide avenues through which we are placed before God so that our inner spirit can be touched and freed.[17]

There are various Hebrew words to describe praise:

1. *halal*: to be clear (of sound); to shine; hence to make a show, <u>to boast</u>; and thus to be (clamorously) foolish; to rave; to celebrate; to stultify. "Praise [*halal*] ye the LORD. Praise

[*halal*], O ye servants of the LORD, praise [*halal*] the name of the LORD. From the rising of the sun unto the going down of the same, the LORD's name is to be praised [*halal*(ed)]" (Psalm 113:1, 3, KJV).
2. *tehillah*: to sing *halals*; to sing praises extravagantly; to celebrate with song. From the root word *halal*. "Praise [*halal*] ye the Lord, for it is good to sing praises [*tehillah*] unto our God; for it is pleasant, and praise [*tehillah*] is comely" (Psalm 147:1, KJV).
3. *zamar*: to touch the strings (of an instrument); to celebrate with song and music. "My heart is fixed, O God, my heart is fixed: I will sing and give praise [*zamar*]" (Psalm 57:7, KJV).
4. *yadah*: to revere or worship (with extended hands). "Let the people praise [*yadah*] Thee, O God; let all the people praise [*yadah*] Thee" (Psalm 67:3, KJV).
5. *towdah*: to extend the hands (usually in adoration); confession; (sacrifice of) praise, thanks (giving, offering). "Whoever offers praise [*todah*] glorifies me . . ." (Psalm 50:23).
6. *shabach:* to address in a loud tone; glory; praise; triumph (to shout [in triumph]) praises to God. "One generation shall praise [*shabach*] your works to another, and shall declare your mighty acts" (Psalm 145:4, KJV).
7. *barak*: to kneel; by implication to bless God (as an act of adoration). "And He shall live, and to Him shall be given of the gold of Sheba: prayer also shall be made for Him continually; and daily shall He be praised [*barak*(ed)]" (Ps. 72:15, KJV). [18]

From these root words and definitions we see again that praise is extremely demonstrative as it expresses worship from the heart. Lifting of the hands is particularly important for it takes humility and surrender of the flesh. Even to have your hands right in front of you, close to your body with palms lifted upward shows a humbling submission of asking the Lord to fill them. When a little child wants attention from a parent, what is the first thing he does? He lifts his hands up to his parents. Apply this analogy to your heavenly Father: Lift up your hands and ask of your Father! Apart from the blessing the believer receives, if we are not taking part in Davidic praise and worship to God, then we are not responding to the many, many commands and calls in the Bible to worship and praise as King David did.[19]

God enthrones Himself in our midst. Look at Psalm 22:3. The Hebrew word for "inhabit" is *yashab*, which translates, "to sit down (specifically as judge, in quiet); by implication to dwell, to remain; to settle, to marry; to abide; to dwell."[20] The New American Standard Bible uses the word "enthroned" for *yashab*. Considering the mercy seat, which is covered by the cherubim in the Holy of Holies, to be a type of God's throne, we could say that praise is God's dwelling place, His throne. In Revelation, where we began this week's study, there is continual praise and worship around the throne of God. But could it be more than that? As we lift our hearts, our hands and our voices in praise to God, He enthrones Himself in our midst. **God's presence evokes worship.**[21]

God's resting-place is our Praise! The Hebrew word *navah* translates "to rest (as at home); to celebrate (with praises); prepare an habitation."[22] In Exodus 15:13 we see this word again, where "habitation" (*navah*) not only means God's holy habitation but a celebration of praises to Him.

Look now at the word *strength*, (also in Exodus 15:13), which in Hebrew is *owz*, and means "strength in various applications (force, security, majesty, praise): boldness, loud, might, power, strength, strong."[23] This is the same Hebrew word that appears in Psalm 8:2: "Out of the mouth of babes and sucklings hast Thou ordained strength . . .," KJV. This is the same verse Jesus quoted in Matthew 21:16, but instead of translating the word "strength" as David did, Jesus put the emphasis on praise: "Have you never read, 'Out of the mouth of infants and nursing babies you have prepared praise for Yourself'?" NRSV.

The surprising correlation here is that *God's strength within us and our praise of Him are one and the same*. They are as closely interrelated as God's dwelling place and praise. This word, *owz*, seems to have a counterpart in the New Testament, the Greek word *dunamis*, which translates "force; specifically miraculous power (usually by implication a miracle itself)."[24] The similarities of these two words are shown in Revelation 4:11 in which the apostle John seems to use the word *power* where *praise* would seem more appropriate: "Thou art worthy, O Lord, to receive glory and honor and *power*," KJV. Can it be that praise and God's miracle-working power are so closely related that they are almost one and the same?

Before we leave this word *owz*, please note that the Ark of the Covenant in the Holy of Holies is also referred to as the Ark of the Testimony, the Ark of God, Ark of the Lord and Ark of Thy **Strength**. The word for "strength" here is *owz*. Thus, the Ark of the Covenant is the "Ark of Strength and Praise." Psalm 132:7–9 beautifully embodies all that has been said about praise and worship, God's habitation and strength: "Let us go into His tabernacle (His dwelling place); let us worship at His footstool. Arise, O Lord, to Your resting place; You and the ark of Your strength." <u>God's resting place is praise and worship</u>! The Ark of God is strength and praise![25] (Isaiah 66:1).

<u>God goes before us in Praise</u>! Look once again at Exodus 15:13. It reads that God did guide them in His strength unto His holy habitation. The word *guided* in Hebrew is *nahal*, meaning "to run with a sparkle, to flow; hence to conduct; to protect, sustain: carry, feed, guide, lead."[26] Here we see an aspect of God's character that is most different from our usual concept of God. We see Him "running with sparkle" ahead of His people, leading them gently on in His "strength and praise" to His holy "habitation and celebration of praise." This one verse gives us deep spiritual insight into the desires of God's heart and character and should make our hearts rejoice![27]

There is one thing we do on earth that we will continue to do in Heaven, and that is to praise and worship God. That is why we view life on earth as choir practice for Heaven. Praise and worship are the most important categories of music today. *There is no more important activity of the human heart than to praise and worship God.* It is the reason we exist – <u>our purpose is to glorify God</u>! Worship the Lord and prepare your hearts to do His will. Many of us may have fallen short of the glory of God! But we can pray:

♥*"Lord, set our spirits free to worship You*
with praise and joyful sound." ♥

Sweet Intimacy of Prayer: Harps, Golden Bowls and "Camel Knees"

Day 3 ~ "Humble yourselves in the sight of the Lord, and He will lift you up" (James 4:10).

Lord God, we bow before You. There is none like You in power or might; Your majesty humbles us at every point. We ask that Your Spirit open our hearts to understand how to know You better through prayer. Amen.

Worship is not about personality, temperament, personal limitations or church background – it is all about God. We are called to worship for His benefit, not ours, yet the irony is that we do indeed benefit greatly when we give ourselves to worshipping God. We've been designed to worship.

Jesus clearly understood the priority of worship, and taught the woman at the well the heart of the Father: "Yet a time is coming and has now come when the true worshippers will worship the Father in spirit and truth; for they are the kind of worshippers the Father seeks" (John 4:23, NIV).

God is calling a people out to worship Him and, in fact, has been seeking worshippers since the beginning of creation. He knows that He is the greatest good in all eternity. Learning this truth and expressing it back to Him causes us to draw near to the source of all blessing:[28] "Draw near to God and He will draw near to you" (James 4:8).

To build on understanding worship, open your Bible to Psalm 95: 1–7a. This Psalm shows that <u>we are invited to worship</u> our great and caring God. Worship is the human response to the divine initiative.[29] Study through as many of the following scriptures as possible, jotting notes about how we are invited to worship:[30]

1. <u>Worship is congregational</u>:[31] Psalm 111: 1; Matthew 26:30; Hebrews 2:12 and 10:22–25.

2. <u>Worship is musical</u>: 1 Chronicles 25:1, 3, 6–7; 2 Chronicles 5:11–14 and 20:14–22; Psalm 100:1, 2, 4; Psalm 150; Ephesians 5:18–19; Colossians 3:16.

3. <u>Worship is celebrative</u>: 2 Chronicles 5 again; Psalms 95, 96, 98, 99, 100:1–2; 105; 138; 147; 148; 149; 150; James 5:13; and others.

4. <u>Worship is responsive</u>. Psalm 28:2; Psalm 100:4; 134:2; 149:3.

<u>God</u> <u>is the reason we worship</u>; remember, ***it's all about God!*** Psalm 95:3–5, 7a.

- Worship is to God and for God (Psalm 105:1–3).
- We are lesser and pay homage to the greater, who is perfect in all His ways (Psalm 77:11). Worship fosters a humble spirit and reminds us to whom we belong (Luke 14:11; Zephaniah 2:3).
- God is the author of everything (Genesis 1; John 1:1–3).

<u>We Must Prepare for Worship</u>. People in the Bible gathered in "holy expectancy." They believed they would actually hear the voice of God. When Moses went into the tabernacle, he knew he was entering the presence of God. The same was true of the early church. It was not surprising to them that the building in which they met shook with the power of God; it had happened before (Acts 2:2; 4:31). When some dropped dead and others were raised from the dead by the word of the Lord, the people knew that God was in their midst (Acts 5:1–11; 9:36–43; 20:7–10). They were keenly aware the veil of the temple had been ripped in two at Christ's death, and like Moses and Aaron, they

were entering the Holy of Holies with no intermediaries. They were coming into the awesome, glorious, gracious presence of the living God, gathering with anticipation, knowing that Christ was present among them and would teach them and touch them with His living power.[32] Have you experienced that kind of worship? Oh, Dear One, I hope you have, but it is often rare in our day. How do we cultivate this holy expectancy?

It begins in us as we enter the **_Shekinah_ of the heart**. Shekinah is the "manifestation of the presence of God"; His divine presence. While living out the demands of our day, we are filled with inward worship and adoration. We work and play and eat and sleep; yet we are listening, ever listening, to our Teacher.[33] Whatever He teaches us He will give us the power to obey. Practice the presence of God. Live throughout the week as an heir of the kingdom, listening for His voice, obeying His word. Claim your inheritance!

Cultivate "holy expectancy" corporately. Since you have heard His voice throughout the week, you know you will hear His voice as you gather for public worship. Practicing the presence of God corporately will then bring a sense of being "gathered" into one mind, becoming of one accord (Philippians 3:15). When we are truly gathered in worship, things occur that could never occur alone. Biblical writers called this *koinonia*, deep inward fellowship in the power of the spirit.[34]

This experience is not the least dependent upon homogeneous units or even knowing information about one another's lives. There comes a divine melting of our separateness. In the power of the one Spirit we become "wrapped in a sense of unity and of presence such as quiets all words and enfolds [us] within an unspeakable calm and inter-knittedness within a vaster life."[35]

Worship leads us to trust God and see His work (Psalm 95:7b–11). We are called to respond to God – to *not* harden our hearts. Remember in the *Wait* chapter, Day 4, when we studied scriptures about hardening hearts? (Review that chapter and day if needed). God's authority operates in us and through us as we submit to His authority through the act of worshipping Him. As we yield our lives to Him, He rules and reigns in us and we come to the realization that there is something much, much bigger happening in the spiritual scene than what we see happening in the natural.

The only way to be a vessel of worship is to submit to His authority. Being a worshipper means placing ourselves under God's authority, which brings in God's blessings and makes us ambassadors of His authority (as we function under it). As we yield to God's authority, through worship, we invite the power of God. Sincere worship of God kills stubbornness and rebellion within us.

All of our obedience is worship. The whole thrust of our life is worship because our only reason for being on this earth is to bring glory to God. If we live a life of worship as well as enter into congregational worship, there will be integrity while the kingdom of God is being invoked and invited. *Worship reveals our hearts.* If you don't get anything else from this chapter, I hope you understand this: *The Heavenly Father desires our obedience – and it is worship to Him*!

We are warned to shun unbelief (vv. 7b–11) and to trust God (v. 7a). To harden one's heart equals sin and unbelief. Remember, worship reveals our hearts (Matthew 7:1–5). The one great message of God to us in worship is "Trust Me." Recall Holly Ogden's story and Kerry Bond's song: *"Trust Me – Simply Trust Me!"* Trusting God leads to wholeness and confirms the basis of our worship: God's unconditional love offered in His grace. In this unconditional love come honesty, transparency and trust.

<u>Worship keeps us in fellowship with God</u>. With the obstacle of sin overcome and with unconditional love bringing forth trust, repentance becomes a normal part of maintaining our relationship with God. If the Lord is to be Lord, worship must have priority in our lives because worship opens our hearts to let Him touch us with His deep love (Psalm 86:15). It reminds us He created us, He needs us, and how much we need Him.

Sweet Intimacy of Prayer: Harps, Golden Bowls and "Camel Knees"

Worship focused on a relationship with Jesus causes one to serve out of loving Him. Our lives are to be punctuated with praise, thanksgiving and adoration:

- The divine priority is worship first, service second. Service flows out of our worship for God.
- If we reverse service and worship and do service without the worship, then we become performance based like Martha. This becomes legalistic instead of worship oriented.
- Service as a substitute for worship is idolatry, and activity may become the enemy of adoration of the Heavenly Father.[36]

<u>Worship changes our perspective of others</u>, because *in worship there comes a clearer understanding of our own sin and gratefulness for His mercy.* Look up Luke 17:11–19 and write out your thoughts about what made "the one who returned" different than the others:

It has often been stated, grace is receiving what we don't deserve; and . . . mercy is **not** receiving what we *do* deserve. We become more merciful, compassionate and understanding of others despite their shortcomings or differences when we become worshippers. We begin to gain perspective on why God places certain individuals in our lives.[37] Look up 1 John 2:9–10 (*abides* in v. 10 means close, intimate relationship with God) and write what it means.

<u>Worship changes us</u>. *If worship does not change us it has not been worship.* To stand before the Holy One of eternity is to change. Resentments cannot be held with the same tenacity when we enter His gracious light. As Jesus said, we will need to leave our gift at the altar and go set the matter straight (Matthew 5:23–24). In worship an

increased power steals its way into the heart sanctuary, an increased compassion grows in the soul. *To worship is to change.*

- If worship does not propel us into a heart of greater obedience, it has not been worship. Just as worship begins in holy expectancy, it ends in holy obedience. Holy obedience saves worship from becoming an escape from the pressing needs of modern life.
- Worship enables us to hear the call to service clearly so that we respond, ". . . Here am I! Send me!" (Isaiah 6:8).
- Worship is deliberate and disciplined. It involves opening ourselves to the life of the Spirit. It makes all the religious paraphernalia of temples, priests, rites and ceremonies irrelevant.[38]

"Lord God Almighty! We have long honored You with our lips but our hearts have been far from You. In vain do we worship You and teach as doctrines the commandments of men. We have lain aside the commandments of God and held to the tradition of men. Full well we have rejected the commandment of God, that we may keep our own traditions. Forgive us and enable us to see the truth. Enable us to cast down imaginations and every high thing that exalts itself against the knowledge of You. Enable us by Your Spirit to bring into captivity every thought to the obedience of Jesus Christ. Not by might, not by power, but by Your Spirit, Lord. Cause our blind eyes to see, our dumb mouths to speak and sing praises to You. Cause our limp arms to reach up to You, our heavenly Father. Cause our feet to rejoice and leap for joy. Cause our hearts to open up to receive the wonderful love of God, the honey from the rock. We want to know You, Lord. We want to please You. Cause Your life and Godly emotions to flow through us to You. Make us worshipers in spirit and in truth. In the mighty name of Jesus, amen.[39]

Day 4 ~ "Love the Lord your God with all your heart, with all your soul, with all your mind, and with all your strength" (Mark 12: 30).

Father, Help us sit at Your feet and learn from You! We ask for Your wisdom. In the name of Jesus, amen.

Christianity is a love relationship with the King. God has made us in His image to have intimate communion with Himself. This relationship speaks of intimacy in spiritual, emotional, volitional, intellectual and physical areas, since we are to relate to God at every level of our being! The second great commandment moves on to our relationships with others: "You shall love your neighbor as yourself" (Mark 12:31). These two commandments are critically connected as we think about the kingdom of God and our participation in that kingdom. Our relationship to God must precede our ministry to others because our communion with our Father affects our ministry to others. So how can we know God versus knowing about God since knowing someone and knowing about them are two different things?

Many Christians today know a lot about God but they do not experience intimacy with Him. Knowing a considerable amount of doctrine or scripture is not the same as personally knowing God. The Pharisees knew scriptures very well yet they did not know the Messiah when He came as Christ of the Bible (John 5:39).[40]

Knowing God, then, goes beyond knowing about Him intellectually. Knowing Him personally extends into at least four areas (study through as many as you can):

1. Knowing God's Thoughts (Isaiah 55:8, 9; 1 Corinthians 2:11, 12) and His Ways (Psalm 25:4, 5):

    a. The Holy Spirit is the Spirit of wisdom and revelation, (Ephesians 1:17).
    b. The Holy Spirit reveals God's thoughts and ways to us (Psalm 62:1–2, 5–8).

c. The Holy Spirit is our teacher (1 John 2:27).

2. <u>Knowing God's Presence</u> (Psalm 16:11; 42:5; 90:8; 1 Thessalonians 1:3; Hebrews 4:16; James 4:10):

   a. Although God is omnipresent, the scriptures speak of times when His presence is acutely sensed or manifested.
   b. When God's presence is manifested it elicits various responses such as joy, shame, exposure of sin, peace, laughter, shaking, etc. (2 Samuel 12:1–14; 1 Chron.15:16, 25–28; 21:16; 2 Chron.29:25–30, 36; Ezra 9:6–Ezra 10:1; Nehemiah 9:1–5; Psalm 16:11; Acts 2:42–43; 3:1–10; 5:1-11; and 9:3–7).

3. <u>Knowing God's Love</u> (John 3: 16; 17: 26; 1 John 3:1):

   a. Jesus' identity and security was totally in His relationship with the Father.
   b. Because our Father has loved us, we can in turn love one another (1 John 4:7, 11, 13, 16).

4. <u>Knowing God's Voice</u> (John 10:3–4, 27; Acts 9:4; 10:13; Rev. 1:10–15, 3:20).

God is always communicating to us in various ways: "God does speak, first one way, then another; yet man may not perceive it" (Job 33:14), as mentioned previously. A. W. Tozer said: "Much of our religious unbelief is due to the wrong concept of and a wrong feeling for the scripture of truth. A silent God suddenly began to speak in a book and when the book was finished lapsed back into silence again forever. Now we read the book as a record of what God said when He was for a brief time in a speaking mood. With notions like that in our heads how can we believe? The facts are that God is not silent [and] has never been silent. ***It is the nature of God to speak.*** The second person of the Trinity is called "the Word." The Bible is the inevitable outcome of God's continuous speech."[41] We must learn to distinguish God's "voice" from other "voices" (i.e. self, demonic). How can we tell the difference? God's voice will always be one of peace, truth, matching with Scripture, and confirming. His voice will not be in anger, non-truth, or a twisting of scriptural truth or principles.

To prepare to hear God we have to want to listen!

    a. God's plea has always been, "Please listen to Me! I love you and I want to be your Father."
    b. God is always trying to get our attention.
    c. Believe that God has something to say.
    d. You won't search for something you don't miss. If you don't miss God, you probably won't seek Him.
    e. A willingness to hear God first about ourselves will ready us to hear God for ministry to others.

While living out the demands of our day we need to be filled with inward worship and adoration, all the while listening to God. We work, play, eat and sleep; yet we need to be listening, ever listening, to our Teacher. Frank Laubach's writings are filled with this sense of living under the shadow of the Almighty: "Of all today's miracles the greatest is this: to know that I find You best when I work listening. . . .Thank You, too, that the habit of constant conversation grows easier each day. I really do believe *all* thought can be conversations with You."[42]

We begin praying for others by first "centering down" and listening to the quiet thunder of the Lord of hosts. Tuning ourselves in to divine whisperings or breathings is spiritual work, but without it our praying is vain repetition (Matthew 6:7). Listening to the Lord is the "first, second and third thing" necessary for successful intercession. Soren Kierkegaard once observed: "A man prayed and at first he thought that prayer was talking. But he became more and more quiet until in the end he realized that prayer is listening."[43]

Having entered into a relationship with our Father, and having prepared ourselves to listen to Him, we are now like a short-wave radio waiting to receive His signals. How does He send these signals? What are the ways God speaks to us?

1. <u>God speaks to us through His word, the Bible</u>, as His foremost way of speaking to us (2 Timothy 3:16–17). Bible scriptures are the most authoritative and sure means by which we hear the Lord. *Any other means that God may use will not contradict the written*

word of God, therefore making it imperative that we who are listening to God know His word! Studying and memorizing the Bible is important because it will lead us into greater intimacy and understanding with God. Place yourself into the text asking, "What are you saying to me, Lord? What do You want me to think, to feel or to do? What does this mean in my life right now? How should I live this out?"

2. God speaks to us pictorially (Acts 2:17).

   a. A vision is a picture communication from God usually while the person is awake, but some Biblical examples have visions taking place while asleep. It may symbolically or realistically represent past, present, or future events and/or problems in a person's life: (Genesis 15:1,3–5; 2 Chronicles 26:5; Isaiah 6:1–8; Ezekiel 11:24; Acts 10:9–14, 16:9, 18:9–10; Revelation 9:17).
   b. A dream is a pictorial revelation from God while asleep. Not all dreams are from God, however. It takes discernment and submission to the wisdom and counsel of other mature believers to distinguish God-given dreams from our own: (Genesis 20:3,6; 37:5–6; 41:1; Numbers 12:6; 1 Kings 3:5; Daniel 7:1; Matthew 1:20, 2:22, 27:19).
   c. Many times *God will use what we see naturally* to communicate His truth. The entire description of materials, ways and craftsmen to create the tabernacle exhibits this (Exodus 26, 27, 30, 35–38). The Passover Lamb in Exodus 12 comes full circle in John 1:29 (and 1 Corinthians 5:7; also Numbers 21:4–9 with John 3:4-16; Acts 17:23; and 1 Corinthians 11:23). The parables that Jesus taught in Matthew 13 use the natural to teach the spiritual. Romans 1:19–20 speaks of this as well. Choose and read several of these scriptures.

3. God speaks to us through thoughts, impressions and by His voice (Isaiah 30:21). Often the Bible will say, "The Lord said to _____." It is not known if the person who received God's communication heard an audible voice or heard a voice in their mind. But they did hear "the voice of the Lord." Great

discernment is necessary when we think we hear God speak. Many people have done crazy and destructive things because they thought they heard from God. Examples of God's audible voice are: (Judges 7:2; 1 Kings 17:8, 9; Psalm 27:8; Acts 8:26 and 9:3–5; 2 Peter 1:17).

An impression is a very subjective, "you just know-that-you-know" kind of occurrence. In the middle of a situation, in ministry to others, in prayer, walking into a meeting – a sense of what has happened, is happening, or is about to happen passes through your mind (a brief impression) or permeates your mind (a strong impression). Since impressions are of such subjective nature they should be shared with others in a highly qualified nature such as: "It just occurred to me that you might be feeling angry with your father;" or, "I just had an impression that may or may not be from the Lord. May I tell you about it?"

4. <u>God also speaks to us by using various spiritual gifts and by visitations</u>. Visitations include the presence of the Lord who speaks and angels who deliver messages from the Lord. Having lived in and traveled in some Middle Eastern countries, it is thrilling to hear reports of many in these countries telling of dreams and visions of Jesus coming to them, holding out His hands and saying, "Come." They awake in full knowledge and confidence of who He is and immediately call Him "Lord."

The beginning point, then, in learning to pray for others is to listen for guidance.[44] As we quiet ourselves and remove the distractions, we can begin to distinguish His voice because *God is always speaking to us.* Hearing Him will not only bring us personal spiritual growth but will enable us to be more effective ministers of His kingdom work. May we cultivate that close kind of relationship with our Father and the Lord Jesus out of which we hear His voice and obey His word.[45]

*If we are still, we will learn not only who God is,
but also how His power operates.*[46]

♥ We only need faith the size of the grain of a mustard seed. ♥

Daddy, God, we cry out to You to hear You clearly. Reports of ones who have not known You trust You immediately when You come to them. Please forgive us when we have stubbornly stood aloof to You. We bow before You; we sit at Your feet. We long to be still in Your presence. Teach us we pray, amen.

Sweet Intimacy of Prayer: Harps, Golden Bowls and "Camel Knees"

<u>Day 5</u> ~ *"Be sober, be vigilant; because your adversary the devil walks about like a roaring lion, seeking whom he may devour" (1 Peter 5:8).*

*Father, Thank You that Your power within us is stronger than **anything** our adversary can bring against us. Help us to stand firm in the power of your might! Amen*

Years ago our church sang a song about walking into our enemy's camp and laying our weapons down, shedding our armor as we walked and laying it on the ground. The song instructed us to keep our armor on and be strong in the power of His might to effectually prove to our enemy that we truly are the "Army of the LORD" and we *have* won the victory!

We have learned that the beginning of learning to pray for others is to listen for guidance; that success in the small areas of life gives us authority in the larger matters; that if we are still, we will learn not only who God is but also how His power operates.[47] We *must* have God's power in our lives to enter into the battleground of intercession or else we *will* be entering into the enemy's camp laying our weapons down!

Meditation is the necessary prelude to intercession. The work of intercession, sometimes called the prayer of faith, presupposes that the prayer of guidance is perpetually ascending to the Father. *We must hear, know and obey the will of God before we pray it into the lives of others.* The prayer of guidance constantly precedes and surrounds the prayer of faith.[48]

If we have God-given compassion and concern for others, our faith will grow and strengthen as we pray. In fact, if we genuinely love people, we desire for them far more than is within our power to give, and that will cause us to pray. The inner sense of compassion is one of the clearest indications from the Lord that *this* is a prayer project for you. In times of meditation there may come a rise in the heart, a compulsion to intercede, an assurance of rightness, a flow of the

Spirit. This inner "Yes!" is the divine authorization for you to pray for the person or situation. (If the idea is accompanied with a sense of heaviness, then probably you should set it aside. God will lead someone else to pray for the matter).[49]

<u>What is Intercession</u>? Biblical intercession is prayer made on behalf of someone else for the other person's best good. It is an act of love in which the intercessor names the person before God – sometimes with a specific request for God to do a particular thing for that person – at other times just asking for God's love.[50]

Jesus Himself always lives to make intercession for us (Hebrews 7:25; Romans 8:34). John 17 records a beautiful prayer of intercession that Jesus prayed for His disciples and for all of us the night before He was crucified. Several additional New Testament references to pray for others include James 5:13–16; 1Timothy 2:1; Ephesians 6:18–19.

Although Jesus taught that if we asked we would receive (Matthew 7:7–11), most of us have found that we don't always get what we have asked for. That is partially because we are uncertain as to whether we have asked only according to our own desires, or whether our request is according to the will of God. Here are two suggestions to help in this area of doubt:

1. <u>When you pray for yourself</u>: Pour out all your heart's desires because He is interested in every detail of your life. As you tell God your desires, you will discover that things have a way of sifting themselves out, permitting you to receive God's answer through circumstances. Then be quiet and wait, confident that God is at work.
2. <u>When you pray for others</u>: Remember that you are not the judge, nor the accuser, nor the arbitrator of another's fate. Never confess another's sins before the Lord God – only your own. It is critical in spiritual warfare to know where the battle is being fought. It is *not* the bedroom, in the kitchen, with your mother-in-law, etc. Spiritual warfare is being fought in the spiritual realm. You are not fighting the person in the physical flesh and blood, but the devil in the spiritual realm. Be Alert!

Know Conduct of Warfare and to How to use Weapons of Warfare:

1. Resist the devil by submitting to God (James 4:7). Ephesians 2:2 & 6:10–12 tell who we are resisting. Remember 1 Peter 5:8–9 tells us to watch & pray.
2. Know the Word of God: Read it, memorize it, and learn it.
3. Rebuke the enemy with "It is written. . ." as Jesus did (Matthew 4:4, 7, 10) using scripture to rebuke by authority of the spoken word. This makes Satan a defeated foe. Pray *to* the Lord: 2 Kings 6:15–17 shows who is on our side.
4. By intercession: (1 Timothy 2:1; Hebrews 7:25; Romans 8: 34).
5. Binding and Loosening: (Mark 3:27; Matthew 16:19 and 18:18–19).
6. *Praise!* The devil cannot stand praise (Acts 16:22–26). The object in these verses was not release, but praise (2 Chronicles 20: 12, 15, 17, 21–22; Ephesians 5:15–21).
7. Agree with another believer (Matthew 18:19).
8. Take initiative. Keep your sword sharpened; don't wait until the devil attacks.
9. Take defense instead of offense.
10. Stay in good physical condition so therefore you will be in good mental condition. Prayer is hard work!
11. Don't let your armor slip: "Take heed lest you fall" (1 Corinthians 10:12; Ephesians 6:13–18). Keep your antenna up and always be alert.
12. Mental pictures for intercession: When a person cleans house or rearranges furniture, there is usually an idea – a picture in the mind – of how the result of the work ought to look. A business person can see potential in a wavering firm, so it is purchased. An architect has a mental picture of the finished building being designed and draws up the blueprints accordingly. These are illustrations of something all of us do every day – how things ought to be or could be.

This act of seeing something mentally can be employed in prayer as an aid to intercession and enables us to be led by the Spirit in our asking. Jesus taught us to make mental pictures. In Mark 11:22–24 Jesus told His disciples to picture the moving of a mountain into the sea – to picture it without doubt and it would happen. Each person who came to Jesus to be touched and healed saw himself whole again even before the miracle took place (Mark 5:28; 10:46–52).

The mountains that confront us may not be made of earth and stones, but they are the same impossible types of situations; ones that we cannot change or move, ones that no one can do anything about. We have to learn the balance between facing our responsibilities and trusting God to work it out in His way.

What is your mountain? Don't pretend it isn't there. Don't rationalize and call it by another name. Face it openly; then speak to it. Speak in authority. Jesus encourages us to call it by name and tell it to disappear into the sea. Picture it moving, falling into the sea, leaving behind the large open space for God to fill. In Christ's presence no power can harm us (Romans 8:31–39).

✪ Set aside some time to pray for a while.

Is the ministry of Jesus our ministry?

- He said we would do His works, and greater works! (John 14:11–13).
- He commissioned us and gave us authority to proclaim the good news, and heal: (Matthew 10:1 and 28:18–20; Luke 10:1; Acts 1:8).
- His ministry is to the church corporately: (1 Corinthians 12–14; 1 Thessalonians 5:19–21; James 5:14–16).
- He said we must be filled with the Spirit: (Acts 2:4; 4:8, 31; 7:55 and 13:9; Galatians 5:16; Ephesians 5:18 and 6:18; Jude 20). As ministers of the Kingdom of God, we are to demonstrate the presence of God by the power of the Holy Spirit (1 Corinthians 4:20).

So how do we carry out Jesus' ministry? Maintaining our intimacy with God is crucial. We must know Him, know what He is doing and what He wants to do. The Father prepares us during our times alone with Him, encouraging us, training us in His Word, will, works and ways. He confronts us, molding us and shaping us into the image of His Son, developing our character and producing the fruit of the Spirit in our lives! He gives us compassion for others, the same compassion that moved Jesus so many times to minister to the multitudes.

Ask for His presence and power in your life and in the lives of others. In short: *pray, pray, pray!* We accomplish this by:

1. <u>Emptying ourselves</u>. We can't be filled with the Spirit if we're full of the world and our self. Confess your sins openly, repent, and lay down your life.
2. <u>Being filled with His presence</u>. Let the Holy Spirit fill you, as the above scriptures indicated.
3. <u>Believing that God will use you</u>. Expect it! Believe and trust God to give you wisdom and revelation (Ephesians 1:16–18).
4. <u>Becoming involved in the various areas of Jesus' ministry</u> like evangelism, physical healing, inner healing, deliverance, encouragement, comfort and hope.
5. *<u>Doing the stuff!</u>* (Matthew 10:7–8). List the prayer possibilities of these verses:

Praying for others, "doing the stuff," must be an inner reality and not a mechanical tool. Jesus said, "I only do what I see My Father doing" (John 5:19). This model of prayer should definitely be used by all Christians. Do you see a need? Do you feel compassion? Do you have wisdom in this area? The Father is showing you. It cannot, should not *ever* be our agenda, but always praying from the heart. God is a "heart-checker." Write out or paraphrase Hebrews 4:12 to help understand this concept:

✪ Ministry should be a large part of our life as we live as God's people. Jesus' urging to the twelve echoes down through the centuries to us: *"Freely you received; freely give"* (Matthew 10:8b, NASB). Giving ourselves – our time, money, energy and the gifts the Holy Spirit gives us – is the essence of loving our neighbors and loving this world for which God gave His only Son. Ministry must be our lifestyle. Pray for it! Look for opportunities to minister the power and presence of our Lord wherever and whenever possible. This ministry may come in crisis, as an ongoing process or as a combination of both. In any case, it is our privilege to participate in ministry in the Kingdom of God.[51]

Lord, teach us to pray. We have studied Your Word, Your holy scriptures and even practiced praying this week. Lead us in the direct paths to which You are calling each one of us. Examine our hearts, our heavenly "Heart-Checker," and show us where we are off course. Guide us to You. Train us up to be prayer warriors. To our God who listens, we pray, amen.

~ Chapter 6 ~

Trust without Borders

OCEANS (Where Feet May Fail)

You call me out upon the waters.
The great unknown where feet may fail.
And there I find You in the mystery.
In oceans deep my faith will stand.

I will call upon Your name
and keep my eyes above the waves.
When oceans rise my soul will rest in Your embrace,
For I am Yours and You are mine.

Your grace abounds in deepest waters.
Your sovereign hand will be my guide
Where feet may fail and fear surrounds me.
You've never failed and You won't start now.

<u>Spirit lead me where my trust is without borders</u>.
Let me walk upon the waters
wherever you would call me.
Take me deeper than my feet could ever wander
and my faith will be made stronger
In the presence of my Saviour.

I will call upon Your name.
Keep my eyes above the waves.
My soul will rest in Your embrace.
I am Yours and You are mine!

United, Zion CD by Hillsong, 2013
License Permit #552711, EMICMGMUSIC [1]

Day 1 ~ *"Trust in the LORD with all your heart, and lean not on your own understanding; in all your ways acknowledge Him, and He shall direct your paths" (Proverbs 3:5-6).*

LORD, with all our heart we want to trust in You. Please help us to not lean on our own understanding so that You are free to direct our paths. It is in Your name that we pray, Amen.

This book was birthed while on an innocent morning walk one spring. I was "minding my own business" and enjoying the beauty of the countryside when I felt God spoke to my heart: "Write a book." It was unsettling to me because, first of all, it was an unusual request (in my mind), and secondly, I don't consider myself a writer. I "told" God that, of course, but in my life's experiences He doesn't listen to me when I tell Him things like that. For over three years I questioned God's instructions to me to write a book on *trust*, or any book for that matter. His challenge caused me to examine my life, my ways of living, my entire purpose and everything I know about Jesus Christ and to honestly ask myself if I did truly, honestly and fully trust Him.

Several months into the "write-the-book" instruction I explained it to my husband and told him I needed to obtain a laptop computer to be able to work on this project since the bed and breakfast computer was older and used for the reservations and bookkeeping. "No, you can use mine," he answered, with both of us each insisting from of our viewpoints for well over that first year. A new computer was finally purchased, but then parents, our business, grandbabies and life interrupted any writing for the next several years before *finally* arriving at dedicated writing time. I basically had worked through the fears of writing, attended several writing conferences, learned the computer and began to speak of this book to others by the time I sat down to write. It was *so* exciting and *so* amazing how details and scriptures, thoughts and references all began to come together! The timing was perfect.

Trust without Borders

Trust is our gift back to God and the beauty of a heart which trusts that it is loved gives God immense pleasure. It pleased God that I obeyed Him in the decision to write this book. God finds our gift of trust in Him so wonderful that Jesus was willing to die for the love of it![2] Our trust in Him is like a childlike surrender to the love of God; an uncompromising trust in the love of God. Sounds simple enough, doesn't it? But is it? Look at what Jesus said in Mark 10:15: "Truly I say to you, whoever does not receive the kingdom of God like a child shall not enter it at all," NASB. What do you think Jesus meant by that verse?

To me it means living with and loving Him with a childlike surrender, trusting uncompromisingly in the love of God. Not easy, but requested by Jesus! The opening verses beginning today's lesson teach about intimacy with the LORD, having relationship with Him *with all your heart.* They instruct us to lean not unto our own understanding. Whoa! That *is* trusting Him! When we *acknowledge* Him in ALL our ways, He directs our paths, opens wide the gates, opens "blind" eyes, makes things more clear to us, and sets captives free. But, it is imperative that we constantly renew our trust in God.

Trust, *chasa,* (chah-sah): To trust; to hope; to make someone a refuge.[3] Remember we previously studied that Psalm 57:1 illustrates this verb picturing David as nestling under God's wings for refuge, similarly as a baby bird is sheltered under the feathers of its parent: "Be merciful to me, O God, be merciful to me! For my soul trusts in You; and in the shadow of Your wings I will make my refuge, until these calamities have passed by."

In earlier chapters we discussed *faith* as being conviction, confidence, *trust,* belief, reliance, and trustworthiness. In the New Testament, the word "faith" is the divinely implanted principle of inward confidence, assurance, *trust,* and reliance in God and all that He says.[4] Let's examine and write out a few scriptures that speak of putting our *trust* in God:

Trust without Borders

Psalm 118:8

Psalm 5:11–12: "But let all those rejoice who put their *trust* in You; let them ever shout for joy, because You defend (cover) them; let those also who love Your name be joyful in You. For You, O LORD, will bless the righteous; with favor You will surround him as with a shield."

Do you remember that Day 4 of the *Inheritance* chapter taught us about God being a shield over and around us? What a perfect picture of protecting us, the righteous, with favor. "The LORD also will be a refuge for the oppressed, a refuge in times of trouble. And those who know Your name will put their *trust* in You; for You, LORD, have not forsaken those who seek You (who trust in You)" (Psalm 9:9–10).

It has been mentioned many times previously how hard it is for us to let go and let God defend us. The grace to release and let God be God flows from trust in His boundless love.[5] Without fail, personal experience of the love of Jesus Christ initiates trust.[6]

"But I have *trusted* in Thy lovingkindness; my heart shall rejoice in Thy salvation" (Psalm 13:5, NASB).

Trust defines the meaning of living by grace rather than works. Trust is like climbing a fifty-foot ladder, reaching the top and hearing someone down below yell "Jump!" The trusting disciple has this childlike confidence in a loving Father. Trust says, in effect, "Abba, just on the basis of what You have shown me in Your son, Jesus, I believe You love me. You have forgiven me. You will hold me and never let me go. Therefore, I trust You with my life."[7]

Here is a related story that captures the above essence of biblical trust: "A two-story house had caught on fire and the family – father, mother and several children – were on their way out. The smallest boy became terrified, tore away from his mother and ran back upstairs. Suddenly he appeared at a smoke-filled window crying like crazy. His father, now outside, shouted: 'Jump, son, jump! I'll catch you.' The boy cried: 'But, Daddy, I can't see you!' 'I know,' his father called, 'I know. But I can see you!'" [8]

The only way for this boy to be saved was for him to jump. In John 14:1 and 6, Jesus said, "Let not your heart be troubled; you believe in God, believe also in Me. . . . I am the way, the truth and the life. No one comes to the Father except through Me." He was outright blunt about *trust in God and trust in Me*. We have studied that faith walks hand in hand with love and evidences itself in obedience. Faith approaches God boldly to receive from Him; hope gives us confidence of the future, and love is the greatest of these three. Jesus put them all together in His basket instructing us to *trust* Him. There is none other!

"See, God has come to save me. I will TRUST in Him and not be afraid. The Lord God is my strength and my song; He has given me victory" (Isaiah 12:2, TLB). There is none greater! Is there anyone greater to you? Explain what this verse means to you:

"Miracle Heidi"
~by my friend, Vickie Watson

"*It's a girl*," Dr. Guthrie pronounced as he placed a bloody, squirming little body on my stomach. Standing to my right, my husband Chuck cut the umbilical cord. Then everything changed. Feeble squeaks rather than healthy cries. Shades of blue, then bluer; then purple rather than pink. Alarms buzzed ... People dashed in and out ... Tense faces ... A blaring silence of human voices. She was whisked from the room.

This could not be happening – not after the promises from God during my pregnancy. Not after the illness of our first child. This had to be a nightmare! But it was painfully real and we had just entered the fight of our lives—the fight for our daughter's life! My next glimpse of her was an hour later for a brief goodbye before the transport team rushed her to Cook Children's Hospital.

Later that evening the words from the pediatric cardiologist by phone were not encouraging. Malformation of the tricuspid valve... Ebstein's Anomaly...<u>a heart swelled to six times its normal size</u>... a 17% chance of survival! We hung up the phone and wept.

When Chuck returned to my room at 2:00 a.m. after visiting our daughter twenty-five miles away, he brought video footage taken at her bedside over the past few hours. The picture before me was painfully ironic. I saw my newborn struggling for life as a respirator did the work of breathing for her. In the background I heard Sandy Patti quoting Psalm 139:13–16: *"You made my whole being; You formed me in my mother's body. You saw my bones being formed as I took shape in my mother's body. When I was put together there, You saw my body as it was formed. I praise You because You made me in an amazing and wonderful way."* The cassette player then sent forth her beautiful voice singing, "You are a Masterpiece." "Not now, God; that's far too painful." That was the promise verse and song which the Lord had given me six months earlier for this child. Chuck was playing it by her bedside. At the moment the timing felt like a cruel joke.

Trust without Borders

Ten days later on a Monday afternoon as I sat by her bedside, I felt the weariness of the battle. I had been singing the first verse of her song to her each day, but that day there was no music left within me. I flipped on the tape and listened anew as the words of the second verse jumped out at me:

**'And now you're growing up, your life's a miracle
Every time I look at you, I stand in awe** because I see in you a And you'll always be my little Lamb from God
And as your life goes on each day,
How I pray that you will see just how much
your life has meant to me . . . .'

There it was! He had already told me what I needed to know about Heidi! It was right there in her song! The second verse said, 'Now you're growing up, your life's a miracle.' That was my answer! God told me that she would grow up! He had given me the word long before I even knew I needed it. God would not tell me that she would grow up if she were going to die.

"At that moment, I knew that Heidi would live. I didn't know how we were going to get from Point A, 'she's dying' to Point B, 'she's a miracle.' But I knew God had given me my answer. She would live! ...

"What do you do when what you see with your eyes is so vastly different from what God has told you beforehand about the situation? I had two clear choices:

(1) To believe what I saw with my eyes and heard from a skilled medical community, or (2) To believe what God had told me about her, months before her birth. I chose the latter."

We were told multiple times that she would not live—an accurate assessment in the physical realm. We were told that if she did surprise us all and live, she would be a vegetable due to the extended lack of oxygen during the first month. There were no surgical options.

Daily, hourly, I had to gird up my mind. My focal point had to be what God had told me about her. A masterpiece. A miracle. "God,

Trust without Borders

either I trust You or I don't. I choose to trust You and Your Word about the situation."

The journey was very long. And our God was very faithful. <u>After 85 days in intensive care</u>, we brought her home. At one year old she was medication free. At four years old, Heidi stood on the hospital conference table and sang "Jesus Loves Me" to her medical team. The cardiologist's response? "She's a miracle." At age twenty-one, she ran a half-marathon to raise money for water wells in Africa. In four months Heidi will graduate from college. Our God is trustworthy.

(Quotations from <u>Miracle Heidi: When Doctors Couldn't ... God Could!</u> by Vickie Boone Watson, 1996; Used by permission of Sterling Press International.)[9]

✪ It would show evidence of your trust in God if you committed to memory the verse that began today's lesson:

"Trust in the LORD with all your heart, and lean not on your own understanding; in all your ways acknowledge Him, and He shall direct your paths" (Proverbs 3:5–6).

Memorizing God's word not only strengthens us, but brings encouragement, healing in numerous ways and helps in battle against our enemies. You are to be commended! After committing the verse to memory, close in prayer to end your day:

Heavenly Father, what magnificent attributes You exhibit to us in Your Word. Please continue to reveal them to us, explain them to our finite minds and enlarge them within our spirits. We come as little children with our baskets full of love. Please share more with us, we pray. Amen

Trust without Borders

Day 2 ~ *"The LORD is my strength and my shield; my heart trusted in Him, and I am helped; therefore my heart greatly rejoices, and with my song I will praise Him" (Psalm 28:7).*

O, LORD, our strength and our shield! Our hearts are learning to trust in You and we thank You that You are helping us. We do rejoice in You, O King, and our hearts sing praises to You! Lead us today we pray, Amen.

From Judah, one of the twelve sons of Jacob, from whom the twelve tribes of Israel originate, comes this prophesy: "The scepter shall not depart from Judah" (Genesis 49:10). Into this lineage of Judah was born David, of the House of Jesse, the Bethlehemite. Jesse was the grandson of Ruth and Boaz and so was in the line of the covenant with Abraham that we studied in earlier chapters. David was the youngest of eight sons and was the sheepherder of the family, the lowest on the family totem pole!

It had come about at that time in Israel that the people cried out for a king they could "see" (since they couldn't see God), and though the prophet Samuel tried to talk them out of it, a man named Saul was chosen by God and anointed as the first king over Israel. As shown in 1 Samuel 15, King Saul failed to be obedient to the LORD and God stripped him of his anointing as king. He remained reigning king for nearly 15 more years, but the blessing of the LORD had been removed from him. Take some time today to read these three chapters in 1 Samuel 15, 16 and 17 to understand the story of King Saul and the future King David.

God had instructed Samuel to go to the house of Jesse and there he would find the one to anoint as the next king of Israel. As the first seven sons of Jesse passed before Samuel, the LORD rejected all seven. When fifteen-year-old-David was brought in from shepherding in the fields, the LORD spoke to Samuel saying, "This is the one... and the Spirit of the LORD came upon David from that day forward" (1 Samuel 16:12b and 13b). However, it was many years before David began his reign as king over Israel.

Obviously David was born to become king, but as years passed and he still served in the fields tending sheep and fighting off bears and lions, he probably didn't think he would ever reign as a king! Don't you think he wondered if he really was anointed king? Maybe he thought Samuel and God forgot him . . . or had he just missed the whole message about kingship? And to confuse the fact of being anointed king, Saul, who was still reigning as king, asked David to serve in the palace by playing soothing music for him. "What? I'm supposed to be king!" How confusing that must have been for David. What a mature level of trust from such a young man – truly anointed of God!

Most of us can relate on some level to David's experience. Great lengths of time can pass between instructions and actual occurrences. It took almost fourteen years from the time God spoke to my husband and me about starting a bed and breakfast before we actually moved to our land to begin building. Much had happened in those fourteen years, but I can say with 100% assurance that those years trained, taught and prepared us for what lay ahead for us!

Those were years of learning to put our trust in the God who speaks. They were years of aligning our lives with God's word, adjusting our attitudes, of learning to sit in His presence. *God doesn't waste time*: "And we know that all things work together for good to those who love God, to those who are called according to His purpose" (Romans 8:28). Can you journal of a time or two when this scripture applied to your life?

Our attitude should be shaped "while we are keeping our sheep in the field;" while devoting time sitting in His presence and meditating on His word. David did that often, writing many of the psalms of the Bible. He didn't leave the sheep to go look for a position, but worked to develop his skills while he was on the job. He slayed attacking predators, learned how to pray and come before the LORD, learned

Trust without Borders

that he was larger than insults pitched his way from siblings and a giant; and, he learned that tending physical sheep is how to handle people who act like sheep.

Therefore, when his father sent him to take food to his brothers who were away at war fighting the Philistines, he was ready to fight the giant who bellowed against the Israelites! How did such a young teen like David have the courage and confidence to take a stand against a giant? Because *he trusted in God* who had anointed him to be a king! He was empowered by God spiritually, physically, emotionally and mentally.

Did you like the passages in 1 Samuel 17:38–39 when Saul had his personal armor placed on David? He couldn't even walk! We can't put our trust in the ways of the world and try to wear armor that is not of God, armor not suited for us. We must trust only in the God who goes before us. David took off the heavy, unfamiliar armor and picked up what he was used to: his familiar slingshot. I wonder if he prayed as he picked up the five smooth stones from the brook and put them in his shepherd's bag.

It strikes me that David must have walked over stones the whole way there. How many times do we do the same thing? We walk over the very weapons, the very strengths we need to slay the giant we are facing. God isn't asking for us to pick up amazing, huge strengths or to be something or someone we are not. Scripture says David grabbed smooth stones, not big or sharp stones. God wants us to use the smooth, well-worn strengths that have been chiseled and developed over time. That's why it's so important to develop our strengths . . . they could be the very things God chooses to use to slay our future giants.

And, he knelt down to pick up the stones. Proverbs 16: 3 says to "Commit your works to the Lord and your thoughts will be established." The word *commit* comes from a word used to describe "roll." For instance, when a camel's load became too heavy, it would kneel down and the weight would roll off its back. In order for David to pick up the stones, he had to kneel and let the burden of the battle roll off. We, too, in necessary times of trust, need to take a moment to kneel down so the burden can roll off our backs and we can pick up the very strength we need to carry on.

Then David ran to the valley, or a low place, to meet Goliath. He could run to a low place because he knew he was merely running through it to get to the next high point. Secondly, he knew who he belonged to and had complete faith and trust in Him. He could run straight towards the giant knowing God already had the victory. What a mature place of trust!

If you are in a season of having to *trust* God, embrace it, because it is what will carry you all the way to the palace. No position comes without first being in the field. The route to our destiny requires that we prepare by developing our strengths in the field. Take a stand and choose to clothe yourself with a righteous attitude. We can run toward our giants because we know whose we are and God has given us the victory![10] We can do so because we *trust* in Him!

"For in the time of trouble He shall hide me in His pavilion; in the secret place of His tabernacle He shall hide me; He shall set me high upon a rock. The LORD is my strength and my shield; **my heart trusted in Him**, and I am helped; therefore my heart greatly rejoices, and with my song I will praise Him. Wait on the LORD; be of good courage, and He shall strengthen your heart; wait, I say, on the LORD!" (Psalm 28:5, 7, 14).

✪ Ask God to strengthen you as you choose five, smooth stones to fight off whatever may be your need today. Kneel down before Him and stay in His presence for a while.

Trust without Borders

<u>Day 3</u> ~ *"Trust in the LORD and do good; dwell in the land and feed on His faithfulness. Delight yourself also in the LORD, and He shall give you the desires of your heart" (Psalm 37:3-4).*

LORD, we have been learning how to delight ourselves in You, and You have begun to give us the desires of our hearts. Thank You for the relationship we have in You. Help us, by Your Spirit, Lord, to let that be what we live for. To You we pray, Amen.

Trust is foundational for any relationship whether parent to child, child to parent, spouse to spouse, teacher to student, doctor to patient, business partner to partner, friend to friend, and so on. We have all experienced some kind of relationship that fell short of a solid, relational foundation. It is never a pleasant thing, proving once again that our firm foundation must always be built upon God and His truth. It reminds us: "Is it trust only when we get our way?" No, it is trust when we are hanging on by our fingernails in the tightest grip on the slimmest rope that we have grasped at the last minute as we slipped off that slippery slope.

It is imperative that we look beyond what we can see in the natural, peering where impossibilities are reality, and lingering there until what is impossible is not only possible but tangible. It is *never* easy, but that is *trust*. In every uttered breath of every grateful Christian saved from sin by God's grace is an unshaken trust in Jesus and His refreshing promise of eternal life. Uncontaminated trust in the revelation of Jesus allows us to breathe more freely, to dance more joyfully and to sing more gratefully about the gift of His salvation![11]

Living with experiences of faith and determined hope provides depth to our relationship with the *Abba*. Jesus is the one who introduced us to praying intimately to Abba, the colloquial, Aramaic word meaning "Daddy." He respectfully addressed God as Abba in intimate prayers, teaching His disciples of a closer relationship with their heavenly Father. To address God in this way is the boldest, simplest expression of the absolute trust that God is good, that He is on our side, and that

"The LORD is like a father to his children, tender and compassionate to those who fear him" (Psalm 103:13, NLT). I want a relationship with the Abba of Jesus, who is infinitely compassionate with my brokenness and at the same time is an awesome, incomprehensible, unwieldy Mystery of the ages![12] Often when I am overwhelmed and feel I cannot even breathe because of currents of despair swirling around me, I literally hold out my hands and ask the LORD if I can crawl up into His lap. I promise, before the words are out of my mouth He is saying "Yes!" to me. I call this my "overwhelming" prayer. I cry out – He says "Yes!" – and He enfolds me in His majestic arms. Sometimes I cry; sometimes I just sit. It is *never* rushed . . . and I *always* feel more secure, more stable, and refreshed with answers, or satisfied with none when my time with Him is ended.

Our relationship of faith with our Daddy should reveal a lifestyle of reaching out to and trusting in God, even in the face of previously unknown experiences and seemingly insurmountable odds. Our opening scripture today said to *trust in the Lord* which will help us remember His faithfulness to us in the past. We should not fear opposition even when it seems stronger or better supported. We should be confident that God can use what we have at hand to overcome any obstacles we face.[13]

It is in faith that we step out in trust, in spite of our circumstances. God never failed to provide all that was needed in each situation, sometimes in unusual and miraculous ways! Know that the times when things look impossible are the times to praise, pray and look expectantly to the Lord. Then step out with faith and obedience to the Lord,[14] like the young anointed King David did with Goliath and this young missionary mom did with her family:

"Called to missions in a foreign land with four small children and one soon on the way, Celia Dodge packed up her kids, and with her one-year-old baby strapped to her back, she and her husband set out for Tibet via the steep, narrow and treacherous Silk Road where thieves waited in the night for their prey. As she traveled on a donkey down that narrow path with hairpin curves and watched her children disappear around each terrifying bend, the stark reality of

Trust without Borders

her situation confronted her – she was helpless. Her only choice was to trust in God's protective hand.

"They finally reached the top of the Himalayan Mountains, which was as far as they could safely go by themselves. Before continuing, they needed to join with a larger caravan to ensure protection from thieves. But the hope of continuing their journey grew dim as caravans came and went, each guide demanding more money than they had. Days of freezing temperatures and dwindling rations turned into weeks. The path ahead looked bleaker and even darker than the ebony smoke that filled the tiny dung hut they had temporarily settled in.

"Knowing the first blizzard would be impossible to survive, Celia was once again pressed to look up from her dim circumstances. Stepping out of the dung hut one morning, she lifted her eyes for what seemed like the first time, overwhelmed by the exhilarating scene before her. She stood at the top of the world! As far as she could see, there was nothing but the beauty of the whole world at her feet.

"Sinking into the warmth of God's gentle voice, she was engulfed by the sweetness of His love and all-surpassing peace. The realities of her situation wafted away as she was submersed in the tranquility of a single word from Him – "patience."

"Finally, after one month, a caravan arrived! This time, they were determined to leave with them no matter what it cost. A few days into their journey, the caravan came to an abrupt halt. Slowly making their way down the path, a stilled hush rolled over the convoy. Ice sculptures were in the snow before them . . . it was a trail of men still on their horses. They were all frozen! Chills ran through Celia's body as the full impact of waiting patiently dawned on her. By *trusting* God's word, He had spared them from a vicious band of thieves. Once again, in the tranquility of the moment, she was engulfed by God's love and faithfulness."

Each of us travels down our own Silk Road. In facing thieves and fears we each have a choice: We can keep our eyes on the hairpin turns and threatening shadows of our treacherous mountain paths, or, we can look to God and luxuriate in the warm presence of the One who made the Silk Road and designed the way through. Choosing to submerge yourself into a place of trust will bring an eternal view where the impossible becomes possible.[15]

"See, God has come to save me. <u>*I will TRUST in Him and not be afraid.*</u> The Lord God is my strength and my song; He has given me victory" (Isaiah 12:2, TLB). Journal your thoughts of this Isaiah 12:2 verse we have previously studied and how it relates with Celia's occurrence and one or more close calls in your life:

✪ In the opening chapter of this book, Day 1, we memorized Psalm 37:5. Read over it again today, speaking it from your heart and closing with it in prayer:

"Commit your way to the LORD; trust also in Him and He shall bring it to pass."

Lord, Thank You for being a light to our paths. Thank You for whispering to us, "This is the way; walk in it." Continue to lead us, Lord. Amen

Trust without Borders

A Bump in the Road

We are in economic hard times with more signs occurring every day to prove it. When my husband purchased his first motorcycle years ago it was against my better judgment. God did usher it in, however, with several confirmations, only 300 miles on it, and a great price. In order to assuage my doubt he said I could get anything I wanted. After thinking it over for about two years, I decided "my motorcycle" was to be a red turbo diesel Volkswagen with a sun roof. We lived on a dirt road so the pretty yellow VW with the black convertible top just didn't seem too practical. Standing my ground on the decision just as he had stood his on the motorcycle took a few months while he tried to talk me out of the purchase. Eventually we did get a shiny red VW, which he loved as much as I did.

But now lower to the ground with smaller tires than my former, taller Tahoe I cringed when I hit ridges driving over bridges, or deeper pits and ruts in the roads. There are several on the way to our main shopping sources and I made mental notes to remember them to avoid being swallowed up by the road-pit monsters. We have many heat-wave summers here in Texas with excessive days of 100+ degree temperatures – nationwide as well – like God may be trying to burn us up to get our attention. Newscasts have shown entire highway medians, sidewalks, and such that have buckled up from the intense heat, so hoping to have repairs on my highways and roads close to home seems unlikely.

Other results of the excessive heat are roadway signs with letters, numbers or arrows just curling up on the sign boards. Early spring rains and heavy straight-line windstorms knocked over many signs on nearby highways – often taking great lengths of time before being repaired or corrected. It is a sign of the economic times, with budgets being cut all over the country, in every business, every home, and every governmental agency. Budgets are hurting . . . and yet it seems we are all living in denial. There are signs of closed businesses, properties for sale, empty buildings, foreclosures and bankruptcy signs everywhere. Observations seem to indicate that it will be harder to drive everywhere and in every way we go because of so many "bumps" in the roads.

This is a time to make decisions of where our trust and hope truly lie. The entire world is spiraling out of control and living in denial that we can control our little part of it will certainly result in heartache and despair. The shaking of earthly things is not to be a problem to any Christian but a promise that was given to us long ago. The Bible tells us that as the time draws near for Jesus Christ the Messiah to return, the earth will cry out in labor pains. The earth *is* in travail; the earth *is* in labor. As any woman knows who has birthed a child, it is hard, often painful and not something any woman enjoys going through. But at the end of the hard labor pains is a good thing, a birthing long awaited. Now is the time to *trust* and "to look up, for your Redemption draws near."

Pamela Alexander [16]

Trust without Borders

Day 4 ~ *Psalm 91, Safety of Abiding in the Presence of God,* NASB

¹ He who dwells in the secret place of the Most High shall abide under the shadow of the Almighty.
² I will say of the Lord, "He is my refuge and my fortress; My God, in Him I will trust."
³ Surely He shall deliver you from the snare of the fowler and from the perilous pestilence.
⁴ He shall cover you with His feathers, and under His wings you shall take refuge; His truth shall be your shield and buckler.
⁵ You shall not be afraid of the terror by night, nor of the arrow that flies by day,
⁶ Nor of the pestilence that walks in darkness, nor of the destruction that lays waste at noonday.
⁷ A thousand may fall at your side, and ten thousand at your right hand; but it shall not come near you.
⁸ Only with your eyes shall you look, and see the reward of the wicked.
⁹ Because you have made the Lord, who is my refuge, even the Most High, your dwelling place,
¹⁰ No evil shall befall you, nor shall any plague come near your dwelling;
¹¹ For He shall give His angels charge over you, to keep you in all your ways.
¹² In their hands they shall bear you up, lest you dash your foot against a stone.
¹³ You shall tread upon the lion and the cobra, the young lion and the serpent you shall trample underfoot.
¹⁴ "Because he has set his love upon Me, therefore I will deliver him; I will set him on high, because he has known My name.
¹⁵ He shall call upon Me, and I will answer him; I will be with him in trouble; I will deliver him and honor him.
¹⁶ With long life I will satisfy him, and show him My salvation."

O, Father, open up the words of this Psalm to us to help our finite minds grasp the magnitude of what You have to offer us . . . if we will just trust You. We pray to the Most High God, amen.

Trust without Borders

The beginning lesson of this chapter on *Trust* showed the word trust could be used "to make someone a refuge." It illustrated nestling under God's wings for refuge, similarly as a baby bird sheltered under the feathers of its parent: "Be merciful to me, O God, be merciful to me! For my soul trusts in You; and in the shadow of Your wings I will make my refuge, until these calamities have passed by" (Psalm 57:1).

Make sure you have taken several minutes to read the opening Psalm 91. In this psalm <u>the LORD's promise is conditioned upon making Him our true refuge and habitation</u>. How can we do this? Two Hebrew words in verse 9 give us the answer. The word *makhseh*, translated *refuge*, means a shelter, a place of trust; and derives from a root meaning to flee for protection or confide in.[17] *Maween*, translated *dwelling place*, indicates a retreat. It comes from a root word describing the security of intimately dwelling together (as in a marriage).[18] These key words elaborate a principle: <u>When we make the Lord our refuge and habitation by trusting Him</u> – taking our cares, fears and needs to Him; by seeking His counsel, spending times of refreshing with Him; by loving Him and walking closely with Him through every day – <u>we enter into a sheltered place of promise regarding our lives</u>.[19]

Verse one says if we *dwell* in the shelter of the Most High, then we will *abide* in the shadow of the Almighty. So, if we "come in and stay" in the Most High's shelter, we will abide (live permanently) in the Almighty's shadow. Awesome! That is a very safe place to be . . . *a place of trust*. In John 15 Jesus repeatedly speaks of abiding in Him, just as He abides in the Father, and that by keeping His commandments, we will abide in His love. The abiding, the love, the commandments, the shadow are all interwoven and connected in such a way to provide protection for us – if we choose to abide.

Take some time to read John 15:1–17. How many times is the word *abide* used? _____. Do you see how intertwined it is with the word *love*? Also, do you see how Jesus connects the word *love* with *friends*? Do you remember when we studied that God called Abraham His friend, that *friend* was a covenant word, and that we prayed we could be called friends of God?

Trust without Borders

Almighty, *Shaddai,* means all-powerful and when it appears as *El Shaddai,* it means "God Almighty." Early Biblical patriarchs called God this name, and its origin can be traced to mean "might; unconquerable." It has Akkadian roots also to the word "mountain," indicating God's greatness, strength, or His everlasting nature. *Shaddai* is also a compound of words meaning *all-sufficient God, eternally capable of being all that His people need.*[20] Oh, my Friends, He is all that we need! Why would we trust anyone or anything else?

Verse 2 continues to say to the LORD that He is our refuge and fortress. Scripture is not just referring to God as a safe dwelling for protection, but now He is called a *fortress*, a walled, gated, fortified stronghold! Verse 3 says He delivers us from the snare, or traps of the trappers, allowing us to see the traps before we reach the snares, and saves us from the plague that kills. Verse 4 speaks again of Him covering us with His wings and that His faithfulness is a shield that completely surrounds us. Once again we have the word *shield* that we have studied in previous chapters: an instrument used in battle to protect us from enemies.

In verses 5–7 we see that in God we are secure at all times, in all dangers, and in all circumstances. Verses 8–13 continue with safely watching over all we do; vv.14–16 present six "I wills" that God instructs for us, seven if you read the last phrase as one also. Write out those six or seven "I wills" here:

Psalm 73 begins with a man envious about the boastful, and the prosperity of the wicked. The writer was confused until he went into the sanctuary of God (v. 17). Put into your own words verses 15–28:

Now back up to Psalm 71 and list what this psalm writer calls the LORD:

List several ways David decided to trust in God in Psalm 56:3–11 when he is captured by Philistines in Gath:

List the words of strength David uses for God in Psalm 62:1–8:

"Trust in Him at all times, you people; pour out your heart before Him; God is a refuge for us" (Psalm 62:8).

God, thank You that You are truly a refuge for us; a place we can run to for protection, strength, encouragement and wisdom. Help us by the power of Your Holy Spirit to abide under the wings of Your love. To El Shaddai we pray, amen.

Trust without Borders

<u>Day 5</u> ~ *"The Lord is on my side, I will not fear. What can man do to me? The Lord is for me among those who help me; therefore I shall see my desire on those who hate me. It is better to trust in the Lord than to put confidence in man," (Psalm 118:6-8).*

Whom have I in heaven, but Thee? And besides Thee I desire nothing on earth. My heart and my flesh they may fail, but You are my strength and my portion forever; forever and ever, amen.

I *love* 2 Chronicles 20:1–30 and wanted to write it out completely so we could study it in this book. Unfortunately, space didn't allow it in this chapter, so please read it before we begin today. List five points that impress your heart in a special way (more than five if you want) from these thirty verses:

My special adapted favorites from these scriptures include:

1. Jehoshaphat feared, but set his face to the LORD, called a fast, and prayed a "reminding" prayer to the LORD: "Are You not God in heaven, and do You not rule over all the kingdoms of the nations, and in Your hand is there not power and might, so that no one is able to withstand You?" (v. 6)
2. "Are You not our God, who drove out the inhabitants and gave it to Abraham, Your friend, forever?" (v. 7)
3. "We have no power against this great multitude; but our eyes are upon You." (v. 12)
4. "Do not be afraid nor dismayed . . . For the battle is not yours, but God's." (v. 15)

5. "Stand still and see the salvation of the LORD. . . . Do not fear or be dismayed; tomorrow go out against them, for the LORD is with you!" (v. 17)
6. "And they were three days gathering the spoil because there was so much!" (v. 25)
7. "Then the realm of Jehoshaphat was quiet, for God gave him *rest* all around." (v. 30) (NKJV for all the above)

Did you recognize a few points we have studied in previous chapters? How about Abraham, *Your friend*; "Stand still and see the salvation of the LORD;" "for his God gave him *rest*" (vv. 17 and 30).

Oh, how precious is this chapter to prove to us the fantastic, awesome power of the LORD God, the Almighty God, *El Shaddai*; the One to whom we bow and to whom we place our trust! Trust the Bible as God's living word to you and as the ultimate standard of revealed truth. Battles are won through faith's warfare, but ultimately belong solely to the Lord. We are instructed to pray, praise the Lord, and stand in faith. This is how we will see the salvation and victory of the Lord![21]

Unwavering trust is a rare and precious thing because it often demands a degree of courage that borders on the heroic. When the shadow of Jesus' cross falls across our lives in the form of failure, rejection, abandonment, betrayal, unemployment, loneliness, depression, the loss of a loved one; when we are deaf to everything but the shriek of our own pain; when the world around us suddenly seems a hostile, menacing place – at those times we cry out in anguish, "How could a loving God permit this to happen?" At such moments seeds of distrust are sown. It requires heroic courage to trust in the love of God no matter what happens to us.[22] It takes heroic courage like Jehoshaphat exhibited; heroic courage like Jesus manifested on the cross; and, most likely, heroic courage like you have displayed at certain times in your life.

Many times we presume God will directly intervene to change the course of the horrible or tragic event that engulfs our lives. We presume that by praying, "Lord, Lord," the cancer or bankruptcy or infidelity or untimely death will disappear. Often He does answer;

sometimes He does not. The blunt and brutal truth is that Jesus was mercilessly nailed to the cross, and this side of heaven was left totally alone, away from His heavenly Father. Trust in God does not presume that God will intervene.[23] When we exhaust all our human resources, forgo our control and quit trying to manipulate God, then, at our wits' end, trust happens within us. Then we pray from the heart as Jesus did, "Father, into your hands I commit my spirit."[24]

Trust without borders, in the deepest parts of our heart, aids us to unerringly sense that life is going to be all right. Unspeakable, gut-wrenching, horrible things will happen in our lives, but a certainty persists within us that *God is with us* and loves us in our struggle to be faithful. *Immanuel . . . God with us.* A Holy One who has experienced the pain we feel and through the ultimate healing of heavenly mysteries will inevitably reconcile all things in Himself. Why does our trust offer such immense pleasure to God? Because trusting God without borders is the supremely outstanding expression of love. Thus, it may mean more to Jesus for us to say, "I trust You," than when we say to Him, "I love You."[25] Therefore, we cry out, Abba, Father! "Call upon Me in the day of trouble; I will deliver you and you shall glorify Me" (Psalm 50:15).

A Release to God Who Spoke to Me

We had lived in Teheran, Iran, for almost two years. It had been very exciting, and we had the privilege of traveling to several different nearby countries, but the stress of that culture and its radical religion on our eight-year marriage had taken a toll. From my wife's viewpoint of protecting her and our son, I was often overbearingly controlling and strong-willed about what I would let her do or where she could go. She travelled all over the city, but when she was with me she complained she couldn't "cross the street" without permission. We often fought and disagreed on many, general everyday activities. Looking back later, we were, spiritually speaking, very naïve for late twenty-something's.

We had moved to this middle-eastern, ancient land of Persia wide-eyed and excited about the opportunities provided to us, but never considered that it was a heavily demonic principality in the Kingdom-of-God spiritual realm. We had attended a wonderful, non-denominational church alongside many missionaries who were strong in their love of the Lord and their knowledge of the word of God. But Pamela had been extremely sick with allergies since the week of our arrival, and her poorer health had definitely taken a hit on her normally strong dedication to our family. And, she was very weary of my strong-handed tactics.

We had spent close to a year working on adoption proceedings for two new members who joined our family: a two-and-one-half year old boy and a four-year old daughter. It had not only required numerous visits to two different orphanages, but months of paper work and court dates. A dear Iranian friend, Majid, who worked as an interpreter in my business office, spent months interpreting and negotiating for us on behalf of the children. Months after we thought we would have them in our home, their appearance finally became a reality two days after Christmas. Our oldest son, five at the time, immediately became the official teacher of "English as a second language." In less than the seven months it took to return stateside, the new arrivals spoke perfect English!

Of course, we rolled right from the lengthy proceedings of adoption into the necessity of obtaining American Visas for the children. In January I began weekly trips to the Embassy, waiting in long lines, filling out documentation, and then returning days later to discover even more detailed paperwork required by a female Embassy worker there. Weekly visits and no resulting Visas went on for months, and as time grew nearer for us to leave I increased the Embassy visits to several times a week.

Less than three months before our date of departure for the return trip home to the states, I decided to call my cousin who owned a car dealership about what kind of deal he could offer me for buying a truck. Not able to find his number in any of my files or folders, I began searching through a giant catch-all desk we used for the whole family. Frustrated at not being able to find his number, late one night I pulled out one of the smaller drawers and dug all the way to the

Trust without Borders

back where I found a carefully folded up piece of paper. Unfolding it would turn out to change my life. I sat reading a letter in which Pamela was telling a fellow teacher at the Damavand Girls' College where she taught that she could no longer see him. She had been having an affair with him but was telling him she was ending the relationship. I was numb, re-reading it several times before folding it up and putting it in my pocket.

I went "through the motions" as we put the children to bed; then I waited until they were all asleep to talk with my wife about what I had found. She was surprised that I had found the letter and now knew about her affair, but rather matter-of-fact about it. She didn't seem to care how upset I was and said "sure" when I suggested we get some counseling. Within days a missionary from our church, who was also a teacher at the same school where Pamela taught, began counseling with us. Even though we tried to counsel every week, the counseling did very little to heal any part of our relationship. School soon ended, and the man involved with Pamela returned to the states, the counselor returned to his home, and I continued working on obtaining Visas for our newly adopted children. Instead of any talk of reconciliation, she now said that although the relationship was over with the teacher, she just wanted a divorce. She didn't love me and wanted a divorce as soon as we returned to the states. There was no rationale in anything she said, one day saying all three children would go with her; the next day just our oldest son; the next day just the daughter, then just the two new ones. She just didn't care.

It all made me deeply depressed, and having no luck obtaining Visas for the children was just adding to all the confusion. Homes in Iran are flat-roofed so often at night I would go up the back stairs to the roof and pray. I wasn't sleeping well anyway, so my relationship with God deepened and matured in prayer during those months. One night as I was literally crying out to the Lord, in my heart I felt comforted that if I would stand firm in the marriage and pray for the marriage, my marriage would be restored. It stunned me, but I sat and mulled over the words in my heart. I had nothing: no wife, no home, no furniture, no car, no visas, no support, and no hope. I was all alone. But God comforted my heart that my marriage would be saved if I would stand firm in the marriage and pray for the marriage. I could do that because of the assurance of God to me! I chose right then to *trust* Him.

It was finally the week of departure. Airline tickets were purchased, everything was sold, packed, moved, and we were living in a hotel – but still no visas. The woman Embassy worker was without reason. Worse still, the airlines would not let anyone board the plane without proper documentation because (at that time) they would fine $25,000 per person stateside upon arrival. Pamela didn't care. She just lay around the pool at the hotel with the children. At least she was taking good care of them. But I was beside myself trying to finalize the details with the Embassy. It was now the day before the weekend of our scheduled departure. I sat in the Embassy, with the turn-around of people going in and out of the Director's office being about thirty seconds to a minute each. After thirty minutes it was now my turn.

Behind the Director's desk was a man – not the woman I had been dealing with for months! "What can I do for you?" he asked. I explained I had been working for months with a woman in this office, and I still did not have Visas for two newly adopted children and that we were scheduled to depart in three days. He told me to close the door and sit down, and we talked for 30 minutes. The unreasonable woman had been replaced by this man who finally told me that it was too late to give me regular visas. However, he could give me tourist visas that would allow entry into the United States and then I could apply stateside once the children were there. I could have hugged him!

We had a three-day layover in Majorca, Spain, which was like an oasis after the dry and thirsty land of Iran and my marriage for the past seven months. I took Pamela out to eat one night where we sat on a deck overlooking the beauty of the Mediterranean Sea. She softened slightly as we talked in the moonlight, but her heart was hardened and cold to me. It was very hard to believe God's words to me while looking at her and listening to her anger about our marriage. I made a decision to look at her through God's eyes and always repeat to myself the words He had spoken to me on that rooftop: *If you will stand firm in the marriage and pray for the marriage, I will restore the marriage.*

Once stateside I had us in counseling within three days. The awful, hateful, ugly fights continued over a year. We finally quit going to counseling together and just saw the same counselor separate of each other. I had begun attending some charismatic Catholic meetings some neighbors invited me to and then we would pray at their home every week or so. One night the mother of my friend turned to me and said, "The Lord spoke to me that Pamela will return to your marriage within two weeks." I thanked her for her word but told her Pamela told me daily how much she hated me, and two weeks would be impossible for my marriage to be restored. Nevertheless, she repeated her words to me and I certainly added that hope to my midnight-hour prayers. During one of the midnight sessions, God spoke to my heart and asked if I was willing to give up everything I owned, everything I had. After thinking for a while I answered "yes." He said in my heart, "Even Pamela? Can you give her up? Can you give her to me, even if she leaves you?" That was an excruciatingly long night of prayer, but I released her to Him.

Pamela had walked out mad from one of her counseling sessions when the psychologist had told her if she was really serious about leaving the marriage she would have already gone. "Why keep dragging it on?" he asked her. I was a little upset with him because now she decided since the kids were ready to start school she better interview for jobs so she *could* leave. She was going on interviews all the time and had never had trouble getting a job, ever, in our marriage.

Now, since she told me every morning, "I hate you!" and every evening, "I hate you!" I never came home for lunch. But one day I had some business in the area so decided to stop by the house. Little did I know that she had been pondering over things with God. I found out later that after numerous interviews and turn-downs she had prayed this prayer: "God, I've just received another rejection on a very fantastic job. I've done a lot of dumb things recently, especially in my marriage, but I'm not stupid, so I know You are in this. I don't love Jimmy, but if You will teach me to love my husband, then I will make a commitment to stay in this marriage." She had just finished praying standing there in our bedroom when I walked into the bedroom. She dryly repeated to me: "I don't love you, but I will make a commitment to stay in this marriage if you will work with me." I told her I would take anything that she would give me, but we *would* build our marriage on the Lord. It had been two weeks!

It took months and months of hard work, learning how to trust her, learning how to love her in a way she could accept me. She said one day many months later that she looked at me across the room and knew that she respected me. From that respect grew the love that she had prayed for. As of the writing of this book, we have been married over forty-seven years. I did a lot of things wrong in our marriage and our relationship. I was hard on her, angry too often with her, too harshly controlling and manipulative, all which contributed to the breakdown of our marriage. What I did do right was let my heart be broken before the Lord so there was nothing left of me and everything in it of Him. I called Him, Lord; He called me "friend." He spoke to me and I believed Him. I trusted God and He restored my marriage.

Jimmy Alexander, [26]
A man who obeyed God to pray for his wife and his marriage.

~ Chapter 7 ~

Surrounded by Strongholds

<u>Day 1</u> ~ *"For though we walk in the flesh, we do not war according to the flesh for the weapons of our warfare are not of the flesh, but divinely powerful for the destruction of fortresses. We are destroying speculations and every lofty thing raised up against the knowledge of God, and we are taking every thought captive to the obedience of Christ..."* (2 Corinthians 10:3-5, NASB).

LORD, this scripture reminds us we do not war in the physical, but against unseen forces. Teach us that we must not only gear up as a soldier for battle, but we must put our trust in You, our shield and our fortress; our refuge and our strength. It is in Your mighty name that we pray, amen.

Early in our children's elementary school years a local Christian radio station had an interview about a book of fanciful allegories concerning God's kingdom. I drove immediately to our closest Christian bookstore to purchase it and we began reading it nightly for their bedtime stories. The following is a condensation of one of the tales called *Princess Amanda and the Dragon*, and I want to give heartfelt thanks to David and Karen Mains, authors of <u>Tales of the Kingdom</u>, for their permission to quote and condense this tale in this way:

The book is about a refuge called Great Park, the wonderful land where the King lives. The characters of the different stories represent people like you and me, young and old, all in different phases of life, escaping from the evil Enchanter, all delightfully unpredictable, all pulled in different directions – both toward good or evil. This is an adaptation of a story about one such character in the book described as "you always hear Princess Amanda before you see her." She is a rambunctious tomboy who loved to play in the woods near the lake of Great Park, where there is a posted sign that reads: ***It is Forbidden to Keep Dragon Eggs.***

The two eggs Princess Amanda found one day glowed like amber jewels in the sunlight. Perhaps she meant to carry them to Caretaker, or thought they were shriveled inside; or perhaps she forgot. She chose not to take them to the Caretaker's cottage, but instead she hid the eggs in *My Very Own Place* in her secret wooded location. As the spring sun warmed the eggs only one hatched, turning its big eye on her with a great tear dropping onto its breast. "I must take you to Caretaker because He knows what to do with surprise hatchlings. *I'll keep you for just a little while. Perhaps I can tame you.*"

The Princess nurtured the baby dragon, played and nuzzled with it and watched its bare skin become covered with soft, dazzling scales. Summer was filled with dragonet games, relay races and chasing each other around the secret place of the forest. Soon the dragon won every time. By mid-summer she could crawl on its back between the spikes and they would leap above the meadow, flying in and out of the limbs of old trees. Soon Amanda's pet hated to be left alone and wailed piteously when she left it; particularly being left alone at night so she began to stay away from the Great Celebrations of Great Park. As she stayed with it one night it licked her face and hands gratefully and she felt angry at the stupid law that kept her from sharing her pet with others. *What harm is one small dragon?*

By autumn she had to be more careful about the dragon's deadly tail as it whipped back and forth; and the short bursts of flame had now become long, powerful, torching flames that were scorching the den walls and barely missing her! Once while the dragon was out playing Caretaker stopped by on one of His infrequent visits and asked her about the scorched den walls. She lied saying they had been like that a very long time and thought to herself as he walked away, "You old fool; why don't you just leave me alone?" Caretaker stopped, turned around and sadly said, "If you ever need me, Amanda, just call."

Surrounded by Strongholds

The dragon's scales had now hardened and she knew she could no longer keep him because of the danger to her life. She took it deep into the forest and commanded it to stay. A few days later she woke to a fire in some fallen leaves that had been pushed into a pile by her den door. Suddenly she knew. *Great harm could come from one small tame dragon. Small tame things grow into big wild beasts.* Amanda gasped as she turned to see the huge dragon that had grown even larger. It was waiting for her with its tail flicking slowly back and forth, claws of the paw flexed, tearing the soil beneath it; a thin trickle dripping from its mouth and yellow light was gleaming in its eyes. Dragon had become cunning. Why had she not seen this?

Dragon engaged her in a fight, jumping towards her and shooting flames from its nostrils. She hopped to the side, her heart filled with terror. Flames licked her clothes, her hair and slapped at her hands. "Help! Caretaker! Caretaker!" Although she did not know how, Caretaker was instantly standing beside her. "Kill it! Kill it!" Amanda screamed as the great fiery beast began to lurch.

"No, Amanda, I cannot kill Dragon. Only the one who loves a forbidden thing can do the slaying. Only *you* can slay this dragon." Caretaker pulled his hatchet from the silver belt around his waist and lifted his eyes to the sky praying, "In the name of the King, Amanda, you must slay the dragon!" Then he tossed the hatchet directly overhead. The familiar humming of the hatchet began that the Princess had always loved. It landed right at her feet and as she gripped the wooden handle she felt power begin to enter her. She whacked at Dragon's tail, causing oozing of green dragon blood but also enraging the dragon. Dragon let out a fiery blast that caught Amanda full in the face! She took careful aim, raised the hatchet, sighted the bare white patch on the breast of the weaving dragon – its only vulnerable spot – screaming "For the King!" as she let the hatchet fly.

The beast roared again, catching Amanda's leg with the bleeding stump of its swishing tail and she went down onto the grass. Her aim had hit its mark and the great dragon crashed down covering the Princess. Caretaker ever so slowly raised the edge of the great dragon hulk just enough so that Amanda could inch her way to freedom, then cradled her in His arms and wept. She looked like an outcast, but Princess Amanda had won the battle. She had slain the dragon she loved, *learning that when one loves a forbidden thing, one loses what one loves most. This truth is a hard-won battle for each who finds it and is always gained by loss.*[1]

That was a long allegory with great spiritual significance concerning demonic strongholds. When I began reading those stories to our children, my husband and I were just coming out of great marital stress and just learning the power of demonic strongholds in our lives and how good *and* bad strongholds affect us spiritually. What is a stronghold?

Strongholds of ancient times were fortified dwellings which helped protect someone or a group of people from an enemy. Old Testament times later developed them into fortresses or castles with strong, deep walls, sometimes built into mountainous or difficult, impenetrable areas, such as David hiding from King Saul in wilderness caves or mountain strongholds. I have seen such a stronghold in the high mountainous Arabel Pass in Israel, and it would have been very difficult for any enemy to assault. The point was to hinder and stop the enemy so they could not reach the protected area or the people.

With this in mind, biblical writers adapted the word *stronghold* to define powerful, vigorously protected spiritual realities, both good and bad. Please look up one of my favorites of David's psalms concerning strongholds written after the LORD delivered him from his enemies and from the hand of Saul and read it as a prayer:

> *I will love You, O LORD, my strength.*
> *The LORD is my rock and my fortress and my deliverer;*
> *My God, my strength, in whom I will trust;*
> *My shield and the horn of my salvation, my stronghold.*
> *I will call upon the LORD, who is worthy to be praised; so*
> *shall I be saved from my enemies* (Psalm 18:1–3, NASB).

Surrounded by Strongholds

I absolutely *love* this psalm and that I can call out to all of these names for Him: LORD, my Strength, my Rock, my Fortress, my Deliverer, my Shield, the Horn of my Salvation, my Stronghold . . . and that He is worthy to be praised! When I call out to Him, I shall be saved from my enemies! When we are overwhelmed, petrified with fear, terrified of sickness, lost in not knowing, we can run into His stronghold. How calming is that? In this case, a stronghold is the source of protection for us from our enemy, the devil.

However, a bad stronghold can be a source of defense for the devil where sinful or demonic activity is actually defended within us by our dark thoughts toward evil. These thoughts are the "speculations and lofty things raised up against the knowledge of God . . . ." as read in the 2 Corinthians 10:3–5 scripture. NASB

Often things that happen in the natural are indicative of things that happen or are happening in the spiritual realm. For example, the location where Jesus was crucified was called Golgotha, which meant "place of the skull." It even looks like a skull! To become effective in spiritual warfare, the first field of conflict where we must learn warfare is the battleground of the mind; i.e., the "place of the skull," for the territory of the un-crucified thought-life is the beachhead of satanic assault in our lives. To defeat the devil, we must be crucified in the place of the skull; we must be renewed in the spirit of our minds![2] Dr. Walter Bodine, our friend who translates ancient Sumerian tablets at Yale University, taught us that *the battle is won or lost at the threshold of the mind.*

In the *Wait* chapter we learned that strongholds are first established in the mind, and that is why scripture tells us to *take every thought captive to the obedience of Christ.* We learned that:

- Behind every stronghold is a lie – a place of personal bondage where God's Word has been forced to submit to any unscriptural idea or confused belief that is held to be true.
- Behind every lie is a fear.
- Behind every fear is an idol.
- Idols are established wherever there exists a failure to trust in the provisions of God that are ours through Jesus Christ.[3]

An old European proverb says: "Age and treachery will always defeat youth and zeal." Think about the dragon versus Amanda. Examine that thought by looking up Matthew 10:16, writing the last half of that verse and explaining it in your own words:

Jesus was training and preparing his disciples for spiritual warfare and in this verse was showing how to blend, or fuse, God's wisdom with Christ's innocence which is necessary for *any* victory in *any* spiritual battle. Jesus called Himself our Shepherd and called us His sheep, yet many times we have to do battle in the spiritual realm as warriors. Although that may be new to us, the Bible is full of instances and stories where evil is fought, and we as Christians must be discerning between spiritual issues of light and things of darkness. Just like Princess Amanda, if we tolerate the dark, hidden issues of sin, we leave ourselves vulnerable for satanic assault by that dragon of old.

✪ Let these verses from Colossians be our closing prayer today:

"We . . . do not cease to pray for you, and to ask that you may be filled with the knowledge of His will in all wisdom and spiritual understanding; that you may walk worthy of the Lord, fully pleasing Him, being fruitful in every good work and increasing in the knowledge of God; strengthened with all might, according to His glorious power, for all patience and longsuffering with joy; giving thanks to the Father who has qualified us to be partakers of the inheritance of the saints in the light. <u>He has delivered us from the power of darkness</u> and conveyed us into the kingdom of the Son of His love, in whom we have redemption through His blood, the forgiveness of sins." Amen (Colossians 1:9–13).

Surrounded by Strongholds

Day 2 ~ *"And the LORD your God will drive out those nations before you little by little; you will be unable to destroy them at once, lest the beasts of the field become too numerous for you. But the LORD your God will deliver them over to you, and will inflict defeat upon them until they are destroyed" (Deuteronomy 7:22-23).*

O, Mighty LORD our God, sometimes the numerous beasts of the field are overwhelming to us. Thank You that we can call upon Your name to deliver them to You to inflict defeat until they are destroyed. Thank You that You <u>never leave us nor forsake us</u> in our battle against strongholds. Thank You that You are greater than <u>anything</u> that comes against us. In You we trust! Amen.

Read the following verses that affect us like they did Princess Amanda: "Therefore humble yourselves under the mighty hand of God, that He may exalt you at the proper time, casting all your anxiety on Him, because He cares for you. Be of sober spirit, be on the alert. Your adversary, the devil, prowls around like a roaring lion (dragon!), seeking someone to devour. But resist him, firm in your faith, knowing that the same experiences of suffering are being accomplished by your brethren who are in the world. After you have suffered for a little while, *the God of all grace*, who called you to His eternal glory in Christ, *will Himself perfect, confirm, strengthen and establish you*" (1 Peter 5:6–10, NASB). Write some of your thoughts here about how these verses affect you:

How in the world can we "cast all our anxiety upon Him"? How about trying the last phrase of yesterday's opening verse? *"... taking every thought captive to the obedience of Christ..."* (2 Corinthians 10:5b, NASB). With that in mind, read and write out James 4:7 and keep it in mind as you reflect on the following testimony.

Testimony of Karen Jordan

Being raised Roman Catholic I knew about Jesus as God's son, but in my teen years I became very rebellious and fell away from my upbringing in Catholicism. After I became a true believer of the Lord Jesus Christ and asked Him to become Savior of my life, I was asked to give my testimony. "Lord where do I begin?"

I thought He might want me to start at the point in my life where I was into drugs, being an exotic topless dancer, and prostitution. But instead I felt He wanted me to share who I am in Christ, and how and where God has taken me since I came to know "whose I am."

In my former lifestyle I had a revelation of the demon assigned to me by Satan to take me to hell. I was an exotic dancer, but I never danced for men that I sensed to be evil because extremely vile things always seemed to happen after dancing for them. One day, however, a very well-dressed and groomed man came into the club with fancy sunglasses and a very nice three-piece suit. He looked very rich so I hoped he would tip me well. I met him at the table, got him a drink and proceeded to dance for him. When I made the turn around my dance pole, he had taken off the sunglasses and his eyes stared directly into mine; they were piercingly evil, like the eyes of the devil. I was able to take my gaze off of him only because I called on the name of the Lord Jesus as I circled around my dance pole, but when I circled back around the pole, he was gone. The bartender asked, "Where did that dude go? He didn't pay for his drink!" It was a confirmation to me that the guy *had* actually been there. I knew I had been saved from a demon!

Surrounded by Strongholds

I made a decision to leave that lifestyle but I didn't understand how much bondage I was trapped in! I began visiting all kinds of churches, but I later learned they were mostly cultic types. One I began attending was a Mormon church because I felt secure there. Although I had grown up Catholic, the teaching at the Mormon Church was steady and used scriptures, so I thought it was a good church. The Mormon Church began mentioning a church being built in my town and called it a cult.

I was teaching children's Sunday lessons and loved doing so. But after hearing some teachings from this new church on the radio, I would go early to that church and then to the Mormon Church for the classes I taught. The scriptures taught in the new church gave me such joy that I felt more peaceful than I ever had in my life. I began teaching the scriptures I learned there to the little children in the Mormon Sunday classes. Eventually, someone at the Mormon Church asked me where I heard these scriptures I was using for the children's lessons. After my explanation, I was informed *never* to teach them again. I kept going to this new church and eventually left the Mormon Church to become a member at Victory Life Church.

My marriage began falling apart as I stopped taking drugs and became a godlier, more pure believer. Even though I was seeking the Lord, evil spirits oppressed me, I wrestled with "the spirit of prostitution," and in my marriage I was pretty much treated like I still was one. I became more and more a bother to him, so I granted him the divorce he requested. One night while praying, I asked the Lord why I still felt oppressed by all these evil spirits. I prayed and fasted all that day and deep into the night, finally lying down on the floor screaming to the Lord that I wasn't going to get up until the evil spirits left me. I beseeched Him, recited scriptures, and continued to pray into the wee hours of daybreak. I finally felt them leave as the sun began to rise the next morning. It was through the counseling and teaching of Victory Life Church that I was delivered from many unclean spirits, the spirit of Jezebel, and a spirit of fear.

I decided to go to college in order to be employed in a legitimate job and become self-sufficient. College didn't seem to be the right place for me so I kept asking God what I should do. I sensed His answer was to become a massage therapist because I had always worked out knots, kinks and muscle aches for my children and friends all my life. I questioned that, however, because of similarities to my past lifestyle. Then, amazingly, I received a large tax refund owed to me. With that unknown refund, I was able to go to massage therapy school!

While massaging clients I always prayed over them, and began to see people healed as I massaged. One particular woman had cancerous tumors all over her, and she was down to 86 pounds at 5'8." All the pictures in her home were about her and her horses, and were face-down on her shelves. She had been such a beautiful woman. I finally told her I couldn't massage her anymore because she was so frail and I might injure her. She told me her bones hurt so badly and they always felt better after the massages, and asked me to please "rub her bones." While massaging her, I asked if she was ready to die. "I hurt so badly, but I'm only 45 and I'm too young to die." The power of the Holy Spirit came upon me and I said, "You need to choose to live! You need to go out to those horses and pet them, and call out to the Lord for healing in the name of Jesus!" I remember that power went through me to her and she began to be healed. I told her she needed to forgive her husband because her heart was hardened. She *did change* in her life and she was healed from cancer.

I saw the healing of many people, but then I became very proud of myself and when I became like that, the healings stopped. God spoke to my heart and told me I was taking pride in something that He did through me. I repented and spent much time with the Lord because I had been deceived by a prideful spirit.

One regular client was employed as a money handler at a casino, and when I prayed for her arthritic hands, she had been healed. During another massage I noticed she had an inflamed spot on her back that looked like skin cancer. I needed to pray for her as I massaged, but I felt unworthy because I was so wrongly into pride. I mentioned the spot to her so she could seek medical attention. She lifted her head up and said, "Karen, you laid hands on my arthritic hands and they were healed; you laid hands on my hips and they were healed. So you lay hands on

Surrounded by Strongholds

that spot and ask God to heal it!" I felt so unworthy, but laid hands on her while praying and asked God to heal her. After the massage, she grabbed the spot with her hands and said, "It's healed!" It was now just a circle with a tiny scar in the middle. God had forgiven me, heard my prayer for healing, and healed the spot on this woman.

God has brought me from dark depths of hell and into His glorious light because I have trusted in Him. My life is devoted to Him, and I have used the gifts that He gave me so I can do fruits of good instead of evil.

Karen Jordan, Durant, Oklahoma [4]
Massage Therapist and Prayer Warrior in the Kingdom of God!

As just shown in Karen's testimony, deliverance must not be looked upon as a once-in-a-lifetime occurrence. 2 Corinthians 1:9–10 tells us to "Trust in God . . . who delivered us from so great a death, and does deliver us; in whom we trust that He will still deliver us." That is supernatural delivering that certainly agrees with our opening scripture today from Deuteronomy 7. The LORD our God wants and desires us to *trust* Him, the One who delivered, does deliver and will still deliver us – past, present and future! According to that 2 Corinthians 1:10 verse the believer's deliverance in Christ is:

- A secured fact (free from the penalty of sin)
- A future promise (freed at Christ's coming from the presence of sin)
- A present process (we are still being delivered [in Greek present tense])

Today's opening text from Deuteronomy 7:22–23 provides a picture of this present process of grace in a New Testament believer's life. Though given the land of promise, Israel's possession of it would be "little by little." God will not give what we cannot maintain: we must occupy what He gives, and He will contend with our enemies "until they are destroyed,"[5] (v. 23). Write "little by little" in the margin.

At the moment we choose Jesus Christ as our Savior and become believers, we are covered by His righteousness. He indwells us by the Holy Spirit whom Jesus called *the Comforter.* Why then in Galatians 5:16 does the apostle Paul remind Christians to ". . . walk by the Spirit, and you will not carry out the desire of the flesh," NASB? If we have received Christ's righteousness, why do we still often "walk in the flesh?"

Read on in Galatians 5:17: "For the flesh sets its desire against the Spirit, and the Spirit against the flesh; for these are in opposition to one another, so that you may not do the things that you please," NASB. What does that mean? It means that the flesh and the spirit war against each other – not against you or me – but we often get in the way. The conflict within us is unrelenting, never ending and often fierce, and one in which we can never be victorious by our own strength. Read further in verses 19–21 and list below the many examples of the flesh that get in our way, even as Christians:

My goodness, that's enough to make one want to give up! But then Paul refreshes us with what the Spirit brings to us: "But the fruit of the Spirit is love, joy, peace, patience, kindness, goodness, faithfulness, gentleness, self-control; against such things there is no law" (Galatians 5:22, NASB). When we become Christians, the filling of the Spirit brings into us character; but the fruit of the Spirit show maturity. The Holy Spirit produces *all* of these graces.[6]

Surrounded by Strongholds

What does this have to do with strongholds? Everything! At our birth in Christ Jesus we receive His righteousness. Then <u>we must choose to trust Him</u> in allowing Him to battle for us against the enemy *little by little*, hidden darkness by hidden darkness, deed by deed, of any wrongdoing – taking every thought captive to the obedience of Christ as He purifies us. ***God will make this happen; God will deliver us!*** O, YES! He will make this happen – if we will choose to allow Him to work in us! Name just three things you would like to trust Him with right now:

1.

2.

3.

Numerous times in this study it has been mentioned that when we become believers we are covered with the righteousness of Jesus Christ. We have shown that our salvation is not based upon anything we do, but it is based upon who Jesus becomes to us and in us. As the old, familiar hymn says, "My hope is built on nothing less than Jesus' love and righteousness."[7] Knowing that it is His righteousness – and nothing that we do – should be enough to keep us humble. The strength of humility is that it builds a spiritual defense around your soul prohibiting strife, competition and many of life's irritations from stealing your peace.[8]

"Humble yourself in the sight of the Lord and He will lift you up,"
(James 4:10)

Heavenly Father, We desire to be humble in Your sight. Please lift us up so we can stand against the strongholds of the enemy. In our weakness we ask for Your strength and power. O, Blessed One, hear us! Amen.

Trust without Borders

<u>Day 3</u> ~ "But when Sanballat the Horonite, Tobiah the Ammonite official, and Geshem the Arab heard of it, they laughed at us and despised us and said, "What is this thing that you are doing? Will you rebel against the king?" So I answered them and said to them, "The God of heaven Himself will prosper us; therefore we His servants will arise and build, but you have no heritage or right or memorial in Jerusalem" (Nehemiah 2:19-20).

"I pray, LORD God of heaven, O great and awesome God, You who keep Your covenant and mercy with those who love You and observe Your commandments, please let Your ear be attentive and Your eyes open, that You may hear the prayer of Your servant" (Nehemiah 1:5–6a). Amen.

Speaking of "spiritual defense" at the end of yesterday's lesson, let us review two scriptures again in Numbers 13:28–29 that we just slid over when we read them in a past lesson. These verses speak of the competition the Israelites would come against as they entered the Promised Land to take possession:

> "The people who dwell in the land are strong; the cities are fortified and very large; moreover we saw the descendants of Anak there. The Amalekites dwell in the land of the South; the Hittites, the Jebusites, and the Amorites dwell in the mountains; and the Canaanites dwell by the sea and along the banks of the Jordan."

Scripturally speaking, these *"-ites"* were dwelling in the land that God had chosen to give to the Israelites as their land of promise. Since "the earth is the Lord's" it was by right His to give to whom He wanted. Remember we studied in Numbers 13 that God asked them to spy out the land (v. 2). And, Moses instructed them to *"see what the land is like, whether the people are strong or weak, few or many, the land is good or bad, has forests or not; whether the cities they inhabit are like strongholds or camps; and bring some fruit of the land"* (vv. 18–20). We need to understand that God was asking them to check out what belongs to them; *what I'm going to give you;* and, oh by the way, bring back some samples!

Instead, this is what the "–ites" did to their perspective: ". . . and we were like grasshoppers in our own sight . . .," (v. 33). Let's take a look at these "-ites" because *they are representations of spiritual strongholds in our lives.* Studying them will help us understand who or what is squatting on the land that belongs to us!

The Anakim inhabited Canaan and were greatly dreaded because of their giant size and being extremely evil. They were the later Philistine warriors, such as when Goliath came against the Israelites and was slain by the young shepherd, David.

The Amalekites were a nomadic tribe of descendants of Amalek, a grandson of Esau, brother of Jacob, and thus were not total foreigners to God. Esau was an arrogant, profane, and careless individual who had sold his birthright and his part in God's covenant promise for a pot of stew because he valued his own impulsive appetite over God's promise (Hebrews 12:16). After losing Isaac's blessing as the elder son, *he chose to leave* the family, the promised covenant and to become godless, locating in the arid region between Canaan and Egypt. More than any other nation, the Amalekites tried to eradicate, plunder and destroy Israel from its very inception.

- When the Israelites came out of Egypt and were at their most vulnerable, their first battle was fought against the Amalekites who attacked the weary nation, slaughtering the weak and elderly. Because of that vicious attack, God said that He would utterly blot out the memory of Amalek from under heaven (Exodus 17:14–16).
- Again the Amalekites attacked Israel while they were still wandering in the desert; joined with the Moabites in another attack; often went ahead of the Israelites burning the fields so there was no food for them, and plundered their crops once they inhabited the Promised Land.

- The Israelites, under the leadership of Joshua, later avenged the attack and defeated the Amalekites, but failed to completely eradicate the nation.
- Saul, the first king of Israel, was instructed by Samuel to "strike Amalek and utterly destroy all that he has. . . " (1 Samuel 15:3 NASB). Saul lost his kingship through the disobedience of God's instructions because he spared Agag (the Amalek king) and kept the best of the spoil.
- Years later in the book of Esther one more Amalekite appeared in Persia. A man named Haman, an Agagite, is set to be honored by King Ahasuerus. The name "Agagite" most likely means he was descended from the Amalekite king Agag. Ahasuerus is persuaded to sign a decree inspired by Haman intended to annihilate all the Jews in the kingdom. Haman's plot is foiled by Queen Esther and her cousin, Mordecai, and overturned, thus saving the entire race of the Jewish people. Haman is exposed and executed instead.[9 & 10]

Just as Karen Jordan shared in her testimony, God wants us to forget that *once we didn't know who we were.* The Amalekites showed that generation after generation they were at war with Israel and with God. *As a stronghold, this "-ite" attempts to offer temporary comfort over everlasting peace. As an identity thief it attempts to block your freedom and keep you from your true identity.* Being godless means you forget who you are, and not being who you are in Christ is immoral. It means we trade "God things" for temporary comfort. He definitely wants us to know who we are in Him! If we are godless, then we toil and labor unless we humbly bow before our God and Creator. In Him we know who we are: We are a child of the King! Here are some examples of Amalekite strongholds:

- Satan tempted Jesus in the desert saying He could turn the stones into bread to satisfy His hunger. Satan was attempting to get Jesus to give up His eternal birthright to satisfy what was temporary. But Jesus was no Esau!
- Saul was to utterly destroy the Amalek king Agag, but he settled instead for the temporal comfort and ease of the spoils of riches and animals, and thereby lost his kingship.

Surrounded by Strongholds

- Saul didn't remember he had been anointed as the very first king over Israel, filled with God's Spirit. He instead chose the temporal, chose to be ordinary. Selective obedience is just a form of disobedience.
- Jesus knew who He was and Whose He was: God's only son!

<u>The Hittites</u> were descendants of Heth, the second-born son of Canaan, who was the youngest son of Ham, who was one of the three sons of Noah (so Heth was Noah's great-grandson). The book of Genesis declares them to be one of the twelve Canaanite nations dwelling inside or close to Canaan from the time of Abraham up to the era of Ezra, being mentioned more than fifty times in the Bible.[11]

Joshua 1:4 includes their territory as a great part of the land promised to the Israelites, which is why God commanded the Israelites to eradicate them. The Hittites' religion was a pluralistic worship of nature, believing in various gods ruling over the elements of earth, sky and weather. This nature worship led to despicable practices which brought the wrath of the true God on them. When God delivered Canaan to the Israelites, one of the given reasons for destroying the inhabitants was to eliminate the pagan practices which would ensnare God's people (Exodus 23:28–33), because He didn't want His people following the idolatry of the Hittites. However, they were not destroyed and dwelt in southern Palestine and around Jerusalem with the Hebrews. They also ruled the area of modern-day Syria and eastern Turkey, and battled with Egypt and Babylon for territory.[12 & 13]

Abraham was well acquainted with the Hittites, buying the burial cave for Sarah from them in Genesis 23. Descriptions of land transactions and personal covenants recorded in Genesis bear a strong resemblance to Hittite records discovered by archaeologists.

- Esau took wives from among the Hittites (Genesis 26:34).
- Uriah the Hittite was one of David's mighty men (2 Samuel 11:3).
- Hittites are mentioned throughout the kingdom years and even after the Jews' return from captivity (Ezra 9:1), but it is assumed the Hittites were eventually absorbed into the surrounding cultures and lost their distinctive identity.[14 & 15]

- Hittites were bronze-spear people, and a "Heinz 57" variety of warriors from many locations.
- They were terrorists that based their attacks on their opponent's fears.

As a stronghold, this '-ite' comes against security, from many places, to throw one off-balance. This stronghold also comes against fears from all of your life. It uses "counterfeit worship," knowing we worship what we fear; because we worship whatever it takes to keep us from the fear of failure and rejection. Counterfeit worship is as prostitution because we give ourselves up to the fear instead of trusting in God who is our strength, our shield, our protector and our refuge.

To break counterfeit worship in our lives, all we have to do is humbly bow in worship and release the power of God to come against the enemy for us. Ezekiel 28 is often compared to Satan's fall from heaven, and verse 19 speaks of the terror that has come upon him from God Himself: "All who know you among the peoples are appalled at you; you have become terrified, and you will cease to be forever," NASB.

Doesn't that sound like one of our verses from Psalm 37:10? "For yet a little while and the wicked shall be no more; indeed, you will look carefully for his place, but it shall be no more."

The pulling down of strongholds begins with repentance. When Jesus sent out His disciples, "They went out and preached that men should repent. And they were casting out many demons . . . and were healing" (Mark 6:12–13, KJV). Regarding the deliverance of stronghold spirits that plague the mind, repentance precedes deliverance, and deliverance often leads to healing in other areas. The foundation of our continued success in warfare comes from yielding to the Lord as He reveals these strongholds, and agreeing with Him through repentance in pulling them down.[16] All we need to do is bow to the LORD in worship and ask Him to battle the "-ite" for us!

Surrounded by Strongholds

✪ Look up 2 Timothy 1:7 today for the closing. Write it here and memorize it for battle!

LORD, come minister to our minds and hearts with Your power so that the fears in our lives can be overcome. Please battle with us as You teach us how to battle. Contend for us, O LORD! To our Strength and our Shield we pray, Amen.

Day 4 ~ *"The name of the LORD is a strong tower; the righteous run to it and are safe" (Proverbs 18:10).*

LORD, God, we want to depart from evil and do good so we can dwell forevermore. Please expand Your law within our hearts so that none of our steps shall slide. Amen. (A paraphrased prayer from Psalm 37:27 and 31).

So far in our study of the "-ites" we have looked at the Anakim, the Amalekites and the Hittites. The strongholds that affect us most are those which are so hidden in our thinking patterns that we do not recognize them nor identify them as evil. Jesus revealed in Matthew 12:43–45 that unclean spirits are seeking rest. When our thought-life is in agreement with unbelief, fear or habitual sin, the enemy has rest.[17] Review that scripture and list some thought patterns that might seem unrecognizable at first glance:

The Jebusites were pre-Israelite inhabitants of Jebus, dwelling in the mountains beside the future Jerusalem which was conquered by King David about 1000 years before the time of Christ. The threshing floor was in the center of the village, which in ancient times was not only important for threshing out the grain, a major part of sustenance and economy of a village, but also served as a place of business and government. It so happens that it was in this same location that Abram offered up his son Isaac as a sacrifice.

At the end of 2 Samuel 24, David was instructed to erect an altar to the LORD on this threshing floor of Araunah the Jebusite, so David bought the threshing floor which eventually became the location of the temple of the Lord built by King Solomon, David's wise son.

The threshing floor was the place for winnowing wheat and it could be said that it is an Old Testament example of New Testament "pruning." True worship is *not* protecting ourselves from the healing work of God within us, but pure worship is that which happens when we are being broken of our fleshly nature to become more like Him. When we lay ourselves on the threshing floor of God, He tramples off the husks and chaff of the wheat so that the bread (life) can be made. It must have been a worshipful experience after God spared Isaac's life by providing a ram in the thicket, and then blessed a broken Abraham, who is now called the "Father of our faith." Worship is when you lay the Isaac of your life down, all the chaff is blown away and then is replaced with blessing. *Jebusites are strongholds that separate you from real, authentic worship. They steal your intimacy with God, because <u>all obedience is worship</u>.*

Look up Luke 22:31, paraphrasing it here and journaling what it means to you:

<u>The Amorites</u> were also inhabitants of Canaan and their culture and idolatry lay at the root of their decadence. They often fought Israel, with their history going back before 2000 BC when their settlement in the hill country around Jerusalem helped to set the stage for the revelation of God through Israel.

- Abraham assisted Mamre the Amorite in recovering his land from four powerful kings (Genesis 14:1).
- Later the Amorites were a formidable obstacle to the Israelites' conquest and settlement of Canaan. They preferred living in the hills and valleys that flank both sides of the Jordan River. Two Amorite kings resisted the Israelites' march to Canaan as they approached east of the Jordan, but after the Israelite victory there, tribes of Gad, Reuben and half of Manasseh settled in the conquered area. These two early victories over the Amorites foreshadowed continued success against other Amorites to the west and were often remembered in both history and poetry. West of the Jordan, the Amorites lived in the hills along with the Hivites, Hittites, and Jebusites.

- Five city-states in southern Canaan formed an alliance instigated by the Jebusites and intimidated an ally of Joshua, i.e. Gibeon.[18]

The stronghold of the Amorites is to keep you from humility. They occupied the hilltops because they are "glory thieves," but God doesn't want to share His glory with anyone. He didn't want the Israelites to live among, intermarry, or make covenants with the inhabitants of Canaan. He wanted a people set apart and holy unto Him. Take a peek at Psalm 121:1–2. The author of this psalm looked upward to the hills and asked, "Where does my help come from?" Then the writer answered, "My help comes from the LORD, who made heaven and earth," NCV.

If you want to know what will cause God to draw His sword against you, think back to Day 2 of the *Dirt* chapter: It is your <u>pride</u>. *Amorite strongholds represent the place in your life where you don't need God.* God allows those things to remain that keep you focused on Him. Look at James 4:6b and write it here:

"Humble yourself in the sight of the Lord and He will lift you up,"
(James 4:10)

<u>The Canaanites</u> are descendants of Canaan, the youngest son of Ham, son of Noah. They represent merchants, peddlers and self-sufficiency. *They sold to the Israelites what the Israelites should have been handling on their own but were taking short cuts to get to the things of the Lord.* Write down what Jesus said about this stronghold in Matthew 21:13:

Surrounded by Strongholds

He said His Father's house "shall be called a house of prayer" because that is how to find the answer. There is no short cut. Pray sincerely to God and He will reveal the strongholds of your life. Then ask Him to come against them in Jesus' name.

The Gibeonites are also descendants of the Hivites and Amorites, from Canaan, one of Ham's sons. They occupied the Promised Land before the arrival of Israelites. God ordered the Israelites to avoid making any covenants with the Gibeonites and to expel them from the land. But when the inhabitants of Gibeon heard what Joshua had done to Jericho and Ai, they worked craftily, coming to the Israelites pretending to be ambassadors. They used old sacks on their donkeys, old wineskins torn and mended, old and patched sandals on their feet, and wore old garments. They even showed that their bread was dry and moldy, claiming it had been fresh when they set out. They went to Joshua at Gilgal and said to all the men of Israel, "We have come from a far country; now therefore, make a covenant with us"[19] (Joshua 9). *Gibeonites represent the strongholds of "dealmakers and negotiators."* They didn't want to die so they resorted to a ruse. In this type of stronghold we must constantly resort to an "override." Joshua and the Israelites – without praying or consulting with God – made a covenant with them. So later when the truth became known, Joshua placed the Gibeonites under servitude to the Israelites since the covenant could not be broken. We may not be able to break this type of stronghold in a covenant form, but we can take the "bad deal" to God and allow Him to handle it in the name of Jesus!

These "-ites" represent challenges for all our lives. Did any particular "-ite" come close to home for you? What territory, land or promise has the Lord given to you that these "-ites" may have taken?

Summarize the "-ites" with me:

- Know your identity and remember *whose* you are and who you are in Christ Jesus! Not knowing who you are in the Lord is immoral.
- Don't be terrorized by fears from all of your life.
- Practice and experience the intimacy of worship. Remember that *all* worship is obedience!
- Lay down your pride and practice humility.
- Trust God and lay down your self-sufficiency.
- Avoid impulsive, foolish and wrong covenants in your life. [20]

Our peace in fighting strongholds in our lives comes from being so confident in God's love – of knowing who and whose we are – that regardless of the difficulty and the circumstances of the battle, we can remember that "Greater is He who is in you than he who is in the world" (1 John 4:4, NASB).

"[10] Finally, my brethren, be strong in the Lord and in the power of His might. [11] Put on the whole armor of God that you may be able to stand against the wiles of the devil. [12] For we do not wrestle against flesh and blood, but against principalities, against powers, against the rulers of the darkness of this age, against spiritual hosts of wickedness in the heavenly places. [13] Therefore, take up the whole armor of God that you may be able to withstand in the evil day, and having done all, to stand. [14] Stand, therefore, having girded your waist with truth, having put on the breastplate of righteousness, [15] and having shod your feet with the preparation of the gospel of peace; [16] above all, taking the shield of faith with which you will be able to quench all the fiery darts of the wicked one. [17] And take the helmet of salvation, and the sword of the Spirit, which is the word of God; [18] praying always with all prayer and supplication in the Spirit. . . " (Ephesians 6:10–18).

The word *withstand* in verse 13 suggests vigorously opposing, bravely resisting, standing face-to-face against an adversary with the authority and spiritual weapons granted to us to withstand evil forces – like Princess Amanda throwing the hatchet into the soft belly of her adversary. Our warfare is not against physical forces, but against invisible powers who have clearly defined levels of authority in a real, though invisible, sphere of activity.

In these verses Paul instructs us to take up the whole armor of God so we can maintain a battle-stance against this unseen satanic structure. This armor is not passive, but powerful in the pulling down of strongholds and is to be used offensively. Verse 18 reminds us to always be praying in the Spirit. Prayer is not so much a weapon, or even a part of the armor, as it is the means by which we engage in the battle itself and the purpose for which we are armed. To put on the armor of God is to prepare for battle. <u>Prayer *is* the battle itself</u>, with God's Word being our chief weapon to use against Satan during our struggles.[21]

17-20 But me He caught—reached all the way from sky to sea; He pulled me out of that ocean of hate, that enemy chaos, the void in which I was drowning. They hit me when I was down, but GOD stuck by me. He stood me up on a wide-open field; I stood there saved—surprised to be loved!

21-25 GOD made my life complete when I placed all the pieces before him. When I cleaned up my act, He gave me a fresh start. Indeed, I've kept alert to GOD's ways; I haven't taken God for granted. Every day I review the ways he works, I try not to miss a trick. I feel put back together, and I'm watching my step. GOD rewrote the text of my life when I opened the book of my heart to his eyes. (2 Samuel 22:20–25, MSG)

Revelation 12:11 names three ways to cast down the accuser of the brethren:

1)

2)

3)

Trust without Borders

✪ Let that verse close today's lesson as you meditate on the types of strongholds we studied and how the Lord equips you to pray and battle against them. Don't be afraid! When the strongholds are overcome, you will have such joy and peace it will be amazing to live in the difference!

Lord, we lay ourselves at Your feet, declaring that because of Your power, the weapons of our warfare are mighty to the pulling down of strongholds. We acknowledge that we are Yours, in Christ, and renounce our flawed and earthly old-natured flesh. By Your grace and the power of Your Spirit, we ask You to pull down any strongholds of unbelief that exist in our minds. Help us remember that we are new creatures in Christ and will be continually transformed from glory to glory into Christ's image as we walk with God. To the only true God we ask these things, Amen.

Surrounded by Strongholds

<u>Day 5</u> ~ *"For thus says the high and exalted One Who dwells in eternity forever, whose name is Holy, 'I dwell on a high and holy place, and also with the contrite and lowly of spirit in order to revive the spirit of the lowly and to revive the heart of the contrite. For I will not contend forever, nor will I always be angry; for the spirit would grow faint before Me, and the breath of those whom I have made. Because of the iniquity of his unjust gain I was angry and struck him; I hid My face and was angry, and he went on turning away, in the way of his heart. I have seen his ways, but I will heal him; I will lead him and restore comfort to him and to his mourners'"* (Isaiah 57:15-18, NASB).

O, exalted One who dwells in eternity forever, we bow before You. We ask that You pour Your Spirit into us and wash us with Your light in the dark places of our hearts. Help us put on all our armor today to fight effectively against the evil one. Thank You for being our shield of strength, our refuge, our Stronghold! To You we humbly bow, amen.

Happiness is living on a small farm and running through the alfalfa fields, playing cowboys sunup to sundown, rolling in the freshly cut grass of an enormous front lawn, and racing through irrigation ditches to get to your neighbor's house. I lived on some acreage like this in a house that my parents built until I was in the second grade. Then, because my dad was in the Air Force, we transferred to Japan. We lived off-base for a while, so my two sisters and I continued our exploring in the woods near our home, rode bikes, had fun Christmases, played in heaps of snow, learned Japanese songs and wore beautiful handmade dresses sewn by our mother. One time when I had the mumps, Mom took my sisters to church and Dad took me out riding on his Japanese motorcycle! What a special ride it was to me because I don't ever remember my dad expressing his love for me, and that ride was an expression of that love. I knew he loved me because he built things for me, repaired my broken toys and provided for me; there just wasn't warmth in our relationship, and I don't *ever* remember being told that he loved me.

From the beginning of my relationship with Jesus at age ten, I knew I was special to Him. We attended church regularly where I memorized scriptures, studied and outlined the life of Christ and the apostle Paul in church programs, studied lives of missionaries, taught Bible classes to children in Vacation Bible School and sang in youth choirs. I had great instruction, but I didn't always understand the principles of the scriptures I memorized. Write out Proverbs 29:18:

It is not the legalistic meaning of this proverb to understand, but acquiring the principle of it – like Jesus did. We need to have a vision for our life, who we are and how we want to live in it. We need to seek God's wisdom along with acquiring understanding. We all have choices to make in life, and very early we choose certain strongholds or fortresses in our lives to be our security, and there are only two types: God's strongholds of security, safety and righteous principles; or strongholds of Satan, which are evil, insecure and false. Your stronghold may be different than ones I chose. Yours may be Fear – Legalism – Pride – Anger – Gossip – Immorality – Overeating – Lying –Addictions – Secrets – or other habits.

John 1:16 says, "And of His fullness we have all received, *and grace upon grace*." Because of the graciousness of God and His ultimate, unconditional, loving forgiveness, I can confirm that "All things work together for good to those who love God, to those who are called according to His purpose" (Romans 8:28). Grace is more than God's disposition or impersonal favor. It is God meeting us at our point of need in the Person of Jesus Christ, including all His power and provision.[22]

Early in my teenage years, I began to have fantasies in which I was ill, sleeping, or in the hospital. The man "I loved" was sitting by my side, holding my hand and just loving me for who I was; just stroking my hand, looking at me, and *loving me unconditionally.*

In the middle of my junior year of high school my dad took a job at Texas Instruments in Richardson, Texas, where I met my future husband the first week I was in school. We dated for three years and married when we were 20. Immediately Jimmy began trying to control my independence and creativity that he also said he admired, trying to fashion me to be a quiet, sweet, Mississippi belle like his mother. That didn't sit too well with my scholastic, independent, women's-lib collegiate attitude of that era. Explain in your own words Proverbs 14:1, NASB: "The wise woman builds her house (with God), but the foolish tears it down with her own hands (without God)" (words in parenthesis are mine). What does this verse mean to you?

A wise woman lives by the principle of scriptures, but a foolish woman lives on feelings, emotions and impulses, never searching out the principle of why something happens or continues in her life. Proverbs 4:7 explains it like this: "Wisdom is the principal thing; therefore get wisdom. And in all your getting, get understanding."

Shortly after our first child was born, I was unfaithful to our marriage by having an affair with a former high school boyfriend. Jimmy found out; we talked, prayed, he forgave me, and we determined to go on in our marriage. I sincerely felt his love because he forgave me, as did the Lord. But we were not knowledgeable enough at the time of the "things of the Spirit." We didn't know to pray for inner healing against strongholds, although we did pray for forgiveness. However, *I didn't get the principle of the thing.*

When our son was four we moved to Iran with Jimmy's company. Iran is a difficult country in which to live because of its oppressive religion, and it is definitely Satan's territory, but our spiritual eyes were too naïve to see it. Looking back now, I see what fertile ground it was for the enemy to build on the strongholds in my life.

Three days after arriving in Iran I became sick from allergies which hounded me for the entire two years we lived there. Once every four to five weeks I would get a cold which developed into a sinus infection. Recovery took several weeks, I would have a week's reprieve, and then the cycle would repeat itself. Allergy medication did help, but the colds and sinus infections were relentless.

Fear of all the "unknowns" of living in a foreign country overtook Jimmy, and his controlling nature multiplied intensely. He was grateful that I completely ran the household, shopping and procuring items from all over the gigantic city of Tehran (with a hyperactive four-year-old by my side), traveling by bus, cab, and on foot. But whenever he was with me I couldn't even cross the street without holding his hand. At times he would even lock the door and keep the key to avoid my running an errand if it was too close to sundown. He had to be in total control of everything, including me, because that was his fear.

At the end of our first year I signed a teaching contract with an English-speaking girls' college near our home, got pregnant, and then had a miscarriage during the summer before classes began. My health was not strong and I was exhausted caring for our hyperactive son. In October some adoption proceedings from the previous year began falling into place, and we added two Iranian children to our family right after Christmas: a little two and one-half-year old son and a four-year-old daughter. We were very enthused by the adoption, including five and one-half-year old Jason, who had been praying the entire previous year "for a brother and a sister." God had given us wise discernment, and we were very confirmed about our new family.

I had never read the Bible entirely through and was nearly finished that next spring when I began sensing an unusual strangeness in my life. I repeatedly asked Jimmy to pray with me and for me, but he was often too tired, too busy or too mad at me to do so. I don't use as excuses all the things that have been mentioned: extreme allergies, a

Surrounded by Strongholds

controlling husband, a hyperactive son, two newly-adopted Iranian-speaking toddlers, one of which was handicapped (without his left arm below the elbow); poor health, a job outside the home, and a difficult foreign culture. But now I realize Satan had built a stronghold within me with a wide-opened door, lined me up as an easy target . . . and I walked right in and shut the door.

Proverbs 14:12 says, "There is a way which seems right to a man, but its end is the way of death," NASB. While studying this verse, for the first time I saw the two meanings of this scripture:

1. It seemed right for us to pray, forgive and move on after the affair I had with my old boyfriend early in our marriage. And it was. . . .
2. But we didn't go deeper to examine the *why* of why I risked my marriage to be with another man. We didn't know to delve into the principle, root or *stronghold* of the sin. Because there was no inner healing, no search for the principle reason of why I had an affair, or knowing to search for and break the power of that stronghold in my life, it was going to result in death in our marriage relationship.

There was a teacher at the girls' college where I was teaching, and we would chat, along with many other teachers, as we sat in our lunch area each day. He listened to me and made me feel like I was worth something, and we soon stumbled into an affair. I was again willing to give up everything I had to gain this unconditional love of my fantasy! The affair lasted only a few weeks. I knew it was wrong; that it was impossible. But **_when you are in sin nothing is rational!_** Please understand that. Think about some sin you fight against. When you actually commit that sin, your mind is *not* on God – you are in a selfish, irrational state of mind. I remember praying before it all began while walking down the school hall one day: "Lord, I know this is wrong; please forgive me." Remember – totally irrational!

Finally, I wrote this teacher a letter explaining why we could not see each other anymore and hid it in the very back of one of my desk drawers until I could give it to him the next morning. While I was putting the children to bed that night, Jimmy decided he would call one of his cousins stateside to make arrangements for buying a pickup truck for our arrival home. He hunted all over for the phone number, digging through the desk and found my letter. God had intervened!

What Satan meant for evil and ruin, God began turning around in beautiful ways. Jimmy again forgave me, repented of his sins of control and manipulation, began renewing his life with God, and bathed our marriage in prayer. He got counseling for us before we left Iran *and* within days after we returned stateside. He had gotten "the principle of the thing" and wanted to repair and restore our marriage. However, once my sin was exposed, I decided it was all over. I wanted a divorce.

For the next fifteen months I told him every day how much I hated him. This testimony is really Jimmy's, because during our time of marital stress he was faithful to pray for me and love me through all the tough times. He had people praying for him, me and our marriage; he had meetings with our pastor, and got up to pray in the middle of the night. All these things infuriated me because I was sick of him being a righteous know-it-all. He began attending charismatic prayer meetings where people spoke in tongues and prayed for healing, so I knew he had gone crazy! On Sundays the preacher would "preach right at me" all the things we had fought about during the week which also made me furious because I thought Jimmy had told him all about our fights. It was simply the conviction of the Holy Spirit.

I finally decided that if I was really going to divorce him I needed to leave, so I moved into a rent house of my parent's. But when Jimmy helped me move in, he moved all his belongings in also. Then I decided I needed a job to pull this thing off. With a teaching degree, experience as an executive secretary and being right at 30 years old, nice paying jobs were just waiting for me, since I was usually able to interview for two or three jobs and choose which one I wanted. I interviewed for fifteen jobs and received fifteen rejections. Arriving home after that fifteenth rejection I prayed, "God, I have done a lot of dumb things in my life, but I am not stupid, so I know You are doing this. I do not love my husband, but if You will teach me to love him, I will make a commitment to stay in this marriage. I don't feel any love at all for him, God, so You are going to have to teach me to love this man."

Jimmy never came for lunch because of the frequency and intensity of our fights, but he came home that day entering the bedroom just as I finished praying. I told him of my commitment to stay in the marriage, but that I didn't love him at all. He said he would take anything I would give him. He later told me he almost had a heart attack because I had shocked him so by my decision. He also told me that some neighbors up the street had been praying with him for me and our marriage. One night the grandmother had a word of knowledge that within two weeks I would make a decision to stay in the marriage. That was hard for him to believe, but he held onto it cautiously. God had assured him during these fifteen months that the marriage would be restored if he would be faithful to pray for it. The day I shared that I would stay in the marriage had been two weeks!

Please read in 2 Chronicles 29:16 about how King Hezekiah restored the temple and had the priests clean out and carry the debris to the Brook Kidron. Now back up, reading verses 5–11. Remember studying earlier about the Kidron Valley that for years had refuse and garbage thrown into it? Remember that now it is a lush, beautiful valley in the center of Jerusalem? An example of God's faithfulness! By my commitment to remain in my marriage, I was allowing God to "clean out my temple," and debris was being thrown into the Brook Kidron. God was creating a beautiful "Kidron Valley" in my life!

I prayed my prayer about God teaching me to love my husband every day for six months before one day I looked at him across a crowded room and realized that I respected him. God has since shown me in scripture that this is what He calls the wife to do: ". . .let the wife see to it that she respect her husband" (Ephesians 5:33, NASB). God was faithful to His Word in answering my prayer about loving my husband by first teaching me to respect him. It was from this respect that my love for Jimmy grew and the love we share today in no way compares to what we started our marriage with over forty-seven years ago! We are truly in love spiritually, physically and emotionally, and have a joy that can only come from the Wonderful Counselor. God has blessed us with wisdom, discernment and many happy years, and is now bringing people to us that we pray for concerning their marriages. God is faithful!

The fantasy of my childhood has been healed and renewed in my life by a husband who has exhibited unconditional love for his wife. In whatever areas you are weak, in whatever sin recurs within you, in whatever causes you fear or anger, *study the principle of the thing.* Don't just determine to be good; to not do "it" and go on in your life. **THAT WON'T WORK!!!** Get healing prayer and ask God to reveal to you how to break the stronghold of the temptation or weakness. I never intended to have an affair *or* get a divorce! But Satan knew my weakness and my ignorance, and only God's love coming through my husband kept me from it.[23] Remember:

1. No one is immune from sin. Always be on guard because the liar and the thief roams the earth desiring to snatch us from our walk with God.
2. Satan's lies come when you are in the middle of the circumstance. They always deal with God's intention, His character and His relationship with you. Based on the lie, we begin sinning. If and when we decide to fight Satan's strongholds, *we cannot overcome the fruits of destruction without going back to the base.* If the destructive fruits of Satan are not dealt with, they increase in power, force and control. Remember Princess Amanda's dragon.
3. God loves us unconditionally – That is NO fantasy. His grace and love can cover ANYTHING that we confess to Him (and to others) to break the darkness by His light.
4. Love never fails.
5. Loving involves forgiving.
6. "The effective, fervent prayer of a righteous man can accomplish much" (James 5:16, NASB).

"Jesus is the author and finisher of our faith" (Hebrews 12:2), and we can be ". . . confident . . . that He who has begun a good work in you *(us)* will perfect it . . ." (Philippians 1:6, NASB). <u>God will do this</u>, because:

- Light is more powerful than darkness and truth is stronger than error.
- There's more grace in God's heart than sin in men's hearts.
- There's more power in the Holy Spirit to convict men of sin than there is power of satanic forces to tempt men to sin.
- There's more power in one drop of the shed blood of the Lord Jesus to cleanse men's hearts from the stain of sin than there is in the accumulated filth of men's sin since Adam and Eve![24]

"The salvation of the righteous is from the LORD; He is their strength in the time of trouble. And the LORD shall help them and deliver them; He shall deliver them from the wicked, and save them, because they trust in Him" (Psalm 37:39–40).

~ Chapter 8 ~

Perfect Peace

Day 1 ~ *"And you, (Jesus) child, will be called the prophet of the Highest; for You will go before the face of the Lord to prepare His ways, to give knowledge of salvation to His people by the remission of their sins, through the tender mercy of our God, with which the Dayspring (the Messiah) from on high has visited us; to give light to those who sit in darkness and the shadow of death, to guide our feet into the way of peace"* (Luke 1:76-79).

Heavenly God, thank you for Your tender mercy in sending us the Dawn of creation as a little baby to live among us – Immanuel, "God with us." Thank You for the Light that brought us out of darkness to guide us in the way of peace. To You we pray, amen.

Don't we all want our feet guided in the way of peace like the above scripture states? Of course we do! Some of us do seem to generate more stress than others, but in our hearts we all desire peace. What is this Greek word for peace?

Peace: *eirene*; a state of rest, quietness and calmness; an absence of strife; tranquility.[1] It generally denotes a perfect well-being. *Eirene* includes harmonious relationships between God and men, men and men, nations and families. Jesus as Prince of Peace gives peace to those who call upon Him for personal salvation.[2]

This same word for peace is used in Romans 5:1–2: "Therefore, having been justified by *faith*, we have *peace* with God through our Lord Jesus Christ, through whom also we have access by faith into this *grace* in which we stand, and rejoice in *hope* of the glory of

Perfect Peace

God." We have previously studied all of these words – faith, peace, grace, hope – and what a glorious way to bring them all together! Because we have been made right through our belief in Him by our faith, we have peace. And, because we have peace with God through Jesus Christ and have sure access by faith into His unmerited favor of *grace*, we rejoice in hope. Amazing, just amazing how with God all things work together for our good!

Now, to one of my favorite scriptures, Romans 15:13. Would you look it up please, writing it here and paraphrasing it for your life?

Did you catch the phrase ". . . by the power of the Holy Spirit."? It is a prayerful request: ". . . <u>may</u> the God of hope . . . ." <u>May</u> He fill you with all joy and peace in believing; and, by His power. We ask Him to strengthen us in the peace of believing, and He will by His Spirit. Remember our well-studied scripture: "Now may the God of peace *Himself* sanctify you completely" (1 Thessalonians 5:23). You didn't think I would let you forget that verse did you? Never! It is the same word for peace that we just studied above.

Now let's combine those two verses with this one from Hebrews 13:20–21: "Now may the God of peace who brought up our Lord Jesus from the dead, that great Shepherd of the sheep, through the blood of the everlasting covenant, make you complete (perfect) in every good work to do His will, working in you what is well pleasing in His sight, through Jesus Christ, to whom be glory forever and ever. Amen."

What does it say in verse 21 that the God of peace will do for us?

Could we ever do that on our own? Could we in our own strength in any way, shape or form make ourselves complete or perfect in anything we do? Of course we could not. Although we have the righteousness of Christ within us, we cannot do these things in our own strength. When we try in our own capacity we will have no peace. The peace comes when we submit to the God of creation and allow Him to work in and through us by the power of the Spirit.

To allow Him to work in and through us <u>we need to know who we are</u>: (1) I am nothing. (2) I have nothing. (3) I can do nothing. (4) I know nothing.[3]

1. <u>Without God we are nothing</u>. When we become believers, we are blessed with the gift of the Holy Spirit who comes to indwell us, not only as our Comforter, but to empower us to do the works that Jesus desires us to accomplish in His Kingdom here on earth as it is in heaven. But there should be no glorying or putting confidence in our own flesh. Most of us, after we receive salvation in Christ Jesus and receive His power through the Holy Spirit, then take over and try to do everything ourselves, in our own strength. So, "how's that working for you?"

An excellent story of putting one's full trust in the LORD and of coming to the realization that "you are nothing" is the story of Saul of Tarsus, the extremely successful, highly educated Pharisee that was struck blind while on the road to Damascus to persecute some of the early Christian church members. Take a look at Acts 9:1–20 with me before we continue.

We serve a God who is not just in pursuit of nice people, but who uses every type of personality and type. In verse 5 Jesus basically says to Saul, "If you're pickin'on them you are pickin' on me!" How can that be? Because Christ is in every believer! *With God we are everything!* Saul has been struck blind, which is what he has been experiencing spiritually, and God "sits him in the corner" on Straight Street for three days without sight, food or drink. God has even shown him in a vision a man named Ananias coming in and putting his hands on him so that he might receive his sight.

So, even before God called Ananias to go minister to Saul, God had spoken to Saul about Ananias. The important part of *trust* for Ananias was that he had to walk by faith – not by sight – looking to no one but Jesus. He trustingly said, "Yes, Lord!" without concern for his

Perfect Peace

own person, following the voice of God. With God he facilitated the power of the Spirit and was able to fellowship with Brother Saul as he laid hands on him and baptized him. With God he was everything.

2. <u>Without God we have nothing</u>. Read 1 Corinthians 4:6–7, and explain verse seven in your own words:

Why do we boast as if we had not received it? There is no peace in acting as if we possess gifts that we created. Read and review Deuteronomy 8:18 and paraphrase it here:

Finally, read 1 Timothy 6:6–7 and paraphrase it also:

3. <u>Without God we can do nothing</u>. There is no glorying in might or holiness in our own strength. In John 15:1 and 5 Jesus says, "I am the true vine and My Father is the Vinedresser. . . ." "I am the vine, you are the branches. He who abides in Me, and I in him, bears much fruit; for *without Me you can do nothing.*"

4. <u>Without God we know nothing</u>. There is no glorying in our own wisdom. 1 Corinthians 8:2 says, "And if anyone thinks that he knows anything, he knows nothing yet as he ought to know." But, in Christ we do know: "For 'who has known the mind of the LORD that he may instruct Him?' But we have the mind of Christ" (1 Corinthians 2:16).

Let's end today with Proverbs 3:5–6: "Trust in the LORD with all your heart and lean not on your own understanding; in all your ways acknowledge Him, and He shall direct your paths." Write what "in all your ways acknowledge Him" means to you:

In Isaiah 61:3 God says He will give us beauty from ashes. God uses the total breakdown of our flesh to enrich the beauty of our new selves in Christ. A special prize and benefit to every gardener is the compost pile. Compost piles use all the waste and refuse of the kitchen and yard (except meats or oils). To that junk is added heat, moisture and air. Over time, and with frequent turning of the composting materials, the waste decomposes, forming a rich, fertile, wonderful soil to add to the garden. Remember the compacted soil of Day 1 of the *Dirt* chapter? Composted soil added to compacted clay equals a bountiful and beautiful garden!

✪ Re-read and work on memorizing Proverbs 3:5–6 we just studied above.

Heavenly Gardener,
Thank You for turning the ashes of our composting life into beauty. Help us remember when pressure, turning turmoil and heat make life seem unbearable to us, that You have a purpose and You have not forsaken us. Thank You that You will provide for us a garment of praise for the spirit of heaviness, that we may be called the oaks of righteousness. In Your glorious name we pray, amen.

Perfect Peace

<u>Day 2</u>~ *"You will keep him in perfect peace, whose mind is stayed on You, because he trusts in You. Trust in the LORD forever, for in YAH, the LORD, is everlasting strength"* (*Isaiah 26:3-4*).

We lift up holy hands to Yah, the LORD, praying You will inhabit our praises and be our everlasting strength. Help us to keep our minds and thoughts on You as we continue to grow, and keep us in perfect peace. Amen.

The word *peace* used above comes from the Hebrew word shalowm or shalom, from the root word *safe*, meaning: well, happy, friendly; also health, prosperity and peace.[4] Israelis have been signing treaties of peace since Joshua led them into the Promise Land. Peace treaties have been signed between Israel and many surrounding countries only for many to be broken, re-negotiated and often re-written. Yet the world still clamors for the peace process to continue. Scriptures tell us that the world will never know peace until the Prince of Peace comes. Who is this Prince of Peace? _____.

"For unto us a Child is born, unto us a Son is given; and the government will be upon His shoulder. And His name will be called Wonderful, Counselor, Mighty God, Everlasting Father, Prince of **Peace**" (Isaiah 9:6).

Peace comes *from* God (Romans 1:7) and is an evidence of the rule of the Messiah – whose character as the Prince of Peace waits to instill the settled-ness of His own rule in our souls. Just as the saving power of His death and resurrection makes it possible for us to have peace <u>with</u> God (being reconciled to Him, as we studied yesterday in Romans 5:1), the indwelling of His life and character through the Holy Spirit's work in our lives is intended to help us learn to abide in the peace *of* God. Jesus said to His disciples, "Peace I leave with you, My peace I give to you" (John 14:27).

Surrender to His will and submission to His Word will bring inner rest, as we allow "the peace of God to rule in our hearts" (Colossians

3:15). That is: Let God's peace act as umpire (1) over decisions that would trouble you; (2) overruling doubts that would disturb you; and (3) overthrowing the Adversary's lies that would defeat or deter you. Perfect peace is available when the heart and mind keep focused on God's promise, power, and presence. Trust Him.[5] Remember the opening verse of Isaiah 26:3.

In the Hebrew language words can grow; mainly growing from a root word:

> Practically all words . . . go back to a root, and this root must have in it three consonants. You can do anything you want to the root: you can use it in any verb form or tense, you can turn it into . . . twenty or more nouns. You can make it an adjective, adverb, preposition or what you will. *No matter what you do you will always see staring you in the face the three consonants of the root. You can never escape them.* And equally important: *No matter what you do with the root, no matter into what word you turn it – that word must carry in it something of the meaning of the root.*[6]

The Hebrew language uses mainly consonants; vowel sounds are often only markings – so the root is easy to see. A family of words can be portrayed something like a wagon wheel: At the hub is the three-letter root. Just by adding vowel sounds you create the words in that family which can be pictured like spokes going out from the hub. One wonderful family grows from the root *shelem*: be whole, complete. Just by changing a vowel sound we have one of the "spoke" words: *shalom*, peace. The Hebrew word *peace* literally means "the peace that comes from the whole."

> Jews often greet each other with "Shalom!" Sometimes they say, "Ma Schalomcha?" or, "What is your peace?" When someone says inquiringly, "Ma Shlomcha?" he is actually asking you whether you are whole, complete, in one piece. They want assurance that no part of you – fingers, toes, legs, arms, etc. – is missing or broken. The root meaning of this familiar greeting word is whole,

Perfect Peace

complete. If you are whole, you're probably well and at peace.[7]

Jesus was literally "the *peace* that comes from the whole," as read in the Isaiah 9:6 opening verse. With a play on words, Jesus was "the *piece*" that came from the whole: "The virgin will conceive and give birth to a son, and they will call him **Immanuel**" (which means '**God with us**') (Matthew 1:23, NIV). What does "God with us" mean to you?

When Jesus stood in the midst of His disciples after He arose triumphant over death, hell and the grave, He said, "Peace to you" (Luke 24:36). He brought the peace that comes from being whole. If Jesus bought and brought us such peace, how do we walk in it in such a wild and crazy world? As we have seen from numerous scriptures we have studied, it requires our doing something with our minds. To examine that thought, look at two scriptures:

"You will keep him in perfect *peace*, whose mind is stayed on You, because he trusts in You. Trust in the LORD forever, for in YAH, the LORD, is everlasting strength" (Isaiah 26:3–4). What does it mean to "keep our mind on the LORD"?

(Philippians 4:6–8): "Be anxious for nothing, but in everything by prayer and supplication, with thanksgiving, let your requests be made known to God; and the *peace* of God, which surpasses all understanding, will guard your hearts and minds through Christ Jesus. Finally, brethren, whatever things are true, whatever things are noble, whatever things are just, whatever things are pure, whatever things are lovely, whatever things are of good report, if there is any virtue and if there is anything praiseworthy – meditate on these things." Explain in your own words several things to do according to these scriptures to experience the peace of God.

These verses in Philippians are like a checker game: You have a move, and then God has a move. God never moves out of turn, but He never fails to move when it is His turn. Verse 6 is your move; verse 7 is God's move. Verse 8 is your move. When studying powerful people of scripture or powerful people of God, you will realize they all share something in common: they kept or keep their minds on God. Scripturally speaking, they prayed conversationally without ceasing.

✪ In closing today read two verses from our Psalm 37: vv. 11 and 37. Write them here if you want, but pray over them to close out the lesson.

Father, we desire our future to be one of peace, no matter what happens or what the circumstances are. We ask that You grow us in the supernatural rest that You have to offer us. We believe, Lord; help our unbelief. Amen.

Perfect Peace

<u>*Day 3*</u> ~ *"But the wicked shall perish; and the enemies of the LORD, like the splendor of the meadows, shall vanish. Into smoke they shall vanish away" (Psalm 37:20).*

O, God of Creation, we ask today that You will grow us up in the gift of discernment as we travel through this earthly life. Help us discern evil from the good, things that are righteous from things that are sinful. Some of these things are blatantly obvious; while some are stealthily subtle. We ask for Your wisdom to know the difference. To You, O LORD, we pray, amen.

Every spring I heartily embrace the ageless phrase, "hope springs eternal." I clean up my garden plot, pulling the largest, peskiest weeds and as many of the little ones as I can before Jimmy arrives with his tractor to till the plot. The dirt looks so loose and fresh after the plowing, and I use Granddaddy's plow to make rows, preparing to plant the newly purchased seeds. After drawing out my plans for which vegetables will be planted in which area, I begin the process of planting. I always find myself praying, asking God to watch over the garden and to bless it bountifully. Within just a couple of weeks, if I am not out there frequently, those troublesome weeds are back with a vengeance! I know where I've planted the seeds because of my garden layout plan and am looking for them to sprout – but sometimes it is so difficult to discern them from the weeds. Some are very obviously different, but it is *amazing* how similar to the real plant those pesky weeds are. Let's study what Jesus said about discerning the weeds from the true plants in Matthew 13:24–30.

The servants noticed early in the growing season that the tares (weeds) were growing up alongside the wheat. But the owner, in verse 29, said to leave them to grow beside the wheat until the harvest. I used to wonder why until a missionary to Israel who stayed at our bed and breakfast clarified it for me. Tares look like wheat on the top but the stalk has thorns on it and is hard to handle. If you pull up the tares, the uprooted roots cause the wheat around it to be dislodged and damaged. I can completely understand because some weeds that have grown up around my plantings have huge root systems that really can spread out all around the other plants and when pulled up actually do dislodge roots of the good plants.

Take some time to read Galatians 6:7–9 and paraphrase it here:

The law of sowing and reaping applies to everyone's life. We should always sow only those things we desire to reap, but God does guarantee that harvest will come.

God has a timetable for every seed we plant, but His timetable is not always our timetable. Sometimes the "due season" means a quick return. Sometimes it means a slow return that may take years – even a lifetime. We can count on three things: (1) God will cause a harvest to come from our seeds. (2) God is never early or late. He is exquisitely punctual with our best interests at heart. (3) Our harvest will have the same nature as our seeds sown: good seeds bring good harvests; bad seeds bring bad harvests. What are we to do during the growing time of our seeds?

- Refuse to become discouraged.
- Determine to keep our faith alive and active.
- Give and keep on giving; love and keep on loving.
- Know this – a harvest is guaranteed. Continue in an attitude of expectancy.[8]

When we put our trust in God's timing of anything, we can be sure that He will be standing side by side with us. In that lies the peace that surpasses all understanding. It is out of our hands and into His; what better place for any of our concerns? In that is peace.

We function in a visible world but interact with an invisible, spiritual world, so we must develop discernment – the ability to recognize the movements of things not seen. Being led by God's voice, recognizing unseen opportunities and opposition, leading in prayer and spiritual warfare, are all crucial elements to being an effective, discerning Christian.

Perfect Peace

Discernment is like wearing night vision goggles in the dark. Isn't it true that you cannot walk where you cannot see? If the terrain and movement surrounding you remain outside your scope of awareness, you can be paralyzed. The ability to hear God and respond to and in the invisible world, while still operating in the visible realm, is not only important but necessary in our Christian lives.

The highest level of discernment doesn't lie in recognizing the movement of opposition, but in recognizing the movement of God. Jesus said His primary strategy for ministry was to only do what He saw His Father doing (John 5:19; 6:38). It is important to know "what is just a good idea" and what is God's will for you.[9] Part of the distinguishing of that purpose is in the verse of Romans 15:13 we studied that spoke of being "empowered by His Spirit." His discernment brings peace.

Scriptural examples abound of faith in God in spite of circumstances. Though overwhelming situations arise that seem hopeless, oppressive and fearful, scriptures always point to God as our refuge. Know that God can give you hope when circumstances indicate there is none. Hope in God, for you shall yet praise Him. He has promised to be present with you both day and night.

Set your heart on the Lord, your refuge and shelter in every trouble. Cast, throw and fling your burdens on the Lord. Do not hold onto them for dear life! God is able to take them and desires to carry your troubles for you. Recognize that everyone feels afraid at times. Faith can turn fear into trust. Each time you feel afraid, choose to trust in the Lord. Set your eyes on the Lord; He is greater than anything you fear.[10] Journal your feelings as you read the next several verses:

"Whenever I am afraid, I will trust in You" (Psalm 56:3).

"I will both lie down in peace, and sleep; for You alone, O LORD, make me dwell in safety" (Psalm 4:8).

"The LORD will give strength to His people; the LORD will bless His people with peace" (Psalm 29:11).

Oh, to be blessed with His peace! The Prince of Peace desires that we experience the rest that God has offered us. It is our choice, as we trust Him more each day, to choose to receive that peace, Beloved!

"Mercy and truth have met together; righteousness and peace have kissed. Truth shall spring out of the earth, and righteousness shall look down from heaven. Yes, the LORD will give what is good; and our land will yield its increase. Righteousness will go before Him, and shall make His footsteps our pathway" (Psalm 85:10–13).

O, Father, may the righteousness You poured into us through Jesus Christ kiss Your peace! Thank You that Your truth reaches down to grab hold of the mercy You extended to us! We are overwhelmed by Your love! Thank You that You never leave us nor forsake us. In that we feel peace. In that we are forever Yours, Amen.

Perfect Peace

<u>Day 4</u> ~ *"As for me, I shall call upon God, and the LORD will save me. Evening and morning and at noon I will complain and murmur, and He will hear my voice. He will redeem my soul in peace from the battle which is against me, for they are many who strive with me. God will hear, and answer them - even the one who sits enthroned from of old -Selah- with whom there is no change, and who do not fear God. He has put forth his hands against those who were at peace with him; he has violated his Covenant. His speech was smoother than butter, but his heart was war; his words were softer than oil, yet they were drawn swords. Cast your burden upon the LORD, and He will sustain you; He will never allow the righteous to be shaken" (Psalm 55:16-22, NASB).*

Father, thank You that Your word tells us You will redeem our souls in peace from the battles that rage against and all around us, for they are many. Thank You that Your peace is in us, You abide in us, and You promise to never leave us nor forsake us. We are holding on for dear life! Help us to trust You and never let go. In Jesus' name, amen.

Bad things happen. Most often they arrive unannounced and without planning. You never *plan* to be the victim of a crime, lose your job, suffer illness, or watch your house burn to the ground; experience marital infidelity, live through unspeakable abuse, or suffer the grief of losing a loved one. Most certainly we would *never* choose to live through anything unpleasant if we were given any choice in the matter!

Faithfulness to God does not guarantee that a person's life will be free of trouble, pain and suffering.[11] Jesus said it even more clearly: "<u>In this world you will have trouble</u>" (John 16:33, NIV). Be sure to review your "hall pass" if you think you are exempt; most certainly it will read differently than you recall.

In our lives things will happen that we just do not understand, even as Christians. We simply won't know why they occurred. These difficult instances often become the crossroads of our personal Christian faith. During those difficult times we must focus on the basic truths of God's nature: God loves us, God is good, God wants to have an intimate relationship with us, God is in covenant with us as Christians and He will never leave us nor forsake us; His ways are higher than our ways and His purpose is always greater than what we can ever imagine. He lifts us up out of the mire; He "lets" us find Him. If, however, we get stuck striving to find an answer to *"Why?"* then erosion of our faith will silently begin. May this song help us keep that erosion from beginning:

Find You on My Knees

Troubles chasing me again, breaking down my best defense.
I'm looking, God; I'm looking for You.
Weary just won't let me rest and fear is filling up my head.
I'm longing, God; I'm longing for You. But I will . . .
Find You in the place I'm in,
Find You when I'm at my end,
Find You when there's nothing left of me to offer You
except for brokenness.
You lift me up. You never leave me thirsty.
When I am weak, when I am lost and searching,
I find You on my knees.
So what if sorrow shakes my faith? What if heartache
still remains? I'll trust You. My God, I'll trust You
'cause You are faithful. And I will . . .
Find You in the place I'm in
Find You when I'm at my end
Find You when there's nothing left of me to offer You
except for brokenness.
You lift me up. You never leave me thirsty.
When I am weak, when I am lost and searching,
I find You on my knees.
When my hope is gone; when the fear is strong;
when the pain is real;
when it's hard to heal; when my faith is shaken
and my heart is broken and my joy is stolen.
God, I know that You lift me up.
You never leave me searching.

Find You On My Knees, Used with permission from the copyright owner. Words and music by Kari Jobe, Ben Glover/, Matt Bronleewee; Copyright © 2012: Songs From the Science Lab (ASCAP)/All Essential Music (ASCAP) (Both admin. by Essential Music Publishing LLC)/ Worship Together Music (BMI) 9t One Songs (ASCAP) Ariose Music (ASCAP) (Admin. at CapitolCMGPublishing.com, License Permit #552711). All rights reserved. Used by permission [12]

Perfect Peace

It isn't wrong for us to ask God why. He knows our innermost thoughts and desires anyway and there is nothing we can hide from Him. Take a moment to look up Psalm 139:2, writing it here and journaling what it means to you:

Biblical scriptures are full of questions directed to God, especially the psalms and books of the prophets. But many times we will not understand God or His reason for doing specific things or allowing things to happen.[13] I do know "God is not the author of confusion, but of peace. . . " (1 Corinthians 14:33a).

Journal your thoughts below about Galatians 5:22–23: "But the fruit of the Spirit is love, joy, peace, patience, kindness, goodness, faithfulness, gentleness, self-control; against such things there is no law," NASB:

These virtues are characterized as *fruit* of the Spirit and not as "works." Remember that when we are abiding in Christ and allowing Him to work within us, then we are empowered by His Spirit. Only the Holy Spirit can produce the fruit within us, not our own efforts. When we accomplish things on our own it is called fleshly works. When the Spirit empowers us, He produces *all* of these graces. Colossians 3:15 says, "Let the peace of God rule in your hearts...." That means, let His peace control your thoughts and emotions.

In John 14:26, Jesus tells the disciples that the Father will send the Holy Spirit to "teach you all things, and bring to your remembrance all things that I said to you." Now write out what He told them in verse 27:

Not as the world gives – it's not works of the flesh, but by His Spirit. When we are trusting in Him, there is peace. When we trust in Him we will not be troubled; we will not be afraid. I have to admit there have been times in my life when I have been deeply troubled, anxious about things or events happening that were totally out of my control. There were times I wanted answers for my children or for marriages being prayed for; answers for my parents, relatives, my spouse, health, or jobs. But answers didn't come. Peace didn't come until I relinquished my hold on the situation and allowed God to take over. Reality was that I couldn't control any of it anyway! Why did I keep trying? But peace completely encompassed me when I let go.

Job of the Old Testament was very confused when everything he had was wiped out in a day, including his ten adult children. His health was then attacked and he lived in pain and misery. He questioned God as to why all this suffering had come upon him and God answered him not with direct answers, but by raising Job's awareness of His character and position of authority in the world. Actually, the answer God gives Job is . . . *Himself*! Job realizes he is neither in control of anything nor able to understand well enough ever to be in control. He replies to God, "I know that you can do all things" (Job 42:2, NIV).

There will be times when God will not answer your "whys." Even though He doesn't give you the answer you want, He will always give you Himself. We don't have the capacity to understand the mysteries of God, but we can accept His loving presence with faith. It is therefore important for you to build your relationship with God during the good times so you are prepared when the bad times come.[14] Look up and journal your interpretation of Ephesians 6:13:

Perfect Peace

I want to be a strong specimen that can stand in the day of adversity! In this life we *will* have trouble, but be of good cheer, He has overcome this world.

"Grace to you and *peace* from Him who is and who was and who is to come, and from the seven Spirits who are before His throne, and from Jesus Christ, the faithful witness, the firstborn from the dead and the ruler over the kings of the earth. To Him who loved us and washed us from our sins in His own blood, and has made us kings and priests to His God and Father, to Him *be* glory and dominion forever and ever. Amen" (Revelation 1:4–6).

The above verses bring to my mind The Chronicles of Narnia by C. S. Lewis. In these chronicles some older children are playing hide and seek during some perilous war times and end up being transported through a clothing wardrobe where they had hidden into an adventurous land where an evil kingdom is fighting against a good kingdom. The fighting of good and evil goes back and forth for quite a while, with the "sons and daughters of Adam and Eve" eventually becoming kings and queens in the Kingdom of Aslan, who represents Jesus. I love to watch them mature in the story, how they are humbled at times under the gentle words of Aslan; and how they fight for the victory of Aslan's Kingdom and grow in their wisdom. Eventually they are transported back to their earthly lives, but with a maturity much greater than when they departed. When they re-enter Narnia again in future chronicles, they enter with the wisdom they had previously gained. Re-read Revelation 1:4–6 above and picture yourself as His King or Queen, as His priest serving God the Father. Give Him the glory and dominion forever and ever. Enter His peace.

✪ Read Job 38–41 in closing to see the majestic aspects of God Almighty. Enjoy being in the presence of our mighty God!

Trust without Borders

Day 5 ~ *"Mark the blameless man, and observe the upright; for the future of that man is peace" (Psalm 37:37).*

O Mighty One of All, we are beginning to understand that our honest struggle in this journey of faith and trust is more honoring to You than anything we can do on this earth. Help us to be blameless and upright before You because we desire the peace that You offer. Help us to settle and just sit in Your presence. In Your holy name we pray, amen.

The world loved Mother Teresa because she was the reality of living for, loving and serving the needy. She is quoted to have said, "In the West we have a tendency to be profit-oriented, where everything is measured according to the results, and we get caught up in being more and more active to generate those results. In the East I find that people are more content to *just be*, to just sit around under a banyan tree for half a day chatting to each other. We Westerners would probably call that wasting time. But there is value to it. Being with someone, listening without a clock and without anticipation of results, teaches us about love. The success of love is in the loving – it is not in the result of loving."[15]

Many times we yearn for a simplified lifestyle so that our communication with God can be uninterrupted. But I think He challenges us to relinquish the fantasy of an uncluttered world; to accept each day just as it comes, and find Him in the midst of it all. A successful day is one in which we stay in touch with Him, even if many things remain undone at the end of the day.[16]

At times in my life I have prayed with great urgency and expectancy, but the only answer was silence. This is always frustrating and perplexing to anyone who prays in urgency, because we need an answer NOW! At least we think we do. Sometimes I have wondered if I prayed wrong, without enough passion or eloquence; maybe I asked for the wrong thing or in the wrong way. Did God just not care about my problem? Surely He was paying attention because scriptures say, "He shall neither slumber nor sleep" (Psalm 121:4b).

Perfect Peace

As I matured in my Christian walk, I realized it had nothing to do with how eloquently I prayed or even my insistence on the speed of the answer. It had everything, however, to do with God's purpose for that particular instance and His perfect timing. As we saw from reading the last several chapters of Job yesterday, we *do not* control God and are presumptuous if we think we can.

When our Heavenly Father is silent it is for good reason, but it has nothing to do with what we're doing right or wrong. Only He knows the answer to our situation and because only He knows what we need and when we need, it, He waits for just the right time to respond. He may also wait until our *faith* in Him kicks in and overrides our emotional meltdowns. Sometimes this is a teaching moment in the matters of trust and in our faithfulness in waiting for God to answer our prayers. When we learn to trust, wait and listen expectantly, then He will move, and always in His concise, perfect timing. Remember the "chess game" of Day 2?

Where are you in this particular and most difficult aspect along your journey of faithful trust? Can you lean into the truth of the message of this moment of your life? The discipline of waiting is a true matter of trust, of faith, and of knowing that the God of the universe loves you and cares for you deeply. Pray that your faith will be strengthened so you can trust His power that is always yours![17]

Malta

I had lots of errands to run that day: the grocery store, drug store and cleaners were all calling my name. And now I had to add one more inconvenience to a busy day. Having recently had my annual mammogram, I had just received a call that I needed to redo it. "It's probably just a fold on the film," the woman told me. "I don't think it's anything to worry about." Annoyed, but not worried, I planned the retake.

It wasn't a fold on the film! A quick stop by the clinic evolved into a blur of sonograms, biopsies, agonizing waits and an emergency call to my husband. Words from the doctor hung in the air like an ominous storm cloud. It was a large breast tumor with several tentacles reaching for new places to lodge. As we learned later, the tumor had been present the year before, but had gone undetected because the films erroneously were never read or sent to the doctor. It felt as though my life was at the mercy of negligence.

Shock waves rolled over me that evening with fear arriving in its wake. The struggle to find sleep finally gave way to exhaustion and I drifted off into an uneasy rest. The nether land of a dream began to unfold. There I was, on the shore of the Eastern United States with a backpack secured across my shoulders. Next to me was a woman with a similar backpack who explained to me that we were about to fly to Europe by means of the jet packs within our backpacks. She assuaged my skepticism with one simple statement: **Trust me!**

I slept through the flight and awoke as we were nearing land. Suddenly the jet packs stopped operating and we both fell into the foamy abyss. Efforts to swim to land were challenged by a huge whirlpool that seemed to suck us in, but we both made it to the beach. Fighting to move through thick vegetation, we looked for anything that might give us a clue about our location. Before us appeared a hut-like shop, and we anxiously asked the man there to tell us where we were. "Why, don't you know?" he asked cheerfully. "You are in Malta!" Delight overtook us, but the leaps of joy gradually faded into the sobering reality of the morning light.

Reflecting on the dream, I felt certain that it was from the Lord. My heart began to grope for the hope that the God of Life, not neglect, would have the final say about my life. It seemed He was saying that, like the ominous whirlpool, a struggle was ahead of me, but that the destination was embodied in "Malta." What could I understand about that distant land?

Remembering the story about Paul's shipwreck and arrival on Malta in Acts 27–28, I re-read it with hungry interest. The storm had captured Paul's ship, and death seemed imminent to all on board. But the God of Heaven broke into the moment and spoke. Paul gave

Perfect Peace

specific instructions, assuring all on board that no one would die if they trusted his words, and death was averted.

As they began their time on the island an unfortunate snake found that his resting place had become kindling for the fire. Not at all in a good mood, the poisonous asp clasped his mouth around Paul's hand, and the prognosis for Paul was, again, certain death. Shaking off the snake like an annoying mosquito, Paul shakes off death as well because there is One who has conquered death on his behalf. There is no evangelism recorded from that excursion, but there is the report of their events while there: "…the rest of the people on the island who had diseases were coming to him and getting cured." NASB

So there you have it. Malta was about two things: escaping death and healing. Eagerly looking up the meaning of Malta, I found that it meant *refuge*. Indeed it had been that in this account.

My research continued on the amazing history of Malta. Crusaders, who were called the Knights of St. John of the Cross, had originated from Jerusalem and had established houses for healing. They were called "hospitalers," and thus, the first hospitals were launched and the knights were dubbed "healing warriors." When they arrived on the island of Malta, they pursued their dual calling by successfully averting the Muslims from overtaking Europe and by establishing hospitals. Malta was about warring against the enemy and healing.

I wish I could say that solid faith for healing anchored my heart, but I cannot. I struggled to get to that place, but felt as though I was running only three quarters to the finish line. The mastectomy report found cancer present in lymph nodes. Rounds of chemotherapy and radiation followed surgery. Somewhere in the mix we received a call from our friends in the Czech Republic who invited us to come and offered to pay for the trip. Although uncertainty loomed over me that I was recovered enough to go, desire overtook reason and we were on our way only a few weeks after the last radiation treatment.

The turrets of ancient cathedrals and the maze of endless medieval architecture presented a wonderland of mystical beauty in Prague.

Amidst our time with our friends, I shared my dream with them. The last night that we were to be in this magical place was our friends' anniversary and we made plans to go to dinner. As we rounded the narrow cobblestoned street, the restaurant that my friend had carefully selected came into view.

There on the front door was the visage that had become quite familiar to me: the sign of the Knights of St. John of the Cross. It was the Maltese cross. I looked at Kelsey for understanding. What was that sign doing on a building in Prague? She explained to me that the Knights of Malta, as they have come to be called, made their way to Prague and settled on the very square before us. On the far side of the square was their cathedral, and the restaurant that we were entering had been the hospital.

In storybook fashion, we descended the stone galley to the level below and were seated at a table by an archway that had been sealed at some point in its history. The waiter explained that the tunnel had been used to take the sick from the hospital across to the cathedral so they could have prayer for healing. With the history surrounding me and the crosses adorning the ancient walls of the restaurant, I felt as though I was in that land of Malta.

But it was only when I returned home and was reflecting on that evening when suddenly faith seemed to wash over my heart. "God, You actually fulfilled my dream! You took me there!" It was as though I heard His tender voice say, "Didn't I tell you?" And suddenly I felt _I could trust Him_ for that complete healing. I leaped to my feet and in a loud voice declared, "In the name of Jesus, I am healed!"

No! My life was not at the mercy of negligence; but it was at the mercy of a God who heals, who speaks, and who is willing to go to an extravagant extent to reassure my faltering faith.

Suzanne Wallace [18]
Community Director, *Behind Every Door*
www.behindeverydoor.net

Perfect Peace

(My former neighborhood friend and mentor at Redeemer's Fellowship in Old East Dallas; later co-pastoring at Redeemer's with her husband, John Wallace, then transitioning into the startup of Vineyard Christian Fellowship Church of Dallas in the late 80's. She and John worked for years with Blood and Fire Ministries, Int'l, followed by Kingdom Culture Ministries, Dallas, Texas.)

"Now may the God of Peace be with you all. Amen"
(Romans 15:33)

Closing Thoughts

Working on this book of *Trust* has been a *precious privilege and an absolute joy* to me! God wants us to trust His word. He walked with me through the Word and showered me with His wisdom as I have never experienced before! It has been a guarded responsibility and indeed a privilege to pray for each and every person who studies or peers through this book. My prayer has been that each one will meet God in the way that their heart is crying out to Him.

Jeremiah 29:11–14a says: "For I know the thoughts that I think toward you, says the LORD, thoughts of peace and not of evil, to give you a future and a hope. Then you will call upon Me and go and pray to Me, and I will listen to you. *And you will seek Me and find Me, when you search for Me with all your heart*. I will be found by you, says the LORD. . . ." If that is not inviting enough, then Jeremiah 33:3 continues: "Call to Me, and I will answer you, and show you great and mighty things, which you do not know."

He answers in the *instant* of a heartbeat! He desires relationship with us, especially as Christians, but He also desires the hearts of those still lost to Him. Would you be willing to place your hand in His and choose to give Him your heart? It would instantly give you His forgiveness in this life and begin a peace through His salvation of grace that will follow you into eternity. Trust Him, God's only Son, as the Savior of your life. There is no other way.

I love each of you who have "studied to show yourselves approved unto God, a workman who does not need to be ashamed, rightly dividing the word of truth." And, God loves you even more. I will see you soon! Even so, come Lord Jesus!

Pamela Johnson Alexander
The grace of our Lord Jesus Christ be with you all. Amen

Teaching Suggestions

- Pray about opening your church, home or other location for a class to study <u>eight weeks</u> of *Trust without Borders* in your area. Decide on a day and time that works for your locale, and if there will be any type of child care available for those requests. Pray often asking God to strengthen you or one to whom He will lead you to teach the Bible study.
- If possible, have a back-up teacher available in case of illness or other event that may take the main teacher away from a scheduled class.
- Approximately one month ahead of the first class, begin announcements, listing in church bulletins, calling, sending emails to secure members for the Bible study.
- Plan on 2 hours of class time including an opening prayer and time to close in prayer, feeling free to read any of the opening and closing prayers from any of the days of the particular week you are studying. Be especially attentive to anyone who may need prayer, but keep any sharing or requests brief and discreet. Most of us schedule our times closely, so beginning and ending promptly is very important.
- Purchase the *Trust without Borders* books ahead of time or instruct members where they can obtain them.
- **<u>Prior to the first class</u>, have the members read the Preface, Introduction, Foreword and Psalm 37 and complete the first week's study (The "Dirt" on Dirt). This will keep the weeks of study to eight. *If* nine weeks are acceptable to your group, the first week can be spent covering the Preface, Introduction, Foreword and Psalm 37, getting to know one another, and prayer.
- Always arrive or be ready at least 30 minutes ahead of class time. Light refreshments and/or some types of tea, coffee or lemonade are always a nice touch of hospitality for the class times. Delegate someone to help with this so one person is not burdened with all the details of the class.
- Have some paper or a journal for members to sign in with their names, addresses, phone numbers and emails in case notification needs to be made concerning any kind of emergency, important prayer request or weather cancellation. Encouraging notes are always a nice touch mid-way through the eight classes (if the class is not too large).
- Always feel free to ask if anyone has any specific questions. If you don't feel you know the answer, you can say that you will get back with them later.
- *<u>Always open and close the class in prayer</u>.*
- Greet class members as they arrive and have the information sign-in sheet and name tags available (if needed). If members were not able to read the

Preface, Introduction, Foreword or Psalm 37 ahead of class, encourage them to do so now or do so together to begin the class. Encourage everyone to write out Psalm 37 by hand to "get it in their hearts." This extra step helps open up the mind to understand this psalm and would be wonderful in the memorization of many of the verses.

Chapter One: The "Dirt" on Dirt – Cultivating the Land

Day 1:
1. In view of the opening word, *cultivate*, discuss that word and the answers members wrote for the Hosea 10:12-13 verses. Ask if anyone wants to share about "sowing in righteousness" or "reaping in mercy or in accordance with kindness."
2. Discuss why it is important to break up fallow ground. Follow that discussion with "how long to wait for the LORD" (relating to #4 on that page's study).
3. Take some time to read, review and discuss *1 Thessalonians 5:23-24. *These two scripture verses will be mentioned in *every* chapter of *Trust without Borders* so please study and acquaint yourself well with them. Emphasize that we must exhibit responsibility, but it is the grace of Christ that makes us righteous.

Day 2:
1. Discuss how the LORD was going to clear out the nations, and how does that relate to us? How do our answers relate to Philippians 2:5-13? Discuss some of the class's lists of things that interfere with humility. Discuss pride and how 1 Thess. 5:23 is important to our changing.
2. Are there any specific insights gained from this Day's scripture studies?
3. Finalize this day discussing 2 Thess. 1:11-12, Heb. 10:23 and Jude 24-25.

Day 3:
1. Consider this thought: "The presence of anxiety means the absence of humility." Give ample time on that thought before moving on to, "Is it trust only if we get our way?"
2. Ask if there are any questions on the words researched from 2 Cor. 4:8-10.
3. Feel free to discuss any other verses, questions, or read from other versions.

Day 4:
1. Share about spiritual places they would like to abide.
2. Allow the class freedom to share thoughts on Holly Ogden's *Shattered Pieces*. Then lead from *Shattered Pieces* into Kerry's song *Restored*. Discuss the ease or difficulty of the phrase "Trust Me, Simply Trust Me."

3. Ask if anyone is changing viewpoints on the 1 Thess. 5:23-24 verses? Is it harder? Easier? Is their understanding changing?

Day 5:
1. Ask for any thoughts about the Hebrew word for *land* (erets). Discuss the process of confessing and repenting in relation to that.
2. Encourage members to share "dirt" being swept under their rugs (but do not ask individuals unless they offer).
3. Read Psalm 37:1-11 in closing prayer time. Ask if anyone would care to quote any from memory. Encourage members to memorize any or all of the Psalm 37 verses. Close this week with prayer requests, insights or any further sharing. Encourage them to continue!

Chapter Two: Hurry Up and Wait – It "shouldn't-oughta" be this Hard!

Day 1:
1. Ask if anyone is willing to discuss any cookies they are needing at this time.
2. Would anyone share about how they think God might want them wait on Him?
3. Dig into the scriptures studied for this day's lesson. Receive comments, suggestions, and thoughts.

Day 2:
1. Discuss the definitions of *rest*. Receive answers on how members rest in the LORD.
2. Discuss the point that "No matter what is happening around us, trusting God gives the foundation needed for a condition of restfulness." How do the verses of 1 Thess. 5:23-24 apply to that restfulness?
3. What part of Zechariah 4:6b puts the responsibility upon our shoulders? Compare, in discussion, those verses to Ex. 14:13-14. Ask if any group member memorized and can quote those verses.

Day 3:
1. Ask the class if they had ever considered that strongholds of sin were first established in the mind (2 Cor. 10:4-6). Then discuss the accompanying paragraph in the lesson about "Behind every stronghold is a lie."
2. Discuss the *Red Sea Moment* idea.
3. Explain the meaning of *anapauo* and ask if anyone would be willing to share their experience with this new word. Discuss Matthew 11:28-30 in correlation with *anapauo*.

Day 4:
1. Discuss responses to the list of *all that Christ is and what He has done for us*, and how He fulfilled all that Moses foreshadowed.
2. Using Heb. 3:7-11, share and discuss God's wrath toward the Israelites. Going further up to v. 19, discuss what "hardening of the heart" means in a person's life.
3. How does obedience discussed in the above verses bring rest to our soul? Review and discuss the scripture study of this lesson.

Day 5:
1. Discuss the promise of God in Heb. 4:1-13 of entering His rest through Jesus Christ. How do *trust* and entering this *rest* co-mingle?
2. What is the important challenge of Heb. 4:11? How does knowing God's word bring us rest? Ask if anyone would be willing to share a memorized scripture from this study. If not, discuss the Isaiah 43:2 scripture (and any other part of this printed scripture) and receive comments.
3. Discuss Majid's testimony. Close with the prayer that ends this week's lesson (or pray your own).

Chapter Three: Inheritance: Blessings of the "Now and Not Yet"

Day 1:
1. Encourage discussion of Habakkuk 2:1-3 and talk about setting that as a goal for their lives.
2. Talk about how class members would have reacted or have reacted when asked to "Go to a land that I will show you."
3. Have members share thoughts about the Heb. 11:1 verse, and that "Faith is a firm belief or conviction in something for which there is no visible proof." How often do we show doubt? How often can we believe?
4. Ask if someone would be willing to recite Heb. 11:1. Encourage members to "hide the Word" in their hearts.

Day 2:
1. Discuss "journaling stones of remembrance." Read through and discuss 1 Samuel 7:10-12.
2. Ask if members could more easily take on a "piece of the mountain" instead of the entire mountain? Review the points 1-7 of this day's section about entrusting our lives to God. Could they relate to the "changes of names"?
3. Review Numbers 13, especially vv. 1-2 and 18-20; would it encourage you if vv. 1-2 were given to you personally? Continue discussion on these topics and verses if members are well engaged.

Day 3:
1. Review the definition of *meekness* and discuss how Joshua and Caleb used their meekness in view of the other 10 Israelite spies.
2. How do the verses in Numbers 14:10-25 relate to our study of Psalm 37:12-15? How did the meekness of Caleb's response of faith keep division out of the Israelite camp? How was he encouraged in his patience and faith for the next 40 years, even with thousands dying around him daily?
3. Close this Day out reading Psalm 37:16 -22 and discussing the wicked vs. the righteous.

Day 4:
1. Ask for participants to share practices to form as habits to reach or maintain peace. Discuss why it matters if we live by the standards of His Word as studied in Philippians 4:6-7.
2. Discuss Shadrach, Meshach and Abed-Nego, and what to do when we feel "God doesn't show up." Ask if anyone felt they often went to others instead of "bending their knee" and calling upon God?
3. Spend some time reviewing the studied scriptures of this day's lesson. Zero in on the eight listings of Phil. 4:6-7 if you have not already done so; discuss and compare with Psalm 37:23-31.
4. How do we "display strength and take action" so that we aren't wimpy Christians? Discuss maturing in faith to go boldly before the throne as Hebrews 10:19-23 explains.

Day 5:
1. Read or paraphrase the story of the prodigal son (Luke 15:11-24) and discuss "have you ever come to yourself?"
2. Discuss the word *called* and how it relates to our coming boldly before the throne (as discussed with Hebrews 10). Ask if anyone wants to share about a prodigal experience in their life.
3. There may be questions about how can a person sin and leave the family if they are a Christian? Discuss the verse about "how his father saw him *when he was still a great way off.*" Discuss how our Father's love to us is everlasting. What does *everlasting* mean? Be prepared for special requests as you close with prayer.

Chapter Four: Matchless, Scandalous Grace

Day 1:
1. Compare the word *grace* using the Webster's definition, the Greek and 2 Cor. 12:9. How does that verse mesh with our now famous 1 Thess. 5:24? Can the members imagine any situation in which they would measure up next to Jesus (without His matchless righteousness given to us at salvation)?

2. Discuss worldly reassurance versus God's certainty of trust and relate the discussion to Matt. 11:28-30. How does trusting God relate to *anapauo (rest)*? Review Heb. 4:9-13, discussing what we receive and who receives.
3. Ask if some of the members *went out to play*? Discuss freedom, liberty and grace in Christ as shown in Gal. 5:5 and Rom. 8:15.

Day 2:
1. Review the meaning of *propitiation*, along with forgiveness, grace and how it all relates to John 15:13.
2. Many members may express unhealthy guilt and shame. Engage the group in the awesomeness of God, His infinite existence versus our finite being, His unfathomable wisdom . . . and eventually back to our trusting in His grace! There may need to be a pause in the study to pray for someone struggling with guilt. Feel free to do so. Discuss what He can do, especially in light of Heb. 4:16.
3. There might arise a lively discussion of the Bonhoeffer quote. Work on those thoughts awhile. Lead this discussion into 'the first commandment' quoted in Mark 12:30, explaining how operating in this principle of grace keeps us from distorting the message of grace.

Day 3:
1. Enjoy a delightful discussion on butterflies (bring pictures, samples if possible) and the relation of their life cycle to our Christian lives.
2. Discuss how we become *a new creation* even when we are the same person in the flesh. Mingle these thoughts into our legal standing before God.
3. Examine with participants how we grow in righteousness progressively.

Day 4:
1. Allow open discussion on how we must allow God to see us and love us precisely as we are in order to grow in trust. How can we do that?
2. Compare feelings the class may have concerning the confessional stories versus how God would feel. Can God really love us *just as we are*? Discuss Rom. 5:8 by reading the verse and allow sharing by individuals. Read or sing the hymn *Just as I Am*.
3. What were the two things Paul says that grace is able to do? Close this lesson discussing Matt. 11:29.

Day 5:
1. Make sure all have read the testimony of Jennifer Alexander Wright. If not, read it together in class. Lead into a discussion on gratefulness in light of God's graciousness.

2. Review Luke 17:11-19, discussing why only one returned. How does that relate to Phil. 4:11? Why is gratefulness a foremost quality of a trusting disciple (a follower of Christ)?
3. Discuss their reasons for being grateful. Have closing prayer with members speaking out a word of gratefulness.

Chapter Five: Sweet Intimacy of Prayer ~ Harps, Golden Bowls and Camel Knees

Day 1:
1. Briefly review the 12 points for the power of prayer in a Christian's life. Allow for questions, discussion, and review of any scriptures they studied.

Day 2:
1. Discuss how praise brings us into worship, and how Christ's death did away with animal sacrifices opening the New Covenant for the sacrifice of praise. Discuss what praise is.
2. Study the beautiful Hebrew words for praise.
3. Discuss how God inhabits our praise, His resting place is our praise and goes before us in praise. Don't overlook the Hebrew word *owz*, and how God's strength within us and our praise of Him are one and the same!

Day 3:
1. Discuss how Psalm 95 invites us to worship. Study through the scriptures of the four points about worship.
2. Have conversation about why worship is all about God. Discuss how we prepare for worship and what it means to enter the *Shekinah* of the heart.
3. What does it mean that *all of our obedience is worship*? Discuss the notes of how worship changes us, especially the three bulleted notes at the end of this Day's lesson.

Day 4:
1. Why must our relationship to God precede our ministry to others? Review some of the scriptures about how to know God.
2. On No. 4, Knowing God's Voice, what does it mean: "It is the nature of God to speak"? Review the five "a-b-c" points about wanting to listen.
3. Discuss the four points of God speaking through His word, by pictures, by thoughts and by spiritual gifts. There most likely will be much and varied discussion. Avoid being dogmatic, but welcome scriptural discussion.

Day 5:
1. We have learned and discussed how imperative it is to listen for God's guidance. Now discuss how being still before the Lord is necessary for intercession for others. Discuss what intercession is.
2. Discuss conduct of warfare and using Christian weapons of warfare. Why is knowing God's word so imperative in spiritual warfare?
3. Review the five points toward the end of the chapter about asking for His presence and power in our lives. Close in the power of His prayer.

Chapter Six: Trust without Borders

Day 1:
1. If you have (or can borrow or download) the United Zion CD by Hillsong, play *Oceans* as the opening prayer. Share "Miracle Heidi's" testimony and any from your group that may have a miracle to share.
2. Combine a discussion around Mark 10:15, Psalm 57:1 and the word trust, *Chasa*.
3. Discuss the Isaiah 12:2 verse toward the last page, inviting people to share what it means to them. Ask if anyone would be willing to share Proverbs 3: 5-6 from memory to close this Day's study, or read it aloud.

Day 2:
1. Discuss the feelings of David of exhilaration, exasperation, questioning and doubts of being anointed King.
2. Ask for any to share that may have had to "wait." Discuss the thought that God doesn't waste time; and that time is totally different to God's existence than to ours.
3. Ask what members do to keep a good attitude while "keeping sheep in the field." How do Proverbs 16:3 and Psalm 37:5 figure in to their answers?

Day 3:
1. This lesson taught that trust is foundational for *any* relationship, especially with God, and made us ask, "Is it trust only when we get our way?" Discuss that with the class.
2. Ask if anyone would be willing to share about their intimacy with Abba, Father.
3. Isaiah 12:2 has been discussed before. Have some members share their journal thoughts. See if anyone could share the memorized Psalm 37:5 discussed above.

Day 4:
1. Read Psalm 91, discussing how the LORD's promise is conditioned upon making Him our true refuge and habitation. Comparatively study *dwell* and *abiding*.
2. Discuss their review of John 15:1-17. Remembering the discussion of dwelling in the shadow of the Almighty, continue with the study of *Shaddai*, God being all-sufficient and eternally capable of being all that His people need.
3. Have people share the six *I wills* from Psalm 91:14-16 and discuss what they mean in our lives.

Day 5:
1. Have members share some of the points they listed for the 2 Chronicles 20: 1-30 verses. Did they notice some of the references from previous scriptures?
2. What does it mean, "Battles are won through faith's warfare, but ultimately belong solely to the Lord"? And what about, "Trust in God does not presume that God will intervene." Allow time for discussion.
3. Discuss having *trust without borders* and how that relates to *Immanuel, God with us*. Ask for any discussion on the testimony shared in Day 5.

Chapter Seven: Surrounded by Strongholds

Day 1:
1. Discuss the dictionary version of what a stronghold is and then participants' spiritual definitions. Include explanations of demonic strongholds as studied in 2 Cor. 10:3-5.
2. Discuss what "the battle is won or lost at the threshold of the mind" means and how strongholds are first established in the mind (like we studied in the *Wait* chapter), along with the four bulleted notes. Share ideas about how idols are established when we fail to trust in God's provision.
3. In conjunction to Jesus' teaching to His disciples in Matt. 10:16, discuss being wise as serpents and innocent as doves.

Day 2:
1. Have members share thoughts about 1 Peter 5:6-10. How does the last verse connect with 1 Thess. 5:23-24?
2. Compare 2 Cor. 10:5b with James 4:7: "Submitting to God, resisting the devil and he will flee from you"?
3. Discuss the three points of 2 Cor. 1: 10 from the lesson. Discuss the importance of remembering those points alongside Deut. 7:22-23. Invite sharing of *flesh* that gets in the way as described in Gal. 5:19-21. What does v. 22 have to do with strongholds?

Day 3:
1. Reviewing the Num. 13:18-20 scriptures, discuss understanding that God was asking them to see what belongs to them and what HE *was going to give them*.
2. Discuss some of the 'ites' and why God wants us to forget *that once we didn't know who we were*. In the temporary comfort of our idol or sin, we don't need God. Now that we know God, we know we need God!
3. Have someone share from memory 2 Tim. 1:7. How does this help us in the midst of battle?

Day 4:
1. Take some time to delve into the first paragraph of this lesson concerning Matt. 12:43-45. Share about unrecognizable thinking patterns. Then discuss Luke 22:31 and Peter's warning from Jesus.
2. Discuss aspects of the 'ites' in our lives and their summaries. Allow time for discussion and comparisons.
3. Read Eph. 6:10-18 discussing the armor and the word *withstand*. How is prayer the battle itself?
4. What are the three ways to cast down the accuser in Rev. 12:11 and what do they mean?

Day 5:
1. What does Prov. 29:18 teach about the principles of life? Review John 1:16 and Rom. 8:28 and how they show that God is meeting us at our point of need.
2. Discuss how Prov. 14:12 teaches that it is important to get "the principle of the thing" in life.
3. Discuss the five points at the end of this lesson. Review Heb.12: 2 and Phil. 1:6, comparing them to 1 Thess. 5:23-24. Close with discussion of the bulleted points. Invite discussion of the testimony given, or allow someone to share or comment. Close in prayer.

Chapter Eight: Perfect Peace

Day 1:
1. Review the definition of peace, *eirene*, and have discussion of Romans 5:1-2. Compare and discuss Rom. 15:13.
2. Discuss that word *peace* in 1 Thess. 5:23. O, how that verse has carried us through this study! Combine these verses with Heb. 13:20-21. Discuss what the God of peace will do for us.
3. Discuss the four points of *nothing*. Emphasize we are nothing *without* Christ! With Christ we are everything! Close with Isaiah 61: 3, discussing different member's comments on receiving *beauty from ashes*.

Day 2:
1. Discuss this second definition of peace from Isaiah 26:3 and how it helps us dwell in the peace *of* God.
2. Ask the members what "Immanuel, God with us," means to them. Allow time for sharing before asking what does it mean to 'keep our mind on the LORD'?
3. Invite sharing about Phil.4:6-8 concerning "the peace of God."

Day 3:
1. Discuss how weeds grow up in the middle of proper plantings and what are we to do during the growing time of our seeds?
2. Ask for thoughts about recognizing the movement of God instead of the movement of opposition.
3. Review the scriptures studied and allow time for discussion.

Day 4:
1. Bad things happen – discuss that in light of John 16:33 and Psalm 139:2. Ask members how they deal with the bad things when they come before God.
2. Discuss *peace* being one of the fruit of the Spirit. Allow sharing on Colo. 3: 15 and John 14:26-27.
3. Close discussing Rev. 1:4-6. Our God who created time certainly extends beyond and came before time. That God offers us peace!

Day 5:
1. Discuss why answers to our prayers sometimes do not come. Remind participants that only He knows truly what we need, even though we often *think* we know.
2. Ask "where are you on this difficult journey of trust?" What **can** you trust God for? Then that is where you begin!
3. Either review the testimony of Malta, or read it if enough participants have not done so. Close out the study reading my "closing thoughts" to you, and invite anyone who may not be a believer in Jesus Christ, or anyone who needs compassionate prayer today, to allow prayer over them.

I cannot believe that we are done, but . . .
"Well done, good and faithful servant!"

Endnotes

Chapter One: *The Dirt on Dirt*

1 *Merriam-Webster.com*/help/citing.htm, 2010.
2 *New Spirit Filled Life Bible*, Jack W. Hayford, Litt.D. et al, *Book of Hosea*, Truth in Action #3, (Nashville, Tenn.: Thomas Nelson, 2002), 1158.
3 *New Spirit Filled Life Bible, Epistle of Galatians*, Truth in Action #4, 1641.
4 Brennan Manning, *Ruthless Trust: The Ragamuffin's Path to God* (New York: HarperSanFrancisco, 2002), 7.
5 Holly Ogden, "*Trust Me*," Christian Motorcyclists Assn. Missouri Women's Conference, 2012; Exec. Ministry Support Mgr. and CMA Int'l Liaison, PO Box 9, Hatfield, AR 71945-4278; www.cmausa.org. Permission granted.
6 Kerry Bond, *Restored*, 2012, Permission granted to use Words and Music.
7 James Strong, *The New Strong's Exhaustive Concordance of the Bible* (New York: Thomas Nelson, 1990), Hebrew word #776.
8 *The American Heritage Dictionary of the English Language*, 4th Edition, Houghton Mifflin, ©2000, updated 2009. All rights reserved. www.free-dictionary.com/dirt.

Chapter Two: *Hurry up and Wait*

1 Pamela Alexander, Personal Writings, 1969.
2 *Merriam-Webster.com*/help/citing.htm, 2010.
3 Strong, *Concordance*, Hebrew word #4496.
4 Strong, *Concordance*, Greek word #373.
5 *New Spirit Filled Life Bible*, 2 Corinthians 10:4-6, Kingdom Dynamics, Christopher J. Hayward, 1621-1622.
6 Dr. David Jeffress, KCBI Radio Station, 2013; Pastor/Author, First Baptist Church Sermon, Dallas, Tex.
7 *New Spirit Filled Life Bible, Epistle of Hebrews*, Ch. 2, bulleted adaptation of vv. 8-15 and associated footnotes; 1732.
8 *New Spirit Filled Life Bible, Epistle of Hebrews*, Ch. 3:2-6, footnotes; 1733.
9 *New Spirit Filled Life Bible, Epistle of Hebrews*, Ch. 3, footnote; 1733.
10 *New Spirit Filled Life Bible, Epistle of Hebrews*, Ch. 4, footnotes; 1734.

11 Duane Sherriff, Pastor, Victory Life Church, Durant, Okla.; Sermon Series: *The Power of the Cross*, #5.
12 *New Spirit Filled Life Bible, Epistle of Hebrews*, Ch. 4:10, footnote; 1734.
13 Manning, *Ruthless*, 7.
14 *New Spirit Filled Life Bible*, Hebrews 4:11-13, Kingdom Dynamics; Roy Hicks Sr.; 1734.
15 Majid Babakhanian, Personal Testimony 2014; Permission granted.

Chapter Three: *Inheritance*

1 Alexander, Personal Writings, 2010.
2 Strong, *Concordance*, Heb. Word # 5157.
3 Manning, *Ruthless*, 23.
4 Manning, *Ruthless*, 23.
5 Strong, *Concordance*, Heb. Word #1288.
6 Holly Ogden, Speech at CMA Women's Conference, March 2013; June Hunt Hope for the Heart Center, Plano, Tex.; Permission granted.
7 Manning, *Ruthless*, 9.
8 Manning, *Ruthless*, 9.
9 Manning, *Ruthless*, 177.
10 *New Spirit Filled Life Bible*, Galatians 5:16-17, Kingdom Dynamics; Kenneth C. Ulmer, 1637.
11 D.J. Butler, *I Will Change Your Name,* Mercy/Vineyard Publishing Music, © 1987; Permission granted: License #168482, Music Services, Brentwood, Tenn.
12 Debbie Morris, Co-Pastor, Co-Director and House Parent of the Father's House, Dallas, Tex.; Kingdom Culture Ministry. Permission granted.
13 *New Spirit Filled Life Bible*, Numbers 13:30; 14:6-9, Kingdom Dynamics; Roy Hicks Sr.; 194.
14 *New Spirit Filled Life Bible*, Roy Hicks Sr.; 194.
15 Brennan Manning, *The Ragamuffin Gospel* (Sisters, Ore.: Multnomah, 2000), 78.
16 *New Spirit Filled Life Bible, Gospel of John*, Ch. 1:1, footnote; 1443.
17 Manning, *Ruthless*, 6.
18 *New Spirit Filled Life Bible, Gospel of Matthew*, Ch. 11:12, footnote; 1309.
19 Nathan Alexander, Testimony 2010; Permission granted.
20 *New Spirit Filled Life Bible, Epistle of Galatians* 1:6, Word Wealth, 1630.
21 Manning, *Ruthless*, 15.
22 Manning, *Ruthless*, Preface, xv.
23 James Finley, *The Contemplative Heart* (Notre Dame, IN: Sorin Books, 2000), 57.

Chapter Four: *Matchless, Scandalous Grace*

1. *Scandalous Grace*: Words and Music by Matt Crocker & Joel Houston//©2012, Hillsong Music. Permission granted. EMICMGMusic, License #552711, U.S. and Canada.
2. *Webster's Seventh New Collegiate Dict.*, G. & C. Merriam Co., 1967, 362.
3. Strong, *Concordance*, Greek Word #5485.
4. *New Spirit Filled Life Bible, 2nd Epistle of Corinthians* 12:9, Word Wealth, 1624.
5. *New Spirit Filled Life Bible, 2nd Epistle of Corinthians* 12:9, Kingdom Dynamics, 1624.
6. *Studio G* (Magazine of Gateway Church, Dallas, Tex.; Spring 2010), 33.
7. *New Spirit Filled Life Bible, 1st Epistle of Thessalonians*, Word Wealth, 1684.
8. Manning, *Ragamuffin*, 74.
9. Manning, *Ragamuffin*, 75.
10. Manning, *Ragamuffin*, 114.
11. Dietrich Bonhoeffer, *Life Together* (San Francisco: Harper & Row, 1954); Quoted in Bob and Michael Benson, *Disciplines for the Inner Life* (Waco, Tex.: Word Books, 1985), 60.
12. Mike Bickle, "What's Wrong with Grace?"- *Charisma,* (April 2013): 30.
13. Bickle, "What's Wrong with Grace?"- 30.
14. Compiled and adapted from three Websites (November 2013): www.thebutterflysite.com/life-cycle.shtml www.ansp.org/explore/online-exhibits/butterflies/lifecycle/ and www.aprairiehaven.com/pageid=9860.
15. Compiled and adapted from: www.examiner.com/article/butterfly-life-cycle-versus-the-growth-process-of-a-christian, (November 2013).
16. Kerry Bond, (Unnamed song), 2013, Permission granted.
17. Bara Bloom, Facebook Quote, 2013.
18. Bickle, "What's Wrong with Grace?"- 28.
19. Bickle, "What's Wrong with Grace?"- 30.
20. Donald P. Gray, *Jesus, the Way to Freedom* (Winona, Minn.: St. Mary's College, 1979), 33.
21. Henri Nouwen, www.markandrewnouwen.com/2012/08/we-are-seen-by-god-with-gazing-love.html.
22. Manning, *Ruthless*, 16.
23. Manning, *Ruthless*, 19.
24. Anne Lamott, From a Radio Program, no reference.

25 Manning, *Ragamuffin*, 112.
26 Manning, *Ragamuffin*, 112-113.
27 Charlotte Elliott (Words) and William Bradbury (Music): Hymn, *Just As I Am*, Transferred from www.hymnary.org/hymn/BH 2008/p.599, Dec. 2013.
28 Jennifer Wright, Personal Testimony, 2013, Permission granted.
29 Austin Lewter. Adapted from the editorial, "The Days of Miracles are not Over," *Jefferson Jimpecute*, Jefferson, Tex. (November 2010), Permission granted.
30 Manning, *Ruthless*, 24.

Chapter Five: *Sweet Intimacy of Prayer ~ Harps, Golden Bowls and "Camel Knees"*

1. Mike Bickle, *Introducing the Primary Principle of the Harp & Bowl Model*, Internet Notes, Session 16: Values, pt. 1, Sept. 10, 2004.
2. Beth Moore, *Whispers of Hope*, (Nashville, Tenn.: LifeWay Press, 1998), 5.
3. Richard Foster, *Celebration of Discipline,* (San Francisco: Harper & Row, 1978), 30.
4. Foster, *Celebration,* 30.
5. Foster, *Celebration,* 31.
6. Foster, *Celebration,* 23.
7. Rosalind Rinker, *Prayer: Conversing With God*, Grand Rapids, Mich.: Zondervan, 1959, 19.
8. Foster, *Celebration,* 33.
9. Henry Blackaby & King, *Experiencing God,* (Nashville, Tenn.: Lifeway Press, 1993); 8, 10.
10. John Wimber, *All about Worship*, Vineyard Music Group, 1998, 11.
11. Bickle, Alexander, Sullivant, *Apostolic Intercession*, Internet Notes, Session 13a: 12-Fold Apostolic Prayer Model, Mike Bickle, 1.
12. Christian Fellowship Church Notes/Sermons, VV6, 12-1987, General Notes used in this Chapter 5, 1.
13. Anne Murchison, *Praise and Worship in Earth as It Is In Heaven*, (Waco, Tex.: Word Books, 1981), 77.
14. Foster, *Celebration,* 146.
15. Foster, *Celebration,* 147.
16. Foster, *Celebration,* 146-147.
17. Foster, *Celebration,* 147-148.
18. Murchison, *Praise*, 82.

19 Murchison, *Praise*, 84.
20 Strong, *Concordance*, Hebrew Word, #3427.
21 Murchison, *Praise*, 84.
22 Strong, *Concordance*, Heb. Word, #5115.
23 Strong, *Concordance*, Heb. Word, #5797.
24 Strong, *Concordance*, Greek Word, #1411.
25 Murchison, *Praise and Worship*, 87-88.
26 Strong, *Concordance*, Heb. Word, #5095.
27 Murchison, *Praise*, 88.
28 Wimber, *Worship*, 6.
29 Foster, *Celebration*, 138.
30 John Wallace, *Introduction to Worship* sermon notes, Central Christian Fellowship, VP, March 20, 1988, 1.
31 Wallace, *Worship*, 1.
32 Foster, *Celebration*, 141.
33 Foster, *Celebration*, 141, 144.
34 Foster, *Celebration*, 141-143.
35 Foster, *Celebration*, 143.
36 Foster, *Celebration*, 140.
37 Terry Butler, "*What Worship Produces in Us*," Isaiah 61 Conf. Notes, 1994.
38 Foster, *Celebration*, 148-149.
39 Murchison, *Praise*, 72.
40 Ministry Team Training Notes, Vista Ridge Vineyard, Lewisville, Tex., 1998, 2.
41 A.W. Tozer, *The Pursuit of God*, (Camp Hill, Penn.: Christian Publications, 1982), 81-82.
42 Frank C. Laubach, *Learning the Vocabulary of God*, (Nashville, Tenn.: The Upper Room, 1956), 22-23.
43 Foster, *Celebration*, 34.
44 Foster, *Celebration*, 35.
45 Training Notes, VRV, 2-8.
46 Foster, *Celebration*, 35.
47 Foster, *Celebration*, 35.
48 Foster, *Celebration*, 35.
49 Foster, *Celebration*, 35.
50 Training Notes, VRV, 26.
51 Training Notes, VRV, 11-15, used selectively throughout chapter.

Chapter Six: *Trust Without Borders*

1. *Oceans (Where Feet May Fail)*: Words and Music by Matt Crocker, Joel Houston & Salomon Ligthelm//©2012, Hillsong Music. Permission granted, EMICMGMusic, License #552711, U.S. and Canada.
2. Manning, *Ruthless*, 2.
3. Strong, *Concordance*, Hebrew Word #2620.
4. *New Spirit Filled Life Bible, The Gospel of Mark,* Word Wealth, 1372.
5. Manning, *Ragamuffin*, 117.
6. Manning, *Ragamuffin*, 228.
7. Manning, *Ragamuffin*, 77.
8. Walter J. Burghardt, *Tell the Next Generation* (New York: Paulist Press, 1980), 43.
9. Vickie Boone Watson, Quotations Used by permission of the Author from *Miracle Heidi: When Doctors Couldn't ... God Could!*, (Bedford, Tex.: Sterling Press, 1996).
10. Elaine Fisher, "Born to Be," *Studio G* Magazine, Gateway Church, Southlake, Tex.,(Spring 2012): 26-27.
11. Manning, *Ruthless*, 30.
12. Manning, *Ruthless*, 106.
13. *New Spirit Filled Life Bible, Book of 1st Samuel,* Truth in Action #4, p. 400.
14. *New Spirit Filled Life Bible, Book of 1st Kings,* Truth in Action #4, 478.
15. Lynda Grove, "At the Top of the World in a Dung Hut," *Studio G* Magazine, (Gateway Church, Southlake, Tex., April 2012): 8. Permission granted.
16. Alexander, Personal Writings, July 2011.
17. Strong, *Concordance*, Heb. Word #4268, derived from #2620.
18. Strong, *Concordance*, Heb. Word #4583.
19. *New Spirit Filled Life Bible*, Kingdom Dynamics, Nathaniel Van Cleave, 758.
20. *New Spirit Filled Life Bible*, Psalm 91, Word Wealth, 757.
21. *New Spirit Filled Life Bible, Book of 2nd Chronicles,* Truth in Action #4, 596.
22. Manning, *Ruthless*, 4-5.
23. John Shea, *The Challenge of Jesus* (Chicago: Thomas Moore, 1975), 133-134.
24. Manning, *Ruthless*, 117.
25. Manning, *Ruthless*, 181.
26. Jimmy Alexander, Personal Testimony, 2014, Permission granted.

Chapter Seven: *Surrounded by Strongholds*

1 David & Karen Mains, "Princess Amanda and the Dragon," *Tales of the Kingdom*, (David C. Cook Publishing, Elgin, IL, 1983), 74-80; Permission granted by authors.
2 Francis Frangipane, *The Three Battlegrounds*, (Advancing Church Publications, Marion, Iowa, 1989), 1, 15.
3 *New Spirit Filled Life Bible*, 2 Corinthians 10:4-6, Kingdom Dynamics, Christopher J. Hayward, 1621-1622.
4 Karen Jordan, Testimony, 2014, Permission granted.
5 *New Spirit Filled Life Bible*, Deuteronomy 7:22-23, Kingdom Dynamics, Christopher J. Hayward, 241-242.
6 *New Spirit Filled Life Bible*, Galatians 5:22-23, paraphrase of footnote; 1638.
7 Edward Mote, Hymn, *My Hope is Built on Nothing Less*, 1837.
8 Frangipane, *Battlegrounds*, 13.
9 John Allister, Compiled notes: The Amalekite Genocide, (12 August, 2013).
10 http://matthiasmedia.com/briefing/2013/08/the-amalekite-genocide/.
11 http://amazingbibletimeline.com/blog/the-hittites/
12 http://comegrowwithme.com/documents/Lesson 12_Hittites_10-30-13_notes.pdf.
13 http://gotquestions.org/Hittites/html; *Who were the Hittites?* (July 31, 2013).
14 S. Michael Houdman, CEO, http://www.gotquestions.org/Hittites.html.
15 Margaret Hunter, Compilation by Hunter, (Publishers of The Amazing Bible Timeline), http://amazingbibletimeline.com/blog/the-hittites/ (12 August, 2013).
16 Frangipane, *Battlegrounds*, 18, 22.
17 Frangipane, *Battlegrounds*, 23.
18 Daniel C. Fredericks, *Holman Bible Dictionary*, (Broadman & Holman, 1991).
19 http://amazingbibletimeline.com/gibeonites/.
20 Paige Henderson, Q^I *Notebook*, Fellowship of the Sword Ministries, 2011; Compiled from *Victory at Home: Dealing with the "-Ite's";* 81-85.
21 *New Spirit Filled Life Bible*, *Ephesians 6:13,* Word Wealth; vv.10-18, Kingdom Dynamics, Dick Eastman; 1654-1655.
22 *New Spirit Filled Life Bible*, Use of footnote of John 1:16, 1444.
23 Alexander, Personal Testimony, 2014.
24 *New Spirit Filled Life Bible*, *Isaiah 55:9*, Kingdom Dynamics, A. Joy Dawson, 939.

Chapter Eight: *Perfect Peace*

1. Strong, *Concordance*, Greek Word #1515.
2. *New Spirit Filled Life Bible*, Luke 1:79, Word Wealth, 1388.
3. Sheriff, Sermon Notes, Victory Life Church, March 19, 2013.
4. Strong, *Concordance*, Hebrew Word #7965.
5. *New Spirit Filled Life Bible*, Isaiah 9:6, Kingdom Dynamics, Fuchsia T. Pickett, 885.
6. Edward Horowitz, *How the Hebrew Language Grew*, (KTAV Publishing House), 22.
7. Horowitz, *Language*, 22.
8. *New Spirit Filled Life Bible*, Galatians 6:7-9, Oral Roberts, Kingdom Dynamics, 1639.
9. Bob Hamp, "Leadership in an Invisible Kingdom," *Studio G*, (April 2013): 11.
10. *New Spirit Filled Life Bible*, Truth in Action #4, 742.
11. Donald C. Stamps and J. Wesley Adams, *Fire Bible: Global Study Edition*, 'The Suffering of the Righteous,' (LIFE Publishers, Int'l, 1980).
12. *Find You On My Knees*, Used with permission from the copyright owner. Words and music by Kari Jobe, Ben Glover/, Matt Bronleewee; Copyright © 2012: Songs From the Science Lab (ASCAP)/All Essential Music (ASCAP) (both admin. by Essential Music Publishing LLC)/Worship Together Music (BMI) 9t One Songs (ASCAP) Ariose Music (ASCAP) (Admin. at CapitolCMGPublishing.com, License Permit #552711). All rights reserved. Used by permission. U.S. and Canada.
13. "Why Me, Lord?" *Charisma Magazine*, (July 2010): 67; Bible Study adapted from Principles 4Life (Life Publishers International).
14. "Why Me, Lord?" *Charisma Magazine*, (July 2010): 67.
15. http://www/goodreads.com/quotes/139680-in-the-west-we-have-the-tendancy-to-be-profit-oriented, (August 2013).
16. Sarah Young, *Jesus Calling*, (Nashville, Tenn.: Thomas Nelson, 2004), 92.
17. Chaplain Donna Kafer, "Waiting on God: In His Silence, Have Faith"; *TriVita Magazine*, (April 2013): 25.
18. Suzanne Wallace, *Malta*, Personal Testimony, 2014, Permission granted.